I CHOSE HEAVEN
How to Avoid Eternity in Hell

Charles C. Pringle

Unless otherwise noted, all Scripture quotations are taken from *The New Scofield Reference Bible: King James Version (KJV)*. Scofield, C. I., New York: Oxford University Press, 1967.

I Chose Heaven: How to Avoid Eternity in Hell
Copyright ©2022 by Charles C. Pringle

Cover Design by Alpha Advertising
Interior Design by Pine Hill Graphics

Published by: Advantage Books
               www.advbookstore.com

The views expressed or implied in this work do not necessarily reflect those of ACW Press. Ultimate design, content, and editorial accuracy of this work is the responsi-bility of the author(s).

ISBN number: 978-1-59755-684-2

All rights reserved. No part of this book may be reproduced, stored in a retrieval system, or transmitted in any form or by any means–electronic, mechanical, photo-copying, recording, or otherwise–without prior permission in writing from the copy-right holder except as provided by USA copyright law.

First Printing: August 2022
22 23 24 25 26 27   10 9 8 7 6 5 4 3 2 1

TABLE OF CONTENTS

Dedication 5
Preface 7

CHAPTER ONE:
Searching for the "Spiritual Missing Part" 9
(Prov 25:2; Jn 3:11–12; Prov 3:5–6; Jn 3:3, 5–7; 1 Tim 1:5)

CHAPTER TWO:
Analyzing My Past 47
(Book of Romans; Ps 46:10)

CHAPTER THREE:
My Rationale for Researching the Bible 57
(Jn 3:3–7; Jn 3:15–16; Jn 6:40; Luke 24:25–27: Jn 11:25–26)

CHAPTER FOUR:
My In-Depth Bible Study Considerations and Revelations 67
(Jn 5:39; Luke 24:25–27; Eph 1:12–14; 2 Tim 3:16–17)

CHAPTER FIVE:
Understanding the Value of God's Love 75
(Rom 5:8; Rom 8:32; Jn 11:25–26; 1 Jn 4:13–16; Rom Ch 8)

CHAPTER SIX:
Finding My "Spiritual Missing Part" 85
(Jn Ch 3; Jn 5:24; Rom 10:9–10; Eph 1:13; Jn 14:26; Rom Ch 8)

CHAPTER SEVEN:
How to Obtain Maximum Blessings Daily 97
(Prov 3:6–7; Ps 37:3–7; Jer 9:23–24; Gal 5:13–26; Prov 22:4)

CHAPTER EIGHT:
Adjusting My Life's Purpose Toward God's Love Concept . . . 103
(1 Tim 1:5; Eph 5; 1 Jn 4:1; Thess 5:16–18)

CHAPTER NINE:
Adjusting My Mindset to Follow God's Will............ 109
(Rom Chs 5, 8 and 12; Rom 12:1–2; 2 Tim 1:6–7; Josh 1:8–9)

CHAPTER TEN:
Growing Daily into a Mature Spiritual Being............ 115
(Matt 22:37–40; 1 Thess 5:16–18; Mic 6:8; Jer 9:23–24)

CHAPTER ELEVEN:
Adjusting My Behavior According to God's Love Concept... 119
(Col 3; Matt 16:26; Eph Ch 4; Luke 24:44–49)

Appendices

Appendix 1: References and Acknowledgements............ 127

Appendix 2: Recommended References for Spiritual Growth ... 129

Appendix 3: Books of the Bible Abbreviations.............. 131

Appendix 4: Fundamental Bible Truths................... 133

Appendix 5: 48 Basics Bible Lessons 135

DEDICATION

I dedicate this book to Jesus, my wife Janice, our six children and their children, my sister, my brother, his wife, their children, and their grandchildren. I also dedicate this to my friends who put up with me and encouraged me to persevere in my research to find the answers to my life questions concerning my life's purpose, meaning, fulfillment, and the "spiritual missing part."

I also dedicate this book to all saved sinners who have found their "spiritual missing part" and have re-united their spirit with God's Holy Spirit, avoiding eternal spiritual death in hell and who shared their own eternal salvation story through their love connection to God, Jesus, and the Holy Spirit, in concert with God's Love Concept.

PREFACE

Growing up I felt that I was missing something in my understanding of life, something that was taking away from my life's purpose, meaning, self-fulfillment, and joy. The main purpose of my book is to share the results of my successful research to find the answers for life's purpose, meaning, fulfillment, and questions about the "spiritual missing part," and reuniting my spirit with God's Holy Spirit again forever. Accordingly, I have designed the sequences of the Bible verses in this book to support the rationale of the respective paragraph subjects that they follow.

I have been a spiritually born-again Christian for 51 years. I want to share God's Love Concept (Matt 22:36–40; Gal 6:7–8; 1 Tim 1:5), his love fundamentals (spiritual growth concepts), and Bible lessons that I've learned during my Christian journey. My hope is that Bible teachers can use this book to enhance their evangelistic, missionary, one on one, small group, house church, and counseling training classes (Eph Ch 4; Gal 5:13–18).

The Bible Scripture references identified in this book are from the 1967 New Schofield Reference Bible, KJV. The same Scriptures are in both the Catholic and Protestant Bibles. The purpose of using Scripture is to be in concert with Jesus' use of Scripture. In the book of Luke we read about his interaction with two of his disciples while they were on the road to Emmaus after Jesus' death on the cross: "Then he said unto them, O fools, and slow of heart to believe all that the prophets have spoken: Ought not Christ to have suffered these things, and to enter into his glory? And beginning at Moses and all the prophets, he expounded unto them in all the scriptures the things concerning himself" (Luke 24: 25–27).

Accordingly, at the end of each chapter of this book I have inserted appropriate lists of Scripture verses annotated by the appropriate paragraphs in this book.

My basic research conclusions come from my prayer requests and answers for spiritual enlightenment from God's Holy Spirit, my own rationale, life experiences, and reading. Additionally, I have learned from other Bible scholars' knowledge, understanding, and wisdom [See Appendix 1]. It was important to me that any agreements or disagreements with my rationale and conclusions could be easily resolved by perusing the Bible references listed in this book.

I used the 1967 New Schofield Reference Bible for my Scripture quotations, because it is a comprehensive and well supported Scripture reference source that outlines God's path to spiritual perfection through in-depth study and obedience to God's Word (Prov 25:2; 2 Tim 3:16–17; 1 Jn Chs 3 and 4; 1 Tim 1:5). In addition, the Scofield Reference Bible notes reinforce that God's Agape Love (Jn 21:15–17; 1 Jn 4:12–13) is absolutely and eternally unconditional, enduring, and respectful (Rom 5:5; Rom 8:2; Rom 8:14–17) in contrast to human love's many spiritual shortcomings (Mt 15:1–9; Jn 3:11–12; Jn 5:42). True unconditional, enduring, and respectful "Charity" is equivalent to God's Agape Love (1 Cor 13:4–13; 1 Jn 4:12–13).

I also wanted to share how I obtained eternal salvation by becoming spiritually born-again. It was my free-will faith decision to personally accept Jesus' love sacrifice (2 Tim 3:15–17; 2 Pet 1:20–21; 1 Tim 1:5; Heb 11:6; Rom 10:9–10; Jn 5:24; Eph 1:13; Isa 56:15).

Chapter One

Searching for the "Spiritual Missing Part" in My Life

(Prov 25:2; Jn 3:3–12; Prov 3:5–6; Jn 3:3, 5–7; Jn 5:24; Titus 3:5; Eph 1:13)

During my first 27 years of life, four of my most concerning questions were about life, love, and death. In addition, I felt that I had a "spiritual missing part" in my life. I felt an absence of true, complete, and comprehensive joy, love, and happiness. This book has been written to share my faith journey in life, the answers I've found to these four life questions, and the associated Bible research. In other words, I want to share how to avoid eternity in hell by choosing eternity in heaven through God's simple plan of salvation by trusting in Jesus' love and his love sacrifice on the cross. I have learned to place my trust in the fundamentals of his promises with the pure, trusting faith of a child.[1]

This book reflects my consideration of key relevant life factors, questions, and concerns in my life as well as the rationale, logic, and my conclusions on why I choose eternity in heaven, which is full of God's love, as my eternal destiny in lieu of eternity in hell, where no love exists. The content also presents how I came to understand that God is a God of pure love. This understanding was the key to inspiring me to become a spiritually born-again Christian [2].

The ideas presented in this book revolve around the identification, clarification, and employment of God's concept of love (Matt 22:36–40), basic spiritual growth practices (Eph Ch 4), basic Bible truths, and associated Bible lessons[3].

The Bible states that God is Love. He is pure love that is holy, loving, and just, always (1 Jn Ch 4). Through his love for us, God sent his son, Jesus, to cover the consequences of our sins through his sacrificial death on the cross (1 Pet 3:18). In essence, Jesus suffered an excruciating "hell" experience, totally devoid of love, as the consequence for humanity's sin during the three dark hours on the cross (Heb 10:11–18; Jn 19:30). Jesus set up a free will choice option account for me to stay out of hell if I so choose. From studying the Bible, I realized that I needed to personally accept Jesus' love and his sacrifice for me in order to avoid hell. Giving me a choice was totally in concert with a God of pure and complete love (Jn 19:30; Rom 10:4; Heb Ch 10).

The Bible says that I should show sincere trust in Jesus and my love for him by thanking him. I show this through complete faith and trust, expressing my love, thankfulness, and joy, and looking forward to receiving his many blessings (Gal 6:7–8; Matt 7:2). These grateful, thankful, and humble actions help me to have the right perspective. I have been "spiritually born-again" and I will live in heaven with him for all eternity. Choosing Jesus' eternal salvation provides me with a loving mindset and the opportunity for receiving and sharing even more blessings.[4]

Spiritual Faith and Growth from the Word of God

I have used the Bible verses in this book to provide readers with the opportunity to research for themselves the truth about Jesus' sacrifice and to accept, by their free will, eternal salvation through Jesus' faith promises. I have repeated several key Bible verses in this book for the following reasons:

(1) To increase readers' faith and trust in Jesus through understanding *God's love concept.*
(2) To increase readers' knowledge, understanding, and wisdom of God and *his spiritual mind-set.*
(3) To increase readers' subsequent spiritual growth through use of basic *spiritual fundamental practices.*
(4) To provide readers with a better understanding of the logic of God's truths.

I have also arranged the sequence of the Bible verses listed in this book in various chapters to allow the reader to more easily comprehend and follow God's reasoning and logic for specific spiritual truth subjects. Further, I have italicized key words in the Bible verses to allow the readers to focus on critical truths reflected in the verses. After all, using God's own words as a reference source should be the best way to present God's truths, logic, and love mindset.

The following are examples of my four methodologies for using God's Word in this book to increase the readers' spiritual knowledge, understanding, and wisdom.[5]

Prov 2:6, "For the LORD giveth wisdom: out of his mouth cometh knowledge and understanding."

Prov 3:5–6, "Trust in the LORD with all thine heart; and lean not unto thine own understanding. In all thy ways acknowledge him, and he shall direct thy paths."

Prov 1:7, "The fear of the LORD is the beginning of knowledge, but fools despise wisdom and instruction." (Please note: the word "fear" used here would be more appropriately translated as "reverential trust" in my opinion, which is more in concert with a God of love.)

Rom 10:17, "So then faith cometh by hearing, and hearing by the word of God."

Jn 1:1, "In the beginning was the Word, and the Word was with God, and the Word was God." (Jesus is the incarnate, living Word of God.)

Rev 19:13, "And he was clothed with a vesture dipped in blood: and his name is called The Word of God."

Jn 14:6, "Jesus saith unto him, I am the way, the truth, and the life: no man cometh unto the Father but by me."

Heb 4:12, "For the word of God is quick, and powerful, and sharper than any twoedged sword, piercing even to the dividing asunder of soul and spirit, and of the joints and marrow, and is a discerner of the thoughts and intents of the heart."

2 Tim 3:16–17, "All scripture is given by inspiration of God, and is profitable for doctrine, for reproof, for correction, for instruction in righteousness: That the man of God may be perfect, thoroughly furnished unto all good works."

Prov 25:2, "It is the glory of God to conceal a thing: but the honour of kings is to search out a matter."

In cases of counterfeit money, FBI agents study real money. Why? Because if you know what the real thing looks like it is easier to detect counterfeit money. Similarly, God wants people to decide to sincerely get to know him and his mindset through diligent, persistent, and persevering study of his Word, so that they can make spiritually wise decisions.

Jn 3:5–7, "Jesus answered, Verily, verily, I say unto thee, Except a man be born of water and of the Spirit, he cannot enter into the kingdom of God. That which is born of the flesh is flesh; and that which is born of the Spirit is spirit. Marvel not that I said unto thee, Ye must be born again."

Jn 3:9–12, "Nicodemus answered and said unto him, How can these things be? Jesus answered and said unto him, Art thou a teacher of Israel, and knowest not these things? Verily, verily, I say unto thee, We speak that we do know, and testify to that we have seen; and ye receive not our witness. If I have told you earthly things, and ye believe not, how shall ye believe, if I tell you of heavenly things?" In other words, if we don't seek the spiritual truth of God's words, how could we ever understand the value of his wisdom and eternal love for us?

Jn 6:63, "It is the spirit that quickeneth (gives life); the flesh profiteth nothing: the words that I speak unto you, they are spirit, and they are life."

Jn 4:24, "God is a Spirit: and they that worship him must worship him in spirit and in truth."

Jn 11:25–26, "Jesus said unto her, I am the resurrection, and the life: he that believeth in me, though he were dead [spiritually], yet shall he live. And whosoever liveth and believeth in me shall never die [spiritually]. Believest thou this?"

Eph 1:13, "In whom ye also trusted, after ye heard the word of truth, the gospel of your salvation: in whom also after that ye believed, ye were sealed with that holy Spirit of promise…."

Rom 10:9–10, "That if thou shalt confess with thy mouth the Lord Jesus, and shalt believe in thine heart that God hath raised him from the dead, thou shalt be saved. For with the heart man believeth unto righteousness; and with the mouth confession is made unto salvation."

Jn 15:13, "Greater love hath no man than this, that a man lay down his life for his friends."

Rom 8:16, "The Spirit itself beareth witness, with our spirit, that we are the children of God."

Rom 8:14, "For as many as are led by the Spirit of God, they are the sons of God."

Eph 4:4–6, "There is one body, and one Spirit, even as ye are called in one hope of your calling; One Lord, one faith, one baptism, One God and Father of all, who is above all, and through all and in you all." (Note: all spiritually born-again Christians' spirits are immediately re-united into God's Holy Spirit forever and will live with him in heaven for all eternity).

Questions Concerning My Life, Love, Death, and "Spiritual Missing Part"

Before I was 27 years old, I would often question how I could determine and understand the purpose of my life, love, and death. I would specifically question if "death" was consistent with a God of love. Is the definition of "death" in the Bible addressing the expiration of my earthly body or does it address the "spiritual death" of my spirit and soul?[6] During my search for answers regarding my existence and purpose, it became apparent that I was also missing something in my life relative to my inner joy, peace, and happiness. I questioned if there was some purposeful rationale, meaning, and design for my existence. I also questioned how or where I could search to determine if my existence had some main purpose of which I was unaware. I was also uncertain where to begin to find the answers regarding the "spiritual missing part" in my life.[7]

Bible's Definition of "Death"

Most of all, I was concerned that if there was life after death, would I have the opportunity to make a decision about where I would spend eternity? In particular, I wanted to resolve in my mind the truth of the following Bible verses relative to my four life questions:

Jn 8:23–24, "And he [Jesus] said unto them, Ye are from beneath; and I am from above: ye are of this world; I am not of this world. I said therefore, unto you, that ye shall die in your sins: for if ye believe not that I am he, ye shall die in your sins."

Jn 11:25–26, "Jesus said unto her, I am the resurrection, and the life: he that believeth in me, though he were dead [spiritually], yet shall he live. And whosoever liveth and believeth in me shall never die [spiritually]. Believest thou this?" Note the repetition in these verses, something God uses throughout the Bible to make an important point.

Jn 3:3–7, "Jesus answered and said unto him, Verily, verily, I say unto thee, Except a man be born again, he cannot see the kingdom of God. Nicodemus saith unto him, How can a man be born when he is old? Can he enter the second time into his mother's womb, and be born? Jesus answered, Verily, verily, I say to you, Except a man be born of water and of the Spirit [i.e. Holy Spirit], he cannot enter in the kingdom of God. That which is born of the flesh is flesh; and that which is born of the Spirit is spirit. Marvel not that I say unto you, you must be born again."

Gal 6:7–9, "Be not deceived; God is not mocked: for whatsoever a men soweth, that shall he also reap. For he that soweth to his flesh shall of the flesh reap corruption; but he the soweth to the Spirit shall of the Spirit reap life everlasting. And let us not be weary in well doing: for in due season we shall reap, if we faint not."

Jn 8:31–32, "Then said Jesus to those Jews which believed on him, If ye continue in my word, then are ye my disciples indeed; And ye shall know the truth, and the truth shall make you free."

Rom 5:8, "But God commendeth his love toward us, in that, while we were yet sinners, Christ died for us."

Heb 12:4, "Ye have not yet resisted unto blood, striving against sin."

Luke 22:42–44, "Saying, Father, if thou be willing, remove this cup from me: nevertheless, not my will, but thine, be done. And there appeared an angel unto him from heaven, strengthening him. And being in an agony, he prayed more earnestly: and his sweat was as it were great drops of blood falling down to the ground."

Jn 8:51, Jesus said, "Verily, verily, I say unto you, If a man keeps my saying he shall never see death."

Eph 2:8–9, "For by grace are ye saved through faith; and that not of yourselves: it is the gift of God: Not of works, lest any man should boast." God's grace is a free, undeserved gift not a blessing request before a meal!

Rom 10:9–10, "That if thou shalt confess with thy mouth the Lord Jesus, and shalt believe in thine heart that God hath raised him from the dead, thou shalt be saved. For with the heart man believeth unto righteousness, and with the mouth confession is made unto salvation."

1 Cor 6:17, "But he that is joined unto the Lord is one spirit."

Eph 1:13 "In whom ye also trusted, after ye heard the word of truth, the gospel of your salvation: in whom also after that ye believed, ye were sealed with that holy Spirit of promise...."

Titus 3:5, "Not by works of righteousness which we have done, but according to his mercy he saved us, by washing of regeneration, and renewing of the Holy Ghost [Holy Spirit]...."

Isa 57:15, "For thus says the high and lofty One that inhabiteth eternity, whose name is Holy; I dwell in the high and the holy place, with him also that is of a contrite and humble spirit, to revive the spirit of the humble, and to revive the heart of the contrite ones."

2 Cor 7:10, "For godly sorrow worketh repentance to salvation not to be repented of: but the sorrow of the world worketh death".

Isa 45:22, "Look unto me, and be ye saved, all the ends of the earth: for I am God, and there is none else."

Worldly Wisdom versus God's Love Concept

As I began my research, I considered that a lot of human songs, books, stories, dreams, expectations, actions, poems, dances, movies, commercials, organizations, sports, etc. focus on these questions of life, love, and death and their impact on humans at various stages in life. Apparently, I was not the only one looking for true, fulfilling, and realistic answers. I wondered if a better understanding of God's concept of love would possibly help me in my quest. I discovered that God's "Love Concept" is for everyone to be the best that they can be, to love as God does, to receive his blessings, and to spend eternity in heaven with him.[8]

Additionally, I questioned if God had a better plan for my life than my own plans. Could he answer my life, love, death, and "spiritual missing part" questions? Were the answers based solely upon God's love for me? I concluded that I needed to study the Bible in-depth. My worldly education, religious training, and life experiences up to this point had not provided me with reasonable answers to my four life questions (Rom 1:16–25).

After much in-depth Bible study, I came to the realization that God's love is based upon him sharing his love, blessings, and wisdom with me, not because he wants to exert control over me by requiring re-payment, or exacting a price for his love. Rather, God loves me just for my free-will return of love. In other words, God wants me to obey his commands and directions out of my own free will choices. As a result of choosing to obey in love, I will grow spiritually, I will be blessed for my choices here, and one day I will live with him forever in heaven as his family member.[9]

Life Search Questions and Initial Conclusion

One of my observations was that other people appeared to be as frustrated, confused, and disappointed as I was in seeking answers to their own life questions. I also felt that, like me, others did not know where to search for answers. After further research, analysis, and initial in-depth Bible study; I felt that the below statistical data and pertinent Bible verses respectively supported my conclusion that I needed to study the Bible, not worldly knowledge, understanding, and wisdom, to provide me with direction and answers.[10]

Statistical Data

Suicides in the United States have increased 35% from 1999 to 2018 according to *The National Institute of Mental Health*, Jan 2021. The number is about 48,344 per year now.

Illegal drugs today are used by more than twenty million people in the United States, according to an article in *Newsweek*, Jan 2021.

Church attendance today has reduced by 50% in the USA over the last ten years per Lifeway Research Organization, Jan 2021.

Even though there are 380,000 churches in the USA today, many people are becoming less enchanted with formal churches and are seeking more one-on-one, personal, transparent, and meaningful spiritual relationships according to a National Congregational Study Survey, dated 22 Aug, 2020. People are becoming more involved in individual or small group Bible studies/home churches where there is a greater opportunity to exchange and share ideas, comments, questions, and life experiences and revelations.

While the Bible defines the Church as the people, not a physical church building, Heb 10:25 and Eph 4 respectively advise not to forsake assembling together in order to encourage, uplift, and edify one another in love. The Church can be a great resource for Bible teaching, fellowship, and spiritual growth.

I questioned what organizations and informational sources I had visited in my past, besides a church, that encouraged spiritual knowledge, understanding, and wisdom to answer my four life questions. There were none. I concluded therefore that I needed to do my homework and select a church that followed a faith doctrine that lined up with Jesus' teachings[11.] In addition, the church that I selected would have to provide me with sound spiritual knowledge, understanding, wisdom, and fellowship to enable me to spiritually grow into a mature Christian following Jesus' Love Concept and life examples (Matt 11:28–30; Phi 4; Rom 8:31–32).

Consideration of Pertinent Religious Bible Verses

Some of the pertinent Bible verses I encountered in my initial study appear to be the cornerstone Scriptures for many church denominations' beliefs, training, and life standards. Nevertheless, though the verses are easy to read, at first I did not really understand the meaning of these Scriptures relative to my four life questions. More importantly I did not know how to apply these verses to my life until I started to study the Bible in earnest. Few people could clearly explain these Bible verses and their relevance. In particular, there was confusion among many folks concerning the definitions of many Bible words and spiritual concepts such as life, love, death, law, faith, hope, trust, grace, soul, spirit, heaven, hell, Jerusalem, Christ, Jesus, etc.

Matt 22:36–40, "Master, which is the great commandment in the law? Jesus said unto him, Thou shalt love the Lord thy God with all thy heart, and with all thy soul, and with all thy mind. This is the first and great commandment. And the second is like it, Thou shalt love thy neighbour as thyself. On these two commandments hang all the law and prophets [the Mosaic Law]." Use of the word law in the Bible refers to teachings or instruction. (Ps 19:7–11 and Ps 119). The above verses are God's Concept of Love clearly defined. (See Rom 8:2 and Rom 3:20–25).

Gal 3:10–12, "For as many as are of the works of the law [the Mosaic Law] are under the curse: for it is written, Cursed is every one that continueth not in all things which are written in the book of the law to do them. But that no man is justified by the [Mosaic] law in the sight of God, it is evident: for, The just shall live by faith. And the law is not of faith: but, the man that doeth them [i.e. tries to comply with the Mosaic Law: the ten commandments, social judgments, and worship ordinances] shall live in them [consequences of the Mosaic Law]."

Mark 7:7–9, "Howbeit, in vain do they worship me, teaching for doctrines the commandments of men. For laying aside the commandment of God, ye hold the tradition of men, as the washing of pots and cups; and many other such like things ye do, And he said unto them. Full well ye reject the commandment of God, that ye may keep your own tradition."

Mark 7:13, "Making the word of God of none effect through your tradition, which ye have delivered: and many such things do ye."

Gal 6:7–9, "Be not deceived; God is not mocked: for whatsoever a man soweth, that shall he also reap. For he that soweth to his flesh shall of the flesh reap corruption; but he that soweth to the Spirit shall of the Spirit reap life everlasting. And let us not be weary in well doing; for in due season we shall reap, if we faint not." In other words, the above verses define God's Golden Rule (i.e. God wants us to be all that we can be, so that we can better understand that our decisions require fair, loving, and just consequences if true love and true relationships are be realized, understood, and gainfully employed and enjoyed in our lives).

Matt 7:1–2, "Judge not, that ye be not judged. For with what judgment ye judge, ye shall be judged: and with what measure ye mete, it shall be measured to you again."

Rom 2:1–16 (paraphrased): I will be judged according to my deeds, my knowledge, understanding, and wisdom of the truth; and the gospel, which is the good news of Jesus and his gift of eternal salvation that allows whoever believes and trusts in him to re-unite their spirit with God's Holy Spirit forever.

Matt 7:13–14, "Enter in at the narrow gate; for wide is the gate, and broad is the way that leadeth to destruction, and many there be who go in that way. Because narrow is the gate and hard is the way, which leadeth unto life; and few there be that find it."

Jn 3:3–7, "Jesus answered, and said unto him, Verily, verily, I say unto thee, Except a man be born again [spiritually born-again, or becoming spiritually alive], he cannot see the kingdom of God. Nicodemus saith to him, How can a man be born when he is old? Can he enter the second time into his mother's womb, and be born? Jesus answered, Verily, verily, I say to you, Except a man be born of water and of the Spirit, he cannot enter in the kingdom of God. That which is born of the flesh is flesh; and that which is born of the Spirit is spirit. Marvel not that I say unto thee, you must be born again."

Heb 11:6, "But without faith it is impossible to please him: for he that cometh to God must believe that he is, and that he is a rewarder of them that diligently seek him."

Matt 6:33, "But seek ye first the kingdom of God, and his righteousness, and all these things (life's spiritual and basic needs) shall be added unto you."

Matt 11:28–30, "Come unto me all ye that labor, and are heavy burden, and I will give you rest. Take my yoke upon you, and learn of me; for I am meek and lowly in heart, and ye shall find rest unto your souls. For my yoke is easy, and my burden is light."

Jn 5:24, "Verily, verily, I say unto you, He that heareth my word, and believeth on him that sent me, hath everlasting life, and shall not come into condemnation; but is passed from death unto life." In summary, whoever chooses by their own free will and faith to personally accept Christ's free love gift of undeserved grace and eternal salvation, will live with him in a new body forever. Or people may choose to reject his free gift and live in a place devoid of God's love forever.[12]

Rom 10:9–10, "That if thou shalt confess with thy mouth the Lord Jesus, and shalt believe in thine heart that God hath raised him from the dead, thou shalt be saved. For with the heart man believeth unto righteousness, and with the mouth confession is made unto salvation."

Titus 3:5, "Not by works of righteousness which we have done, but according to his mercy he saved us, by the washing of regeneration, and renewing of the Holy Ghost [Holy Spirit]".

Rom 3:20–25, "Therefore, by the deeds of the law [the Mosaic Law] there shall no flesh be justified in his sight: for by the law is the knowledge of sin [the law of sin and death]. But now the righteousness of God without the law is manifested, being witnessed by the law and the prophets; Even the righteousness of God which is by faith of Jesus Christ unto all and upon all them that believe: for there is no difference: For all have sinned and come short of the glory of God, Being justified freely by his grace through the redemption that is in Christ Jesus: Whom God hath set forth to be a propitiation through faith in his blood, to declare his righteousness for the remission of sins that are past, through the forbearance of God…"

Rom 8:2, "For the law of the Spirit of life in Christ Jesus hath made me free from the law of sin and death." Use of the word *law* in the Bible refers to teachings/instruction. Here it refers to the Mosaic Law, which is made up of the ten commandments and more than six hundred worship ordinances and social judg-ments spelled out in the books of Exodus, Leviticus, Numbers, and repeated in the book of Deuteronomy.

Eph 1:13, "In whom ye also trusted, after ye heard the word of truth, the gospel of your salvation: in whom also after that ye believed, ye were sealed with that holy Spirit of promise…."

1 Cor 2:9–10, "But as it is written, Eye hath not seen, nor eye heard, neither have entered into the heart of man, the things which God hath prepared for them that love him. But God hath revealed them unto us by his Spirit: for the Spirit searcheth all things, yea, the deep things of God."

Rom 8:28, "And we know that all things work together for good to them that love God, to them who are called according to his purpose."

Mic 6:8, "He hath shewed thee, O man, what is good; and what doth the LORD require of thee, but to do justly, and to love mercy, and to walk humbly with thy God."

2 Cor 12:9–10, "And he said unto me, My grace is sufficient for thee: for my strength is made perfect in weakness [i.e. when I follow God's plan in my life, in lieu of following my life plan for me]. Most gladly therefore will I rather glory in my infirmities, that the power of Christ may rest upon me. Therefore, I take pleasure in infirmities, in reproaches, in distresses for Christ's sake: for when I am weak, then I am strong." In my opinion, we receive more blessings, spiritual growth, and spiritual wisdom from trials, tribulations, and arduous growing experiences than from doing nothing and remaining like "baby Christians."[13]

Prov 3:5–6, "Trust in the LORD with all thine heart; and lean not unto thine own understanding. In all thy ways acknowledge him, and he shall direct thy paths."

Ps 37:3–5, "Trust in the LORD, and do good; so shalt thou dwell in the land, and verily thou shalt be fed. Delight thyself also in the LORD, and he shall give thee the desires of thine heart. Commit thy way unto the LORD; trust also in him, and he shall bring it to pass."

Key Eternal Life Bible Verses

After joining a sincere Bible study group, certain key Bible verses sparked my motivation in my search to answer my questions.

Matt 16:26, "For what is a man profited, if he shall gain the whole world, and lose his own soul? or what shall a man give in exchange for his soul?"

Rom 5:8, "But God commendeth his love toward us, in that, while we were yet sinners, Christ died for us."

Rom 3:23, "For all have sinned, and come short of the glory of God." To sin is to have a thought, word, or action that is non-loving.

Rom 3:20, "Therefore by the deeds of the law there shall no flesh be justified in his sight: for by the law is the knowledge of sin."

Jam 2:10, "For whosoever shall keep the whole law, and yet offend in one point, he is guilty of all." Adhering to God's Love Concept (or the spiritual law of life) is to love God first and your neighbor as yourself. Otherwise, my thoughts, words, and actions are sin-motivated: selfish, inconsiderate, and disrespectful, because they transgress God's Love Concept.[14]

Gal 3:10–12, "For as many as are of the works of the law are under the curse: for it is written, Cursed is everyone that continueth not in all things which are written in the book of the law, to do them. But that no man is justified by the law in the sight of God, it is evident: for, The just shall live by faith. And the law is not of faith: but, the man that doeth them [i.e. tries to comply with the Mosaic Law] shall live in them [the consequences of the Mosaic Law]."

Luke 16:10, "He that is faithful in that which is least is faithful also in much: and he that is unjust in the least is unjust also in much." My mindset influences my thoughts, words, and actions. My life decisions and actions are accordingly pursued and identified, therefore, as either being holy, loving, and just (following God's Love Concept), or not. In other words: a liar will lie; a thief will steal; a cheater will cheat; a true Christian will endeavor to follow God's will in their thoughts, words, and actions.

Jn 3:16–17, "For God so loved the world that he gave his only begotten Son, that whosoever believeth in him should not perish, but have everlasting life. For God sent not his Son into the world to condemn the world; but that the world through him might be saved." Note: Jesus Christ, translated, means "God saved his anointed one." A true love relationship requires both parties to have a faith, trust, and reciprocal holy, loving, and just attitudes/thoughts/actions toward one another based upon their own free-will decisions, not because of forced decisions.

Jn 3:3–7, "Jesus answered, and said unto him, Verily, verily, I say unto thee, Except a man be born again, he cannot see the kingdom of God. Nicodemus said to him, How can a man be born when he is old? Can he enter the second time into his mother's womb, and be born? Jesus answered, Verily, verily, I say to you, Except a man be born of water and of the Spirit [Holy Spirit], he cannot enter into the kingdom of God. That which is born of the flesh is flesh; and that which is born of the Spirit is spirit. Marvel not that I said unto thee, Ye must be born again."

Eph 1:13, "In whom ye also trusted, after ye heard the word of truth, the gospel of your salvation: in whom also after that ye believed, ye were sealed with that Holy Spirit of promise...."

Eph 4:30, "And grieve not the Holy Spirit of God, whereby ye are sealed unto the day of redemption."

Rom 1:17, "For therein is the righteousness of God revealed from faith to faith: as it is written, The just shall live by faith."

Jam 4:10, "Humble yourselves in the sight of the Lord, and he shall lift you up." We learn more when we are humble, than when we are proud.

Prov 22:4, "By humility and the fear of the LORD are riches, and honour, and life."

1 Pet 5:5–6, "Likewise, ye younger, submit yourselves unto the elder. Yea, all of you be subject one to another, and be clothed with humility: for God resisteth the proud, and giveth grace to the humble. Humble yourselves therefore under the mighty hand of God, that he may exalt you in due time."

Eph 2:8–9, "For by grace are ye saved through faith; and that not of yourselves: it is the gift of God: Not of works, lest any man should boast." God's grace is a free, undeserved gift!

Rev 20:15, "And whosoever was not found written in the book of life was cast into the lake of fire."

Rom 5:7–9, "For scarcely for a righteous man will one die; yet perhaps for a good man some would even dare to die. But God commendeth his love toward us in that, while we were yet sinners, Christ died for us. Much more then, being now justified by his blood [assurance that my sins are covered by Jesus' love sacrifice on the cross], we shall be saved from wrath through him." But only if I choose him and accept his salvation.[15]

Rom 5:10–11, "For if, when we were enemies, we were reconciled to God by the death of his Son, much more, being reconciled, we shall be saved by his life. And not only so, but we also joy in God through our Lord Jesus Christ, by whom we have now received the reconciliation".

Luke 24:25–27, "Then he [Jesus] said unto them O foolish ones, and slow of heart to believe all that the prophets have spoken! Ought not Christ to have suffered these things, and to enter into his glory? And beginning at Moses and all the prophets, he expounded unto them, in all the scriptures, the things concerning himself."

Titus 2:11, "For the grace of God that bringeth salvation hath appeared to all men." This includes all of God's creation.

Rom 1:19–20, "Because that which may be known of God is manifest in them, for God hath shown it unto them. For the invisible things of him from the creation of the world are clearly seen; being understood by the things that are made, even his eternal power and Godhead, so that they are without excuse."

Jesus' Love and My Reconciliation Bible Verses

After being involved in a sincere Bible study for some months, the in-depth study of the following Bible verses helped me to better understand in my spirit and soul, and how much Jesus loves me. I discovered that our restored spirit helps us to connect to God (Jn 4:24), and our soul is the essence of ourselves—our thoughts, thinking, desires, decisions, etc. These Bible verses helped me to understand how important it was to understand what part Jesus' love played in my eternal salvation in heaven. These Bible verses also helped me to understand that I needed to be spiritually reconciled with God through Jesus by believing or trusting in Jesus' love for me and his love sacrifice on the cross to cover my sins (Col 1:20–22; 2 Cor 5:14–21). These Bible verses also helped me to realize how simple and easy Jesus had made it for me to become a "spiritually born-again Christian." Ultimately my spiritual reconciliation with God through Jesus Christ was achieved when I finally became a "spiritually born-again" Christian (Jn 3:3–7; Jn 3:15–18). My spiritual conversion occurred when I finally understood and chose to accept God's life purpose, meaning, and fulfillment for me. I knew my faith actions, resolve, and mindset needed to be reconciled with God based upon my trust in his actions and promises.

2 Tim 3:15–17, "And that from a child thou hast known the holy scriptures, which are able to make thee wise unto salvation through faith which is in Christ Jesus. All scripture is given by

inspiration of God, and it profitable for doctrine, for reproof, for correction, for instruction in righteousness, That the man of God may be perfect, thoroughly furnished unto all good works."

1 Tim 2:4–5, "Who will have all men to be saved, and to come unto the knowledge of the truth. For there is one God, and one mediator between God and men, the man, Christ Jesus."

Rom 8:32, "He that spared not his own Son, but delivered him up for us all, how shall he not with him also freely give us all things"?

Luke 22:42–44, "Saying, Father, if thou be willing, remove this cup from me; nevertheless, not my will, but thine, be done. And there appeared an angel unto him from heaven, strengthening him. And being in an agony, he prayed more earnestly; and his sweat was, as it were, great drops of blood falling down to the ground."

Heb 12:4, "Ye have not yet resisted unto blood, striving against sin."

Rev 19:13, "And he [Jesus] was clothed with a vesture dipped in blood; and his name is called The Word of God."

Jn 1:1, "In the beginning was the Word, and the Word was with God, and the Word was God."

Heb 4:12, "For the word of God is quick, and powerful, and sharper than any twoedged sword, piercing even to the dividing asunder of soul and spirit, and of the joints and marrow, and is a discerner of the thoughts and intents of the heart."

Rom 3:20–25, "Therefore, by the deeds of the law [Mosaic Law] there shall no flesh be justified in his sight; for by the Mosaic Law is the knowledge of sin (i.e. law of sin and death). But now the righteousness of God apart from the law is manifested, being witnessed by the law and the prophets, Even the righteousness of God which is by faith of Jesus Christ unto all and upon all them that believe; for there is no difference. For all have sinned and come short of the glory of God; Being justified freely by his grace through the redemption that is in Christ Jesus, whom God hath set forth to be a propitiation through faith in his blood, to declare his righteousness for the remission of sins that are past, through the forbearance of God."

Gal 3:10–12, "For as many as are of the works of the law are under the curse; for it is written, Cursed is everyone that continueth not in all things which are written in the book of the law, to do them. But that no man is justified by the law in the sight of God, it is evident; for the just shall live by faith. And the law is not of faith, but the man that does them shall live in them."

Jn 3:3–7, "Jesus answered, and said unto him, Verily, verily, I say unto you, Except a man be born again [spiritually born again], he cannot see the kingdom of God. Nicodemus said to him, how can a man be born when he is old? Can he enter the second time into his mother's womb, and be born? Jesus answered, Verily, verily, I say to you, Except a man be born of water and of the Spirit [Holy Spirit], he cannot enter in the kingdom of God. That which is born of the flesh is flesh; and that which is born of the Spirit [Holy Spirit] is spirit. Marvel not that I say unto you, Ye must be born-again."

Jn 14:6, "Jesus saith unto him, I am the way, the truth, and the life; no man cometh to the Father but by me." In essence, I realized that my spirit must be reunited with Jesus' Holy Spirit to be spiritually born again and to become a child of God forever.

Matt 18:3–5, "And [Jesus} said, Verily I say unto you, Except you be converted, and become as little children [in your faith in Jesus Christ], ye shall not enter into the kingdom of heaven. Whosoever, therefore, shall humble himself as this little child, the same is greatest in the kingdom of heaven. And whosoever shall receive one such little child in my name receiveth me."

Isa 57:15, "For thus saith the high and lofty One who inhabiteth eternity, whose name is Holy: I dwell in the high and the holy place, with him also who is of a contrite and humble spirit, to revive the spirit of the humble, and to revive the heart of the contrite ones."

2 Cor 7:10, "For godly sorrow worketh repentance to salvation not to be repented of; but the sorrow of the world worketh death."

Heb 11:6, "But without faith it is impossible to please him: for he that cometh to God must believe that he is, and that he is a rewarder of them that diligently seek him."

Eph 2:8–9, "For by grace are ye saved through faith; and that not of yourselves: it is the gift of God: Not of works, lest any man should boast".

Matt 22:36–40, "Master, which is the great commandment in the law? Jesus said unto him, Thou shalt love the Lord thy God with all thy heart, and with all thy soul, and with all thy mind. This is the first and great commandment. And the second is like it, Thou shalt love thy neighbour as thyself. On these two commandments hang all the law and prophets" (See Rom 3:20–25).

Rom 8:2, "For the law of the Spirit of life in Christ Jesus hath made me free from the law of sin and death." God's Spirit of Life law through Christ Jesus [God's Love Concept] replaces the Mosaic Law's consequences. Remember that the use of the word *law* in the Bible refers to teachings or instruction. (Ps 19:7 to 11 and Ps 119).

1 Tim 1:5, "Now the end of the commandment is charity out of a pure heart, and of a good conscience, and of faith unfeigned." God wants me to be holy, loving, and just in all my life decisions. I will receive many blessings accordingly and my mindset will also grow more loving and more in concert with God's Love Concept.

Eph 1:13, "In whom ye also trusted, after ye heard the word of truth, the gospel of your salvation: in whom also after that ye believed, ye were sealed with that Holy Spirit of promise…."

Rom 10:9–10, "That if thou shalt confess with thy mouth the Lord Jesus, and shalt believe in thine heart that God hath raised him from the dead, thou shalt be saved. For with the heart man believeth unto righteousness, and with the mouth confession is made unto salvation."

Jn 3:15–16, "That whosoever believeth in him should not perish, but have eternal life. For God so loved the world, that He gave his only begotten Son, that whosoever believeth in him should not perish, but have everlasting life."

Jn 15:13, "Greater love hath no man than this, that a man lay down his life for his friends."

Titus 3:5, "Not by works of righteousness which we have done, but according to his mercy he saved us, by washing of regeneration, and renewing of the Holy Ghost [Holy Spirit]...."

Ezek 36:26–27, "A new heart also will I give you and a new spirit will I put within you: and I will take away the stony heart out of your flesh, and I will give you a heart of flesh, and I will put my spirit within you, and cause you to walk in my statues, and ye shall keep my judgements, and do them." (See also 2 Cor 6:16)

2 Cor 5:17–19, "Therefore, if any man be in Christ, he is a new creature: old things are passed away; behold, all things are become new. And all things are of God, who has reconciled us to himself by Jesus Christ, and hath given to us the ministry of reconciliation; To wit, that God was in Christ, reconciling the world unto himself, not imputing their trespasses unto them; and hath committed unto us the word of reconciliation."

1 Cor 2:9–10, "But as it is written, Eye hath not seen, nor eye heard, neither have entered into the heart of man, the things which God hath prepared for them that love him. But God hath revealed them unto us by his Spirit: for the Spirit searcheth all things, yea, the deep things of God." God's blessings for those who love him are his ever faithful, unending, unwavering love, his assured eternal salvation, re-uniting with God's Holy Spirit, and the eternal joys of heaven now.

Simple Guidelines for My Godly Spiritual Christian Growth

- Pray daily: Talk to God to stay in his Love Concept mindset.[16]

- Listen to God daily: Study your Bible in order to grow in the knowledge, understanding, and wisdom of God.[17]
- Talk, walk, and live within God's mindset.[18]

Key Bible Verses

There are several Bible verses that are the basis of my rationale, logic, and conclusions in this book. These verses support the truth that living in God's Love Concept promotes spiritual growth, a direct personal relationship with God, access to his knowledge, understanding, and wisdom through the Holy Spirit, membership in God's family forever, eternal salvation in heaven, and receiving abundant blessings.

2 Pet 1:20–21, "Knowing this first, that no prophecy of the scripture is of any private interpretation. For the prophecy came not in old time by the will of man: but holy men of God spake as they were moved by the Holy Spirit."

Luke 24:25–27, "Then he [Jesus] said unto them, O fools, and slow of heart to believe all that the prophets [of the Old Testament] have spoken: Ought not Christ to have suffered these things, and to enter into his glory? And beginning at Moses and all the prophets, he expounded unto them in all the scriptures, the things concerning himself."

2 Tim 3:15–17, "And that from a child thou hast known the holy scriptures, which are able to make thee wise unto salvation through faith which is in Christ Jesus. All scripture is given by inspiration of God, and is profitable for doctrine, for reproof, for correction, for instruction in righteousness: That the man of God may be perfect, thoroughly furnished unto all good works."

Heb 4:12, "For the word of God is quick, and powerful, and sharper than any twoedged sword, piercing even to the dividing asunder of soul and spirit, and of the joints and marrow, and is a discerner of the thoughts and intents of the heart."

Rom 1:16–17, "For I am not ashamed of the gospel of Christ, for it is the power of God unto salvation to everyone the believeth; to the Jew first, and also to the Greek. For in it is the righteousness of God revealed from faith to faith; as it is written, the just shall live by faith."

Rom 8:1–4, "There is, therefore, now no condemnation to them who are in Christ Jesus, who walk not after the flesh, but after the Spirit. For the law of the Spirit of life in Christ Jesus hath made me free from the law of sin and death. For what the [Mosaic] Law could not do, in that it was weak through the flesh, God sending his own Son, in the likeness of sinful flesh and for sin, condemned sin in the flesh. That the righteousness of the law might be fulfilled in us, who walk not after the flesh, but after the Spirit."

Jn 8:51, "Verily, verily, I say unto you, If a man keep my sayings, he shall never see death."

Jn 11:25–26, "Jesus said unto her, I am the resurrection, and the life: he that believeth in me, though he were dead [spiritually], yet shall he live. And whosoever liveth and believeth in me shall never die [spiritually]. Believest thou this?"

Matt 22:29–32, "Jesus answered and said unto them, you do err, not knowing the scriptures, nor the power of God. For in the resurrection, they neither marry, nor are given in marriage, but are like the angels of God in heaven. But as touching the resurrection of the dead, have ye not read that which was spoken unto you by God saying, I am the God of Abraham, and the God of Isaac, and the God of Jacob? God is not the God of the dead, but of the living."

Jer 17:9–10, "The heart is deceitful above all things, and desperately wicked, who can know it? I, the LORD, search the heart, I test the conscience, even to give every man according to his ways, and according to the fruit of his doings."

Jn 5:24, "Verily, verily, I say unto you, He that hears my word, and believeth on him that sent me, has everlasting life, and shalt not come into judgment, but is passed from death [spiritual death] unto life [spiritual life]."

Rom 5:8–11, "But God commended his love toward us in that, while we were yet sinners, Christ died for us. Much more then, being now justified by his blood, we shall be saved from wrath through him. For if, when we were enemies, we were reconciled to God by the death of his Son. much more, being reconciled, we shall be saved by his life. And not only so, but we also have joy in God through our Lord Jesus Christ, by whom we have now received the reconciliation."

Jn 1:1, "In the beginning was the Word, and the Word was with God, and the Word was God." The word of God embodies all the treasures of God's knowledge, understanding, and wisdom.

Prov 2:6, "For the LORD giveth wisdom; out of his mouth cometh knowledge and understanding."

Heb 4:12, "For the word of God is quick, and powerful, and sharper than any twoedged sword, piercing even to the dividing asunder of soul and spirit, and of the joints and marrow, and is a discerner of the thoughts and intents of the heart."

Matt 22:36–40, "Master, which is the great commandment in the law? Jesus said unto him, Thou shalt love the Lord thy God with all thy heart, and with all thy soul, and with all thy mind. This is the first and great commandment. And the second is like it, Thou shalt love thy neighbour as thyself. On these two commandments hang all the law and prophets" (See Rom 8:2, Rom 3:20–25).

Rom 8:2, "For the law of the Spirit of life in Christ Jesus hath made me free from the law of sin and death."

1 Tim 1:5, "Now the end of the commandment is charity out of a pure heart, and of a good conscience, and of faith unfeigned." God wants me to be holy, loving, and just in all my life decisions; so I will receive many blessings accordingly and my mindset will also grow more loving and more in concert with God's Love Concept.

Jn 1:12–14, "But as many as received him, to them gave he power to become the sons of God, even to them that believe on his name: Which were born, not of blood, nor of the will of the flesh, nor of the will of man, but of God. And the Word was made flesh, and dwelt among us (and we beheld his glory, the glory as of the only begotten of the Father,) full of grace and truth."

Luke 18:17, "Verily I say unto you, Whosoever shall not receive the kingdom of God as a little child shall in no wise enter therein."

Rom 4:3, "For what saith the scripture? Abraham believed God, and it was counted unto him for righteousness."

Rom 10:17, "So then faith cometh by hearing, and hearing by the word of God."

Jn 3:5–7, "Jesus answered, Verily, verily, I say unto thee, Except a man be born of water and of the Spirit, he cannot enter into the kingdom of God. That which is born of the flesh is flesh; and that which is born of the Spirit is spirit. Marvel not that I said unto thee, Ye must be born again."

Jam 2:26, "For as the body without the spirit is dead, so faith without works is dead also."

Col 2:13–14, "And you, being dead in your sins and the uncircumcision of your flesh, hath he quickened [made alive] together with him, having forgiven you all trespasses; Blotting out the handwriting of ordinances that was against us, which was contrary to us, and took it out of the way, nailing it to his cross."

Eph 1:13, "In whom ye also trusted, after ye heard the word of truth, the gospel of your salvation: in whom also after that ye believed, ye were sealed with that Holy Spirit of promise...."

1 Jn 5:14, "And this is the confidence that we have in him, that, if we ask any thing according to his will, he heareth us."

Titus 3:5, "Not by works of righteousness which we have done, but according to his mercy he saved us, by the washing of regeneration, and renewing of the Holy Ghost [Holy Spirit]...." Our sin separates our spirit from the Holy Spirit, and we need to be re-united with the Holy Spirit to become spiritually alive in God's eyes.

Jn 14:26, "But the Comforter, which is the Holy Ghost [Holy Spirit], whom the Father will send in my name, he shall teach you all things, and bring all things to your remembrance, whatever I have said unto you."

Eph 4:30, "And grieve not the holy Spirit of God, whereby ye are sealed unto the day of redemption."

Eph 4:4–6, "There is one body, and one Spirit, even as ye are called in one hope of your calling; One Lord, one faith, one baptism, One God and Father of all, who is above all, and through all and in you all." All spiritually born-again Christians' spirits are re-united with God's Holy Spirit forever and will never be rejected from living in heaven for all eternity.

Rom 8:14, "For as many as are led by the Spirit of God, they are the sons of God."

Rom 8:16, "The Spirit itself beareth witness with our spirit, that we are the children of God…"

1 Cor 3:16, "Know ye not that ye are the temple of God, and that the Spirit of God dwelleth in you?"

2 Tim 1:7, "For God hath not given us the spirit of fear; but of power, and of love, and a sound [disciplined] mind."

Mic 6:8, "He hath shewed thee, O man, what is good; and what doth the LORD require of thee, but to do justly, and to love mercy, and to walk humbly with thy God."

Deut 31:6, "Be strong and of a good courage, fear not, nor be afraid of them: for the LORD thy God, he it is who doth go with thee; he will not fail thee, nor forsake thee." God will always be there to help me up from spiritual falls; unsaved sinners will not always have this option.

Jam 1:2–3, "My brethren, count it all joy when ye fall into diverse temptations; Knowing this, that the trying of your faith worketh patience. But let patience have her perfect work, that ye may be perfect and entire, wanting nothing." Without tribulations or resistance in my life, I would not have strived to walk, think, talk, learn, make decisions, persevere, overcome obstacles, love, smile, excel, or grow.

Rom 5:1–5, "Therefore, being justified by faith, we have peace with God through our Lord Jesus Christ: By whom also we have access by faith into this grace wherein we stand, and rejoice in hope of the glory of God. And not only so, but we glory in tribulations also: knowing that tribulation worketh patience; And patience, experience; and experience, hope; and hope maketh not ashamed; because the love of God is shed abroad in our hearts by the Holy Ghost [Holy Spirit] which is given to us."

Phil 4:4–7, "Rejoice in the Lord always: and again I say, Rejoice. Let your moderation be known unto all men. The Lord is at hand. Be careful for nothing; but in every thing by prayer and supplication with thanksgiving let your requests be made known unto God. And the peace of God, which passeth all understanding, shall keep your hearts and minds through Christ Jesus."

1 Thess 5:16–19, "Rejoice evermore. Pray without ceasing. In every thing give thanks: for this is the will of God in Christ Jesus concerning you. Quench not the Holy Spirit."

1 Cor 13:13, "And now abideth faith, hope, and charity; these three; but the greatest of these is charity."

1 Jn 4:8b, 16b, "... God is love...."

1 Pet 4:8, "And above all things have fervent charity [love] among yourselves; for charity shall cover the multitude of sins."

1 Cor 13:4–8, "Charity [God's Agape Love] suffereth long, and is kind; charity [God's Agape Love] envieth not; charity [God's Agape Love] vaunteth not itself, is not puffed up, Doth not behave itself unseemly, seeketh not her own, is not easily provoked, thinketh no evil; Rejoiceth not in iniquity, but rejoiceth in the truth; Beareth all things, believeth all things, hopeth all things, endureth all things, Charity [God's Agape Love] never faileth...."

Unconditional, enduring, and respectful Charity is equivalent to God's Agape Love.

Ps 46:10a, "Be still, and know that I am God..." God is always ready to cover my back. The only way for me to come up short in my growth is to not choose to follow God's plan for my life!

Ps 37:3–5, "Trust in the LORD, and do good; so shalt thou dwell in the land, and verily thou shalt be fed. Delight yourself also in the LORD, and he shall give thee the desires of your heart. Commit thy way unto the LORD; trust also in him; and he shall bring it to pass."

Prov 3:5–6, "Trust in the LORD with all thine heart, and lean not unto thine own understanding. In all thy ways acknowledge him, and he shall direct thy paths."

Heaven and Hell

Included in my research concerning life, love, death, and the "spiritual missing part," was the concept that many religions and the Bible assert the concept of an eternal heaven and an eternal hell. According to the Bible, every person will exist eternally in either heaven or hell with a new spiritual body (i.e. my earthly body will eventually die), and our souls and spirits will never die (Rom 8:1–17; 1 Pet 1; Rev 20).[19] In essence, according to the Bible, I will transition some day from my earthly living to either heaven or hell respectively for eternity contingent upon my decision to become spiritually born-again. I have two choices:

1. Ask and accept, by my own free will, Jesus' love sacrifice on the cross for all of my sins, in accordance with my understanding of God's Love Concept, and I will live in heaven forever.[20]

2. I can choose to personally attempt to satisfy all of the Mosaic Law with my life decisions and associated deeds in order to try to cover the consequences of my sins. (Note that the Bible states that it is impossible for any human to cover or redeem their sins' consequences through their own efforts or religion.[21])

In my research about heaven and hell, I questioned if it were possible to personally cover or redeem my sin. Why did Jesus, God's Son, have to come to earth to redeem me? Based on my life experiences with others and with other religions that I researched, I concluded that I was not the only one confused about the true spiritual meaning regarding Jesus' purpose, biblical words, parables, and spiritual concepts.[22]

I considered the Apostle Paul's conversion to Christianity after being reproached by Jesus in a vision from heaven for killing Christians. As a young man, Paul, previously called Saul of Tarsus, had received an in-depth education in the law and the prophets, the Jewish teachings that are contained in our Old Testament. Nevertheless, he did not understand that these Old Testament truths are based upon God's Love Concept (Matt 22:36–40; Jn 3:7–15).

In his vision, Paul was advised by Jesus to seek out Christian teachers in Damascus. He then spent time with Jesus' disciples to learn the true purpose of Jesus' love, his death on the cross, his earthly purpose, his words, parables, and spiritual concepts. These revelations stopped him from continuing to kill Christians. In addition, after his conversion and being filled with the Holy Spirit, Paul planted churches throughout the Mediterranean region and wrote letters to those churches when he couldn't be with them. Those letters now make up the majority of the New Testament books, revealing what he had learned concerning God's Love Concept.[23]

I have found that there is a lot of confusion regarding how to obtain eternal salvation in heaven (Acts 9:17–23; Jn 5:24; Eph 2:8–9). However, the Bible simply states and often repeats that all a person has to do to obtain eternal salvation in heaven is to make a personal decision to ask, accept, and thank Jesus for his love and love sacrifice on the cross by simply trusting him with a child-like faith.[24]

My Eternal Destiny Considerations

During my research and initial Bible studies, I also became more concerned about where I might have to spend eternity: heaven or hell? Would I have a choice, or vote, or have to do something in order to determine or secure which location I would reside for all eternity? After all, eternity is a long, never-ending time! It became apparent to me that my main life concern should be how to become "spiritually alive" as soon as possible. The Bible defines "death" as "spiritual death" (i.e. my spirit being separated from God's Holy Spirit). That spiritual state would prevent me from going to heaven for all eternity (Jn 3:36; Jn 3:3–7; Jn 3:15–18).

In Luke 16:19–31, Jesus presents the parable of the deaths of a rich man and of a poor man named Lazarus. The rich man found himself placed in Hades, or hell. Lazarus went to heaven, to "Abraham's bosom." The rich man requested that Abraham send Lazarus, to earth to warn his kinfolk about the torments of hell. Abraham advised that the rich man's kinfolks had Moses and the prophets to warn them of the torments of hell. However, the rich man stated that if one, who had died, went to his kinfolks and warned them of the torments of hell that his relatives would listen to the warning. However, Abraham stated that if the man's relatives did not hear Moses and the prophets, neither would they be persuaded by someone who had risen from the dead.

This parable indicated to me that there is an individual time period for each person to decide to choose either heaven or hell as their eternal destiny. After this individual time period has passed, a person will not change their final decision no matter what. Consequently, the moral of this parable for me was that I needed to choose heaven as soon as possible in my lifetime, or I would end up in hell forever. In other words, unless I accepted Jesus' gift of eternal salvation, my life on earth would be the only heaven I would know (Eph 2:8–9). Conversely, by accepting Jesus' eternal salvation while living on the earth, my life here on earth would be the only "hell" that I would ever know.[25]

My Purpose, Meaning, and Fulfillment

My conclusion during my 27th year after beginning to study the Bible, was that all of my worldly education, life experiences, and research concerning human knowledge, understanding, wisdom, heaven, and hell were insufficient to answer my life questions. I needed to find another information resource to provide me with a good understanding of my life's main purpose, meaning, and fulfillment. I realized from my research that I had received a good spiritual education, but it was incomplete. After considering my life experiences, researching well-known religions, and my overall formal education, and finding no answers to my questions, I felt that I needed to study the Bible in earnest. The Bible is about Jesus, the only "person" purported to have performed many healing miracles, raised people from death, and personally come back from death. Therefore, it made sense to me to try to better understand Jesus and his reason and motivation to redeem all of my sins out of love (Jn 3:15–16; Rom 5:8; 1 Tim 1:5).

First John 4:8 and 16 state that "God is love." This suggested to me that perhaps understanding God's Love Concept instead of trying to better understand the concept of human love might lead me to the answers I searched for. In particular, Rom 13:10 states "Love worketh no ill to his neighbor: therefore love is the fulfilling of the law." And 1 Tim 1:5 states, "Now the end of the commandment is charity [God's Agape Love] out of a pure heart, and of a good conscience, and of faith unfeigned." (See also Matt 22:36-40; Mic 6:8; Rom 5-6, 8).

What does, "Love is the fulfilling of the law," really mean? Does it mean that God's love was the answer to my four life questions? I felt that I needed to make a serious effort to better understand God's Love Concept, the Mosaic Law, Sin, God's Grace, and their appropriate consequences and correlations before it was too late for me to employ God's Love Concept in my life (1 Cor 2:10–14). After all, I did not want to possibly miss receiving God's eternal blessings such as heaven due to my ignorance of the Bible's messages (Rom 8:1–17; Matt 25:34; 1 Pet Ch 1). In retrospect, when I married my wife, Janice, the joy, happiness, and feeling of excitement of being with her was a little taste, a sneak preview, of God's love and what heaven must really be like (1 Cor 2:9–16). In conclusion, I was now more interested than ever in going to heaven than hell (Rom 14:17). I needed to learn about God's pure love and choosing heaven.

Free Will Choice Versus Mosaic Law Mandates

During my Bible research I considered that if God is really the God of pure and true love, then his solution for me to obtain eternal life in heaven should be very simple and easy to understand. God knows that I am not the brightest light bulb in this life. In addition, this solution should be the same for all people, regardless of their life circumstances. Further, I should be able to understand God's simple plan of eternal salvation and make a decision about his plan with my own God-given, independent free will, or God is not really a God of love.[26] Otherwise, I considered that I might have no other choice than to attempt to comply with God's Mosaic Laws and their consequences as spelled out in the first five books of the Old Testament. But I knew from past experience and my own sin nature that I would not be able—or even want—to comply with all of the Mosaic Law mandates.[27] It was important that I determine my life choice options and their consequences if I expected to make the best decision about the eternal destiny of my soul and spirit.

Decision Consequences

Regarding decision-making, I favor the following thought: "whatever a man sows, that shall he also reap" (Gal 6:7–8). The benefit of having a free will is being responsible for our own decisions. We were created by a God of pure love who expects us to make our own responsible, accountable, and wise decisions. This treats us as valued beings as opposed to simple puppets.

I believed that it would be prudent for my decisions to be holy. I needed to have the right mindset to avoid sin, to be loving and just, in order to make the best decision. I knew that decisions require consequences: otherwise, how could I determine their benefits, quality, and value? Allowing me to make my own decisions and receive the consequences of my choices is fundamental in God's purpose for people. This mindset and subsequent related actions generate true unconditional love. I concluded that a God of love would surely want me to have many blessings; and God would provide encouragement to me by his Word (Eph 4).

God's Love Concept Revealed

God's Love Concept reveals that the purpose and understanding of his Mosaic Law (Matt 22:36–40; Rom 5; Rom 3:20) was to provide loving opportunities for many blessings (Rom 8; Heb 12:1–15) which are directly contingent upon making wise decisions and their consequences, as opposed to me simply becoming an indecisive puppet.[28] In other words, I would receive positive blessings for making spiritually good, loving, and wise decisions in my life. The benefits would come from the rewards of pursuing pure love actions. We reap positive love benefits when we sow positive love goals, actions, life strategies (God's Agape Love).[29]

God's love for me provides me with a permanent spiritual relationship through spiritual re-birth, a positional relationship as a saved sinner going to heaven forever, and self-worth as an eternal member of the family of God. Additionally, I needed to remember that God's Love Concept always requires me to be responsible, accountable, and to deal with the consequences of my life decisions relative to his eternal salvation plan (Gal 6:7–9; Matt 7:2). A true love relationship requires both parties to be considerate, respectful, and caring of each other and to be willing to work through the consequences of their decisions for the benefit of both (Col 3; Eph 4; 1 John 4). I decided to review my life before the age of 27 to determine how much I understood God's Love Concept.

Chapter One
SCRIPTURE REFERENCES

1. Luke 13:3, Matt 18:1–5; Jn 14:6; Jn 11:25–26; Luke 10:25–28
2. Matt 22:36–40, Ex 3:13–14, Jn 3:15–18, 1 Jn 4:7–20, 1 Cor 13:4–8, Matt 22:32, Heb 6:13–20, 1 Cor 13:4–8, 13; Ps 46:10; Hos 11:9
3. 2 Tim 3:15–17, 1 Tim 2:4–5, Jn 11:25–26, Jn 14:6, Jn 5:24, Rom 3:9–30, Rom 5:1–11, Heb 11:6, Jn 3, Eph 2:8–9; Rom 10:9–10, Eph 1:13, Rom Ch 8
4. Jn 3:36; Jn 4:24; Jn 5:24; Gal 6:7–8; Matt 7:2; Gal 5:13–26; Isa 26:3; Josh 1:8–9
5. Heb 4:12; Prov 2; Prov 3; Prov 9:8 to 10; 2 Tim 3:15–17
6. Matt 8:22; Eph 2:1–9; Rom 5:6–11; Rev 20:11–15; 1 Jn 5:10–14
7. Prov 25:2; Rom 5; Matt 16:24 to 28; 2 Cor 5:14 to 21; Rom Ch 8
8. Matt 22:36–40; Gal 6:7–8; 1 Tim 2:4–6; Jn 3; Rom 5:8–11; Heb 11:6; Rom 10:9–10; Jn 5:24; Eph 2:8–9; Rom 3; 1 Tim 1:5; Rom 8:1–16; Gal 3; Eph 1:13; Titus 3:5
9. 1 Tim 2:4 to 6; Gal 5:16 to 20; Prov 8; Rom Ch 8
10. Rom Ch 3; Rom 1:16–22; Rom 4–5; Rom Ch 8; Prov 22:4; Prov 9:10; Heb 4:12
11. Matt 22:36–40; Gal 5:16; Gal 6:2–10; Eph 1:13–14; Eph 4; Jn 3—4; Rom 8:1; Tim 1:5
12. Heb 11:6; Rom 3:23; Rom 10:9, 10; Jn 14:6; Jn 3:15, 16; Eph 2:8–9; Eph 1:13; Titus 3:5; Eph 4:30
13. Rom 5:3–4; Heb 12:2–15; Jam 1:2–12; 1 Pet 1:2–9
14. Matt 22:36–40; Jam 2:1; Jn 2:15–17; Luke 4:1–13; Rom Ch 8
15. Rom 10:9–10; Jn 3:15–18; 1 Pet 3:18; Rev 20:15; Jn 5:24; 1 Pet 2:9; Rom 8:14–17
16. Matt 22:36–40; Luke 18:16–17; 1 Thess 5:16–22; Prov 3:1–13

17. Luke 24:25–27; John 14:26; John 5:39–40; Jn 14:26; 2 Tim 3:16–17
18. 1 Tim 1:5; Rom 12:1, 2; James 1:22–25; Rom Ch 8; Gal 6:7–8
19. Jn 5:24; Ps 16:10; Eph 4:30; Ecc 12:7; Jn 6:63; 1 Thess 5:23; Jn 3:36; Rom 8:14–17; Rev 20:10–15; Matt 23:33
20. Jn 14:6; Jn 6:63; Rom 3:20–31; Gal 5:13–18; Eph 4:1–7
21. Jn 14:6; 1 Tim 2:5–6; Jn 11:25–26; Eph 2:8–9; Jam 2:10; Gal 3:10–12; Gal 3; Matt 5:17–20; Rev 20:15; Gal 2:16; Gal 6:7–8; Rom 1:16–17; Luke 13:3; Rom 2:1–16; Rom 1:18–20; Rom 3:20–31; Titus 2:11; 1 Tim 1:5; Eph 1:13; 1 John 5:10–14
22. Jn 3:1–21; Jn 5:24; Jn 5:39–40; Luke 24:25–27; Jn 4:24; Acts 9:1–23
23. Matt 22:36–40; Gal 3:10–12; Jn 14:6; Eph 2:8–9; Rom 10:9–10; Rom 3:20–25; Titus 3:5
24. Jn 3:11–21; Jn 5:24; Rom 10:9–10; Eph 1:13
25. 1 Cor 2:9–16; 1 Cor 3:11–23; Jn 11:25–26; Rom 14:17
26. 1 Tim 2:4–6; Heb 10:10; Titus 2:11; Jn 3:15–16
27. Gal 3:10–12, 22–25; Heb 10:10–18, James 2:10; Rom 3:20; Matt 22:37–40; Jn 11:25–26; Heb 11:6; Luke 13:3; Rom 10:9–10; Eph 1:13; 1 Tim 1:5
28. Gal 6:7–8; Eph 4; Josh 1:8–9; 1 Tim 1:5; Mich 6:8; Matt 11:28–30; Phil 4:4–8; Rom 8:31–39; Gal 5; Deut 31:6; Jer 9:23–24; 2 Tim 1:6–7; 2 Cor 12:9–10; Prov 3:5–6
29. Prov 3; Ps 37; Josh 1:8–9; Gal 5; 1 Jn Ch 4).

Chapter Two

Analyzing My Past

(Romans 1—8)

In my effort to better understand my life, love, death, and "spiritual missing part" dilemma relative to my Bible research, I decided to re-examine my life experiences, my subsequent conclusions, and my past choices to see if there was a possible correlation between my life's purpose, meaning, fulfillment, "spiritual missing part", and God's Love Concept spelled out in the Bible's messages. I was motivated by the verse in Matthew 16:26, "For what is a man profited, if he shall gain the whole world, and lose his own soul? Or what shall a man give in exchange for his soul?

Past Family Life Experiences

I was raised in a family that was in the lower economic status, humble, with very close family ties, and connected to the same religion. My father had to quit eighth grade and find a job to support his immediate family. His father had died and that made him the "bread winner" for his immediate family. He worked in a combined steel manufacturing foundry and associated machine shop company until age 62. My mother worked in a five and ten-cent store, G. C. Murphy Co., for the better part of her life to help supplement our family's income. Our family of five people lived in a duplex, a two-bedroom home located in southwest Pennsylvania's US Steel manufacturing company "country," fourteen miles southeast from Pittsburgh, PA as the crow flies, during my grade school and high school years.

Religion Versus Direct Personal Relationship

The religion that my family and I were involved in seemed to present some hope of a better current life and after life, and I originally embraced the religion with fervor. However, as I grew older, I found myself looking for something that was "missing" from my life, my heart, my hope. The religion that I was involved in did not provide me with any good answers concerning my "spiritual missing part." As a matter of fact, my Bible research revealed that God, through Jesus (Jn 14:6), wanted reconciliation with me through a direct personal relationship, not through a man-created religion.[1]

Nevertheless, the Bible highly encourages the assembly of Christians to encourage, uplift, edify, and love one another in fellowship. As humans, we need to bond, define and maintain our boundaries, seek the truth concerning our existence and decisions, and mature into adults in order to make responsible, realistic, and accountable decisions.[2] My religion, however, was not providing me with the life answers that I needed.

School Years

I lived an average life during my first 27 years. I attended grade school and high school. I played sports: football, baseball, track, and basketball. I even had a very loving girlfriend who later became my wife for 48 years. Nevertheless, school, sports, and my relationship with my girlfriend did not provide me with any good answers concerning my life purpose, meaning, fulfillment, and "spiritual missing part" questions. My wife was also looking for something that was missing in her life too, but with greater passion than me. She was more driven to find that "spiritual missing part" in her life. Her passion to find answers greatly influenced my desire to discover the "missing part" in my life that was stealing my joy, happiness, and inner peace. She was called to heaven on June 17, 2013 after 48 years of marriage.

College Versus Military Service

After high school, I decided to join the United States Air Force. I did not like going to school, and I also did not have the resources to pay for college or a vocational training education. My girlfriend and I made a pact to not entertain the thought of getting married until after she finished high school. We felt that if we loved one another as strongly as we thought, then our love would carry us to the point of getting married in spite of any physical, psychological, and spiritual life distractions that we would encounter during our period of separation.

Travel

I had always enjoyed exploring creation, so I joined the Air Force in hope that I would not only have opportunities to find the "spiritual missing part" in my life, but also gain training for a lifetime career. My hope was that seeing more of life, creation, other countries, and how other people lived on this planet would provide the answers to my questions regarding my life's purpose, meaning, fulfillment, love, death, and my "spiritual missing part." I enjoyed my many travels, but I did not find the answers I was seeking.

College and Marriage

After some in-depth thought during my first four enlisted years in the Air Force, I decided to take college courses. Being in the Air

Force did not reveal the answers to my life questions. It also became apparent that I needed to have more education in order to secure a career that would provide good pay and benefits. During the second semester of my first year of college, after I was discharged from the Air Force, my girlfriend and I decided to get married. We were married on May 1, 1965.

After some time, it became obvious that everything that I had experienced up to this time in my life, including marriage, had not provided me with any answers. I became very frustrated and disappointed with life overall. I was becoming desperate; I wanted to find my purpose, my meaning, and the missing part in this life more than ever.

College Degree and Air Force Officer Commission

After my first year in college and my recent marriage; I ran out of funds. I decided to re-enlist in the Air Force and apply for the Officer's Candidate School, which would take time, commitment, and perseverance. While in the Air Force during my second enlistment, I applied, and I was accepted into the US Air Force's Airmen's Education and Commissioning Program. I was sent to Widener University in Chester, Pennsylvania for 27 months to obtain my college degree and subsequent USAF Officer Commission.

I hoped that I would find my answers by completing college and becoming an Air Force Officer. Janice and I expanded our family by three children during my second enlistment. That really challenged us.

"Spiritual Missing Part" Research

During my final year of college, I concluded that neither education, religion, travel, military service, nor marriage had provided me with the answers to my questions. Though I was frustrated, I became more open-minded to other possible avenues of research. I began researching psychology books to determine if I was "normal" and had any "personal value." Early in my research, I determined that everyone I had encountered had similar questions concerning their "normalcy" and personal value. I knew any desired positive changes or healing would require a relationship reconciliation with God. In spite of having varying degrees of personal "quirks," I realized that I was "normal" by worldly standards. Therefore, I concluded that my life's value, my self-worth, and my life's meaning would be more relevant, pertinent, and mutually reciprocal if they were more directly related to my spiritual relationship and spiritual position with God the Father through Jesus Christ (Deut 31:6).

Life's Distractions, Diversions, and Misguided Directions Confusion

My self-analysis and psychological research became valuable during my quest to answer my life questions, especially in my Bible studies. I could see how people, the devil and his demons often tried to use bad psychological rationale to confuse me about my life's spiritual purpose, meaning, and fulfillment. In short, it helped me decipher confusing distractions, diversions, or misguided life directions. During those moments, I needed to pray and seek God's guidance. I needed to change my mindset from worldly considerations to seeking God's leading. This helped me to make wise decisions at critical moments according to God's will for my life.[3]

Understanding the Concept of "Spiritually Dead"

During my last year in college, I was married and we had three children. A couple came to our house one evening in August 1970 and welcomed us into the neighborhood. They also invited us to attend their Bible study. I thanked them and bid them good night. I did not trust religious fanatics. I told my wife of the visit. She immediately rebuked me for sending them away. She advised that we needed to befriend these folks and join their Bible study. She hoped that this might help us to discover our "missing part." So we befriended our new neighborhood friends and joined their Bible study. This turned out to be an eternally wise decision. During our in-depth Bible studies, we found the "spiritual missing part" in our lives. James 2:26 says, "For as the body without the spirit is [spiritually] dead, so faith without works is dead also." It appeared from our new Bible studies that we needed to become "spiritually born-again" in order to find the answers to our life questions. We were "spiritually dead" in God's eyes, and we could only become "spiritually alive again" through God's grace, not by trying to comply with the Mosaic Law requirements that only provided us with the knowledge of sin.[4]

God's Grace Versus Works of the Mosaic Law

From my Bible studies, I realized only God's love and grace (i.e. Jesus' love sacrifice on the cross and my faith choice to accept God's simple plan of eternal salvation) could cover the consequences for all of my sins, past, present, and future. My deeds could never accomplish this. The following Bible verses reinforced this declaration:

Rom 3:20–25, "Therefore by the deeds of the law [Mosaic Law] there shall no flesh be justified in his sight: for by the law is the knowledge of sin. But now the righteousness of God without the law is manifested, being witnessed by the law and the prophets; Even the righteousness of God which is by faith of Jesus Christ unto all and upon all them that believe: for there is no difference: For all have sinned, and come short of the glory of God; Being justified freely by his grace through the redemption that is in Christ Jesus: Whom God hath set forth to be a propitiation through faith in his blood, to declare his righteousness for the remission of sins that are past, through the forbearance of God...."

Gal 3:10–12, "For as many as are of the works of the law are under the curse: for it is written, Cursed is every one that continueth not in all things which are written in the book of the law to do them. But that no man is justified by the law in the sight of God, it is evident: for, the just shall live by faith. And the law is not of faith: but, The man that doeth them [attempting to comply with the Law] shall live in them [the law's consequences]."

Jn 14:6, "Jesus saith unto him, I am the way, the truth, and the life: no man cometh unto the Father but by me."

1 Tim 2:5, "For there is one God, and one mediator between God and men, the man Christ Jesus."

Heb 9:28, "So Christ was once offered to bear the sins of many; and unto them that look for him shall he appear the second time without sin unto salvation."

Rom 10:4, "For Christ is the end of the law for righteousness to everyone that believeth."

Rom 8:2, "For the law of the Spirit of life in Christ Jesus hath made me free from the law of sin and death."

Eph 1:13, "In whom ye also trusted, after ye heard the word of truth, the gospel of your salvation: in whom also after that ye believed, ye were sealed with that Holy Spirit of promise…."

1 Tim 1:5, "Now the end of the commandment is charity out of a pure heart, and of a good conscience, and of faith unfeigned."

Eph 2:8–9, "For by grace are ye saved through faith; and that not of yourselves: it is the gift of God: Not of works, lest any man should boast."

Jn 11:25–26, "Jesus said unto her, I am the resurrection, and the life: he that believeth in me, though he were dead [spiritually], yet shall he live. And whosoever liveth and believeth in me shall never die [spiritually]. Believest thou this?"

Jn 3:15–16, "That whosoever believeth in him should not perish, but have eternal life. For God so loved the world, that He gave his only begotten Son, that whosoever believeth in him should not perish, but have everlasting life."

Rom 10:9–10, "That if thou shalt confess with thy mouth the Lord Jesus, and shalt believe in thine heart that God hath raised him from the dead, thou shalt be saved. For with the heart man believeth unto righteousness, and with the mouth confession is made unto salvation."

Heb 11:6, "But without faith it is impossible to please him: for he that cometh to God must believe that he is, and that he is a rewarder of them that diligently seek him."

Jam 2:23, "And the scripture was fulfilled which saith, Abraham believed God, and it was imputed unto him for righteousness; and he was called the Friend of God."

Rom 6:23, "For the wages of sin is death [i.e. spiritual death]; but the gift of God is eternal life through Jesus Christ, our Lord."

Chapter Two
SCRIPTURE REFERENCES

1. Rom 5:10–11; Rom 11:15; 1 Cor 7:11, 2 Cor 5 18–20; Eph 2:16, Col 1:20–21

2. Eph 4; Heb 10:24—25; 1 Jn 4; Jn 15:1–14; Jer 17:10; Matt 7:1, 2; Gal 5:14–16; Gal 6:1–10; Rom 2:1–16; Rom 12:1–2

3. Gal 5; Prov 3:5–6; Matt 11:28–30; Phil 4:4–8; Deut 31:6

4. Eph 2:8–9; Rom 3:9–20; Rom 1:16–17; Jn 5:24; Titus 3:5; Eph 1:13; Rom 8:1–17; Gal 2:16; Gal 3:10–12

Chapter Three

My Rationale for Researching the Bible

(Jn 3:3–7; Jn 3:15, 16; Jn 6:40; 2 Tim 3:15–17; 2 Pet 1:20–21; Luke 13:3)

During my early life, I had considered reading the Bible, but I never made a serious effort to do so. I thought that I could read the Bible in my old age when I had more time and more interest. The curious thing was that I was receiving daily Bible readings from a calendar hanging on the wall in my parent's kitchen. I read it every day while leaning over the sink and snacking. I was also receiving Bible training during the Sunday church services that I attended during my grade school and high school years while living with my parents. I was unaware that I was learning from the Bible, but I am so glad that my faith in God was growing, in spite of my negligence to diligently to read the Bible. Romans 10:17 says, "So, then, faith cometh by hearing, and hearing by the word of God." I remember thinking that the Bible messages that I was casually receiving during my naïve youth were very understandable, relevant, and wise. Now I look back and understand how these two Bible sources helped me to grow in my trust of God and his will for me (2 Tim 3:15–17; Titus 2:11; Josh 1:8–9).

What Is the Value of Bible Study?

When I was young, I felt that I had plenty of time to read the Bible. I did not think that a God of Love would send anyone to hell without allowing them time to read his Word; or would He?[1] I had foolishly ignored the idea that I might die, physically, before I had a chance to study the Bible (2 Tim 3:15–17). Later, when I started to study the Bible in earnest, I knew I had to choose to become spiritually born-again before my body's death and my soul's immediate judgment, or I would not have secured my place in heaven forever.[2] I became much wiser and discerning concerning the value of Bible teachings as I diligently studied the Bible. This greatly enhanced my research concerning my life questions about love, death, and the "spiritual missing part."

In particular, I realized that I was in a daily spiritual battle against principalities, powers, rulers of darkness, and spiritual wickedness in high places (Eph 6:11–20). I needed to employ the whole armor of God daily in order to withstand and combat the devil and his tools of guilt, fear, anger, hatred, peer pressure, distractions, diversions, mis-direction, pride, selfishness, inconsideration of others, disrespect of others, etc. (Gal 6:12–18). I especially needed daily spiritual nourishment and to employ the Sword of the Spirit in my daily spiritual battles. Heb 4:12 states, "For the word of God is quick, and powerful, and sharper than any twoedged sword, piercing even to the dividing asunder of soul and spirit, and of the joints and marrow, and is a discerner of the thoughts and intents of the heart."

It is also interesting that when Jesus was tempted by the devil in the desert by lust of the flesh, lust of the eyes, and the pride of life, Jesus used Scripture, the Sword of the Lord (Heb 4:12), to ward off the devil's attempts to tempt Jesus.[3] This use of Scripture was more than enough justification and merit for me to diligently study the Bible so that I could ward off daily spiritual attacks by the devil and his demons with the help of the Holy Spirit. John 15:4–5 says, "Abide in me, and I in you. As the branch cannot bear fruit of itself, except it abide in the vine; no more can ye, except ye abide in me. I am the vine, ye are the branches: He that abideth in me, and I in him, the same brings forth much fruit: for without me ye can do nothing." I could never presume that I could ward off the devil and his demons without the Holy Spirit (Jn 14:26). Further, 2 Tim 1:7 states, "For God hath not given us the spirit of fear; but of power, and of love, and a sound [disciplined] mind." John 14:26 states; "But the Comforter, which is the Holy Ghost [Holy Spirit], whom the Father will send in my name, he shall teach you all things, and bring all things to your remembrance, whatsoever I have said unto you." The Holy Spirit will come to help you remember God's Word and give you spiritual comfort and guidance. Jesus also said: "But go ye and learn what that meaneth, I will have mercy, and not sacrifice: for I am not come to call the righteous, but sinners to repentance." (Matt 9:13) [4]

Considering my flimsy excuses of the past for not reading the Bible and what I had learned from attending those early Bible studies with my wife, I concluded that I should start studying the Bible in earnest. I had many questions.

- What evidence was there that God really cared about me and loved me? God presents his love for me frequently by his words, actions, and deeds.[5.]
- If Jesus, God's Son, had to endure a love sacrifice for all of my sin consequences, then I obviously could not have accomplished the same results on my own, could I? (Jn 14:6; Eph 2:8–9; Eph 1:13);

- What proof is there that God really exists and will keep his promises? There is plenty of proof of God's love and his promises:
    - Creation and its balance
    - The performance of created creatures' bodies
    - Jesus' character and his many miracles, including raising people from death!
    - The fact that Jesus fulfills over two-hundred prophecies concerning his life, death, and resurrection.[6]

I questioned whether or not my final eternal salvation was "predestined," and that my choice did not matter. During my study, however, I learned my free will choice does matter, because a puppet cannot return love in a personal relationship.[7]

I also felt that I really needed to understand God's concepts and definitions of life, love, and death in order to determine if the "missing part" in my life was connected to God's Word for me. I needed to understand these concepts before I could make a choice that would determine where I spent eternity. The Bible clearly spells out God's simple faith plan to obtain eternal salvation in heaven right now numerous times.[8]

Paul's Conversion to Christianity

As a point of interest, I reminded myself that the Apostle Paul did not understand God's Love Concept message in the Old Testament, in spite of his high caliber education. It was when Paul was on his way to Damascus to kill Christians that Jesus himself spoke to him through a light from heaven (Acts 9; 1 Cor 2:10–14). Paul was blinded by the light. Jesus directed him to go into Damascus and to learn the Old Testament love message from a Christian teacher and the Holy Spirit. Paul had to understand the relevance of the two most important royal love commandments: love God first, and your neighbor as yourself (God's Agape Love).

He needed to become spiritually born-again before he could serve God through planting churches and writing letters of spiritual encouragement—letters that today make up most of our New Testament.[9] Based upon Paul's spiritual conversion, I concluded that I needed to study the Bible's New Testament Books in great depth first before I studied the Bible's Old Testament. This decision allowed me to understand the Old Testament Books more effectively.

Eternal Salvation and Predestination

After considerable Bible study regarding predestination, it was confirmed to me that God did give me an independent, free will, and accountable decision-making capability consistent with his Love Concept. Throughout Scripture I saw a God who values people as independent, relational, and accountable beings, not as puppets or robots.[10] Therefore, I was responsible to make a decision to either accept or reject his simple eternal salvation plan, and receive the consequences accordingly (Gal 6:7–8; Jer 17:10). In relation to predestination, I realized that God could see into my future regarding the time of my eternal salvation decision—even before I was born; even before he created the world (Ps 139). Therefore, God, who is in complete control of his universe, could appropriately prepare my final eternal destiny consequences based on the moment in my life on earth when I made my own free-will decision in faith regarding his gift of eternal salvation through Jesus' love sacrifice on the cross (Prov Ch 3; Rom Ch 8). It was mind-blowing to me to come to the understanding that God is so totally in control of his universe that he developed a plan for all humanity, regardless of their circumstances, that allowed everyone to make their own free will decisions without altering his plan one iota.

Marriage and My Wife's Bi-Polar Condition

Life is often complicated. One week after my wedding, I discovered that my wife had a bi-polar, or manic-depressive, affliction. This subsequently required many hours of counseling, treatments, and prescription testing and balancing to determine how to best balance her body's chemical imbalance and its associated unprovoked, extreme, and alarming psychological actions. Over time, we determined that Janice's father was a true alcoholic. This further complicated her bi-polar condition. These factors were the primary reasons why Janice had a greater drive to find answers to her life purpose, meaning, fulfillment, and "spiritual missing part" questions. With God's help, leading, and chemical imbalance conditioning over time, Janice's bi-polar condition was greatly mitigated and she became a happier, more joyful, and peaceful person. We would often joke that Janice's bi-polar chemical imbalance conditioning was finally mitigated by her last two doctors—Dr. Hitt and Dr. Chop. I attributed our Bible study as our chief motivation, incentive, and success factors, that helped us overcome our marriage struggles, her bi-polar struggles, and our spiritual shortcomings over time with great patience and kindness toward each other and spiritual growth by adhering to Scripture study and employment.[11]

Divine Appointments

In time, Janice said, "Since I am a saved sinner who is going to heaven for all eternity no matter what, why would I not want to share the good news of God's simple eternal salvation plan with everybody that I meet!" This revelation from Janice became my motivation to share Jesus' love, the meaning of his love sacrifice, and the message of eternal salvation with everyone I encountered. Heaven is certainly large enough for everyone and full of God's blessings; so why would I, a grateful saved sinner, not want to share God's Love Concept?

I later learned from my Bible studies that it was wiser to ask the Holy Spirit to set up "divine appointments" with folks who were ready to hear and accept the truth about becoming a spiritually born-again Christian. I am not able to look into folks' hearts like God can, to see if they are ready to hear his eternal salvation plan, so I have learned to trust the Holy Spirit's direction (Jer 17:10).

Tragic Experiences and God's Love for Babies

Another question in my mind was the fate of babies who don't live to the age of accountability (usually around 5 or 6 years old). What happens to babies who are not capable of making a responsible, accountable decision? Are they able to commit sin? My studies lead to this conclusion: if God is a true God of love, then he would have to take these babies straight to heaven to live with him forever, because the babies are not capable of making responsible, independent, free will decisions to sin resulting in their spirit becoming separated from God's Holy Spirit.[12.]

I also considered that God would foreknow what decisions those babies would make concerning their eternal salvation if they had lived a longer life; so He could justly take them to heaven earlier at his discretion to enjoy their blessings. On the other side of this concept, a God of Love might allow babies to be born and to die early in order that the tragedy would prompt others to diligently seek him for understanding and his eternal blessings. As a result of this tragedy, people may come to accept God's Love Concept and his eternal salvation plan.[14]

In conclusion, I realized that the possibility of infant death, a tragic experience, would produce a very sobering thought process, a "no-kidding" reflection on our existence and eternal destiny. I observed that most people I encountered became very sober, very quickly, when any kind of death entered into their lives. I concluded that God would allow the "death factor" to enter our lives in order to help us to become critically aware of him and his plan of eternal salvation. This prompts many people to seek confirmation of where they will spend eternity, whether in heaven or hell, before their body expires.[15]

Fundamental Reasons for Seeking God's Plan for my Life

During my initial Bible studies I discovered God had a plan for my life. This was a driving factor in my decision to study the Bible in-depth. I realized my life's purpose has to come from a relational reconciliation with God's love, Jesus' love sacrifice, and the Holy Spirit and my spirit's reunion (2 Cor 5:14–19; James 2:26).

My life's meaning comes from Jesus and his love-sacrifice for all my sins' consequences. Only after I understood what this meant, accepted his offer of grace, and thanked him with sincere, child-like faith (Matt 16:26; Matt 6:31–33), could I find true meaning in life.

My life's fulfillment is the result of my spiritual rebirth and spiritual growth. Because I am spiritually reborn, I can exercise God's Love Concept daily through a grateful and humble mindset, and acts of faith.[16]

My life's mindset has to come to be humble, contrite, and repentant. I realized that I would learn more with a humble mindset, whereas pride would impede my learning capabilities. Humility helps me to understand, learn, and employ God's Love Concept in my daily life and it helps me to have an open mind toward his spiritual plan for my life.[17]

Chapter Three
SCRIPTURE REFERENCES

1. Luke 13:3; 2 Pet 1:20, 21; Luke 24:25–27
2. Jn 3:3–7; Jn 3:15–18; Jn 5:24; Heb 9:27; 2 Cor 5:6–8; Luke 23:39–43
3. Luke 4:1–13, James 1–15; James 2; 1 Jn 2:15–17; Matt 22:35–40
4. Matt 9:13; Heb 12:1–17; 2 Tim 1:7; Isa 57:15; Isa 40:10; Matt 11:28–30
5. Rom 5:8; Rom 8:32; Jn 15:13
6. Heb 11:6; 2 Pet 1:20–21; Jn 20; Rom 1:19–20; Luke 24:25–27; Deut 31:6; 2 Pet 3:9; Luke 24:44–47; Book of Revelation
7. Rom 10:9–10; Rom 8:28–29; Gal 6:7–8; Luke 18:16–17; Luke 23:39–43
8. Rom 10:9–10; Jn 5:24; Jn 3:15–16; Heb 11:6; Eph 2:8–9; Rom 8:28–29; Gal 6:7–8; Rom Ch 8
9. Matt 22:29–40; Luke 24:25–27; Jn 5:39–40; Jn 14:26
10. Rom 10:9–10; Jn 5:24; Jn 3:15–16; Rom 10:11
11. 1 Cor 13:4–8; Eph 5:18–33; Gal 5:16; Eph 4; Phil 4:4–9; Col 3:12–21
12. Rom 2:1–16; Jer 17:10; 1 Thess 5:23; Gen 1:26; Matt 18:1–6; Rom 4:15; Eph 1:13; Eph 4:30
13. Rom 8:26–30; Eph 1:11; 1 Pet 1:29; Rom 11:1–6
14. Prov 25:2; Rom 8:31–39; Heb 12:6–7, 11; Rom 5:1–11
15. Jn 11:25–26; Jn 3:5–7; Jn 14:6; Eph 1:13; Eph 4:30; Jn 5:24; Rom 10:9–10; Heb 10:10–18; Heb 9:27; Rom Ch 8
16. Mic 6:8; Prov 3:5–6; Ps 37:3–7; 1 Tim 1:5; Eph 4; Mark 16:15
17. Prov 3:5–6; Matt 18:3–4; Matt 11:28–30; Mic 6:8; Prov 22:4; Isa 40:31; Isa 41:10; Deut 31:6; Phil 4:4–9; 2 Tim 1:7; Isa 57:15; 1 Pet 5:5; Ps 113:6; Jam 4:6

Chapter Four

My In-Depth Bible Study Considerations and Revelations

(Jn 5:39; Luke 24:25–27; Eph 1:12–14; Rom 10:13)

I began studying the Bible in earnest and going to Bible studies with our newly befriended neighbors while attending Widener University in Chester, PA in 1968. I was amazed at the plethora of revelations I encountered that directly addressed my questions concerning my life's purpose, meaning, and fulfillment, and my "spiritual missing part." My Bible studies were further supplemented by listening to Dr. J. Vernon McGee during his tenure at the *Through the Bible* radio program. I encountered many key issues during this time in my life.

Reconciliation with God

During my Bible studies, I addressed several relevant subjects associated with reconciliation to God through Jesus by becoming "spiritually born-again" and making better spiritual and wise decisions (2 Cor 5:17–21). These spiritually relevant considerations and revelations, relative to reconciliation with God, are reflected in the remainder of this book.

Playing a Fool's Game

During my initial Bible studies, in particular when I first read the New Testament, I realized that I was playing a fool's game with my life. When I read the New Testament, specifically the Gospels of Matthew and John, and the books of Romans, Ephesians, Galatians, and Hebrews, I realized that God loved me and gave me the ability to make my own independent, unforced choices as proof of his true love for me. It confirmed in my mind that God's love for me required that I receive the consequences of my bad choices. However, my sins were redeemed by Jesus' love sacrifice on the cross. He gave me the choice because he is a God of love (Jer 17:10; Rom 2:1–16). It became very clear in my Bible studies that if I did not accept God's simple eternal salvation plan in pure faith and become spiritually born-again, I would spend eternity absent from God's love in hell (Jn 5:24; Rev 20:15; Ex 32:33). If I became a spiritually born-again Christian, according to the Bible's teachings (Jn 5:39), my life on this earth would be the only hell that I would ever have to experience. Why would I not make a commitment in faith to Jesus and accept his offer of heaven (Heb 11:6), a place filled with God's pure love for all eternity.[1]

Unfortunately, at that time, I needed more faith in God's Word before making a decision about my eternal life destination. My faith had been eroded from living with people who were untrustworthy and and lived according to the world's standards (Rom 10:17; Rom 1). So I continued to study the Bible and my trust in God increased.

Making Better Decisions

My Bible research confirmed that God lets me make my own wise and unwise choices allowing me to experience their consequences in order to become a better decision maker. To paraphrase Hebrews 12:6–11, God allows tribulations for all people so that we will grow spiritually and learn from our decisions, both the good and the bad. To gain this blessing, however, we must seek out the lessons to be learned (see also Prov 25:2; Rom 5:1–11). It was also apparent in my Bible studies that God wanted to reconcile with me concerning my sins' consequences (2 Cor 5:14–19). I concluded that I would choose to accept him in trust, actively consenting in my mind, heart, and will. I not only believed in Christ, but I committed to trusting Jesus, personally accepting his love gift sacrifice on the cross. This gave me the hope of living in heaven with him forever in my new spiritual body.[2]

I concluded that I needed to research and understand specific subjects that are associated with reconciliation with God, becoming spiritually born-again, and making wise spiritual decisions. Most of all, it became very clear that my understanding and striving to employ God's Love Concept in my daily life was the key to my reconciliation and obtaining eternal life with God forever through Jesus.[3]

Understanding Life, Love, Death, and the "Spiritual Missing Part"

My continuing Bible studies ultimately helped me to significantly increase in faith and trust in Jesus Christ. This eventually helped me to determine my answers to my life, love, and death questions and particularly my "spiritual missing part" question (Rom 10:17; Heb 4:12). By diligently studying the Bible, I determined that sin[4.]was doing something that is "non-loving" in my thoughts or actions. Sin resulted in separating my spirit from

God's Holy Spirit: the "spiritual missing part" (Jn 3; Eph 2:1–10). I finally understood that I needed to use God's spiritual viewpoint (i.e. his Love Concept mindset) in order to find answers.

Researching the Concept of "Spiritually Dead"

After a considerable reflection and further Bible research, I concluded that I would lose my soul and spirit and continue to be "spiritually dead" if I continued to live according to my sin nature and the world's sinful standards.[5.] The result would be eternity in hell (Jn 3:36). It became apparent that "death" in the Bible did not mean that I would vanish and exist no more; rather, "death" in the Bible meant separation between my spirit and soul and God's Holy Spirit (Col 2:6, 9–13).

What did I need to do to change my soul and spirit from spiritually dead to spiritually alive and obtain eternal life in heaven through Jesus Christ? After much study, I concluded that my soul and spirit needed to be reunited with God's Holy Spirit to become spiritually alive again.[6.]

Searching for My "Spiritual Missing Part"

The "missing part" I had been searching for was God's pure love in my life (2 Cor 5:16–17). I needed to obtain this pure love connection via the Holy Spirit through reconciliation with God. In an effort to better understand God's Love Concept, Jesus' earthly purpose, my life's purpose, meaning, fulfillment, and my need for spiritual rebirth, I continued searching the Bible. My Bible studies were now beginning to provide me with common sense, realistic, and pragmatic answers as well as showing me how God's Love Concept was the key ingredient in the answer to my questions.[7]

Choosing Heaven or Hell

God wants everybody to go to heaven and be with him for eternity, but he foreknew that not everybody will choose to live by his love standard of being holy, loving, and just (1 Tim 2:4–6; Rom 8:32; Rom 1). The Bible states that folks who do not decide to be "spiritually born-again" through Jesus' are blotted out of God's Book of Life.[8] This infers that everyone's names were initially written into God's Book of Life. God's love will not condemn anyone who has not yet personally committed their first sin.

Nevertheless, a God of love has to allow everybody to make their own personal life decisions and take responsibility for those decisions and their consequences, both good and bad. Otherwise, God would not be a God of pure love and I would not have an independent free will, personal value, or self-worth. Additionally, God provided a way for all people to choose to be forgiven and their sins redeemed. Jesus would not have come to earth to cover my sins' consequences if I could redeem them myself (Jn 14:6; Heb 10:1–18). The name, Jesus, translated means "God Saved." Christ translates as "His anointed One." Jesus' purpose on earth was to provide redemption of our sins' consequences through his sacrifice on the cross.[9.] Only by accepting and trusting in his love sacrifice can we be forgiven, redeemed, and spend eternity in heaven with him.

God's Grace Gift Offers Spiritual Life

God's eternal salvation plan included Jesus' vicarious love sacrifice for me and all people in order to pay for our sins. The Bible states that I still have to choose to accept his grace in pure faith in order to be spiritually born-again (Heb 3:10–18). After all, a gift is not mine until I accept it by my own choice! In my life's journey, I especially relished gifts from folks who gave me a gift out of love, not out of force, tradition, or any other expectation (1 Cor 13:4–8). God indeed was providing this eternal salvation gift to all people because He loves us.

Jesus' Love Sacrifice

My continuing Bible studies revealed that understanding Jesus' love sacrifice was essential to understanding God's love mindset toward me (Rom 5:8–11; Jn 15:13). The Bible spells out, over and over again, that I must choose to confess or acknowledge my sin nature and past sins in order to change my living mindset. Only then can I truly follow God's lead and accept Jesus' love sacrifice for me as payment for the consequences of my sins. In essence, I needed to repent and change my life, confess my sins and sin nature, and trust in Jesus' eternal salvation promise with thanksgiving in order for me to be re-united with the Holy Spirit, born-again spiritually (Rom 10:9–10). I would have to show my faith in Jesus through prayer (Jn 14:6). Thanking God was the necessary faith action for me relative to accepting his simple salvation plan. Thankfulness is a true act of faith in Jesus.[10.] This simple eternal salvation plan made great sense to me. A God of love would not force me to accept his plan because he loved me with unlimited and unconditional love. If God forced people to accept his plan of salvation, that would be in contradiction to his holy, loving, and just character (1 Jn 4:7–16; Ps 145:17). It would undermine my free will, self-worth, and value in God's Love Concept (Rom 2:1–16). This plan also made even more sense to me because it is so simple and loving that anyone could understand it. Even more, it is available to all humans (Rom 1:16–23; Rom 2:1–16), so anyone can employ this simple plan, regardless of their circumstances in life.

Defining Spiritual Terms and Concepts

Proverbs 25:2 states, "It is the glory of God to conceal a thing, but the honor of kings is to search out a matter." After more study and consideration, it became obvious to me that my confusion concerning God's concept of love, life, and death was because I did not correctly understand God's definitions of love, death, life, grace, everlasting life, faith, trust, hope, etc. I concentrated on the spiritual definitions of these concepts and their use in the Bible. As I did these biblical word studies, I discovered that God inserted spiritual messages in names, cities, words, and concepts. This discovery of these messages enhanced my Bible study.[11]

For example, Jerusalem is translated in the Bible as "God's Peace" (Gal 4:26). Death often refers to "spiritual death," or separation from God's love. God's Agape Love, which is unconditional, enduring, respectful charity, is defined in 1 Cor 13:4–8 as patient, kind, protective, trusting, hopeful, persevering, and never failing. This love is contrary to the world's definition of love, which is primarily based upon the question "What is in it for me?" Or, "What will be the consequences from my decision?"

Additionally, I discovered that the exact placement of Jesus, Christ, Jesus Christ, and Christ Jesus in various Bible verses provided different perspectives to saved sinners and to non-saved sinners as appropriate. My effort to obtain God's definition of words in the Bible and their use enlightened my understanding of God's Word.

As I studied, another question came to mind. Was there another factor that affected my understanding of God's salvation plan that needed to be answered? Was my "spiritual missing part" confusion due to not understanding that life, love, death or being born-again spiritually were not just one-time events, but were instead eternally irreversible continued states of being? Continuing Bible study confirmed that the answer to this question was yes (Rom 6).

Chapter Four
SCRIPTURE REFERENCES

1. Rom 5:8; Jn 3:3–5; Jn 14:6; Jn 5:24; Jn 3:15–16; Jn 11:25–26; Rom 14:17; Rom 8:32; Eph 1:13; Eph 4:30; Deut 31:6; 1 Jn 5:10–14
2. Prov 22:4; Rom 10:9, 10, 13; Luke 20:34–38
3. Rom 5:8; 2 Cor 5:16–17; Eph 1:13
4. Gen 2:17; James 2:10; Rom 1; Jer 17:10; Gal 6:7–8; Rom 3:20; Rom 2:1–16
5. Matt 16:24–28; 1 Cor 2:11–14; Col 2:13
6. Jn 3:3–8; James 2:26; Gal 3:10, 22; Jn 14:6; 1 Tim 2:5; Acts 2:38; Acts 4:12; Acts 11:16; Ezek 36:26–27
7. Romans 8:32; Jn 15:13; Jn 14:26; 2 Tim 3:16–17
8. Jn 14:6; Ex 32:32–33; Rev 20:15; Rev 3:5
9. Rom 5:8; Heb 9:11–28; Heb 10:10–17; Jn 5:39, 40; Jn1:25–26; Luke 24:25–27
10. Heb 11:6; John 5:24; Rom 10:9–10; Rom 1:16–17
11. Jn 3:3–18; Jn 6:51, 63; Jn 11:25–26; Jn 15:3–5; Matt 22:36–40; Luke 24:25–27

Chapter Five

Understanding the Value of God's Love

(Rom 5:8; Rom 8:32; Jn 11:25–26; 1 Jn 4:13–16; Gal 6:7–8; 1 Tim 1:5)

I concluded that my life's purpose, meaning, and fulfillment had to be connected to being born-again, spiritually, and growing spiritually (Jn 4:24; Jn 3:3–7; Titus 3:5). I continued my biblical research and analysis to better understand God's purpose, meaning, fulfillment, and "spiritual missing part" for my life. I discovered that the more I studied the Bible the more my spiritual maturity grew, and I would therefore continually increase my understanding regarding the depth of the Bible messages.[1] My understanding of the Bible was greatly enhanced by re-examining Scripture further. I decided at this point to pay particular attention to why I needed the Holy Spirit in my spiritual life.

John 3:5–7, "Jesus answered, Verily, verily, I say unto thee, Except a man be born of water and of the [Holy] Spirit, he cannot enter into the kingdom of God. That which is born of the flesh is flesh; and that which is born of the [Holy] Spirit is spirit. Marvel not that I said unto thee, you must be born again."

Jn 4:24, "God is a Spirit: and they that worship him must worship him in spirit and truth."

Eph 1:13, "In whom ye also trusted, after that ye heard the word of truth, the gospel of your salvation: in whom also after that ye believed, ye were sealed with that Holy Spirit of promise...."

Titus 3:5, "Not by works of righteousness which we have done, but according to his mercy he saved us, by the washing of regeneration, and renewing of the Holy Ghost [Holy Spirit]."

Eph 4:30, "And grieve not the holy Spirit of God, whereby ye are sealed unto the day of redemption."

Ezek 36:26–27, "A new heart also will I give you, and a new spirit will I put within you: and I will take away the stony heart out of your flesh, and I will give you a heart of flesh. And I will put my spirit within you, and cause you to walk in my statues, and ye shall keep my judgements, and do them."

Jn 6:63, "It is the spirit that quickeneth [gives life]; the flesh profiteth nothing: the words that I speak unto you, they are spirit, and they are life."

2 Cor 5:17–19, "Therefore, if any man be in Christ, he is a new creature: old things are passed away; behold, all things are become new. And all things are of God, who has reconciled us to himself by Jesus Christ, and hath given to us the ministry of reconciliation; To wit, that God was in Christ, reconciling the world unto himself, not imputing their trespasses unto them; and hath committed unto us the word of reconciliation."

Gal 5:16, "This I say then, Walk in the Spirit, and ye shall not fulfill the lust of the flesh."

Jn 14:26, "But the Comforter, which is the Holy Ghost [Holy Spirit], whom the Father will send in my name, he shall teach you all things, and bring all things to your remembrance, whatever I have said unto you."

Spiritual Separation caused My "Spiritual Missing Part" Confusion

It was clear: my spirit and God's Spirit were indeed spiritually separated, and I was not connected to God's pure love in my life. This was the reason for my "spiritual missing-part" dilemma. My spirit and God's Holy Spirit were united at my first birth conception in accordance with the Bible.[2] If this were not the case, babies whose bodies expire before they reach the age of accountability would not go to heaven. My spirit and God's Holy Spirit were separated when I committed my first sin.[3] God's Holy Spirit cannot be joined to a sinful person's spirit—God's love and the devil's non-love cannot co-exist (James 4:10). I also concluded that God is not the creator of sin because his love, character, and standard of holiness and justice is totally incongruent with sin. He is not capable of committing sin.[4] I created my own sins.

Avoiding Eternity in Hell

I marveled that my Bible research revealed that I could discount the state of spiritual death forever from my life, according to Jesus' words, by believing, asking, trusting, accepting Jesus into my life and by thanking him for his vicarious love sacrifice for all my sins' consequences (Jn 11:25–26). I am incapable of redeeming the consequences of my own sins. God's salvation plan consists of Jesus' vicarious sacrifice for me to redeem the consequences of all my sins according to his promise. The greatest marvel is that all I had to do in order to secure my eternal salvation was accept Jesus' love sacrifice. Matthew 19:14 states, "But Jesus said, Suffer little children, and forbid them not, to come unto me: for of such is the kingdom of heaven."

Titus 2:11 says, "For the grace of God that bringeth salvation hath appeared to all men." God's salvation plan is for all people. His love is not limited to anyone and is unconditional to everyone forever, regardless of whether a person accepts his love or not

(Rom 8:31–33). However, God does not unconditionally accept sin (Gal 6:7–9; Heb 12:6–8; Heb 13:5). My eternal destiny is contingent upon my acceptance of God's eternal salvation plan, not upon God's love for me. Gal 6:7–8, "Be not deceived; God is not mocked: for whatsoever a men soweth, that shall he also reap. For he that soweth to his flesh shall of the flesh reap corruption; but he the soweth to the Spirit shall of the Spirit reap life everlasting." God can use my unwise decisions to train me to be a better Christian, if I look for the spiritual lessons to be learned from each of my poor decisions. This enables me to grow spiritually and to receive blessings. I finally realized that my past idea of God as an unloving old man with a sharp reaper in his hand racing around the world looking for sinners to send to hell was totally false, as silly as that may seem.

Pondering the Depth of Jesus' Love Sacrifice on the Cross

One thought that I still ponder is how horrifying and excruciating it must have been for Jesus to be without the love of his Father for three hours on the cross as he hung there, dying. Jesus is pure love and has always been full of pure love from his Father (1 Jn 4:7–21). Even though I hope to know the answer to this question, I am also somewhat afraid of the impact this answer might have on me. After all, I am only human and have many limitations. I am trusting that God's love will help me to understand this answer when I arrive in heaven.

Researching My Eternal Destination Options

Even after much study and consideration, I still hesitated to become a spiritually born-again Christian. I had two faithless concerns:

1. Would my spirit and soul never really "die" if I asked and accepted Jesus' sacrifice and promise?

2. Would my spirit and soul really never experience hell (i.e. a place that has no love because of the absence of God's love) if I trust Jesus' concepts of love and spiritual rebirth (Col 2:13)?

Several Bible verses helped me to address and dismiss my "faithless" concerns.

Rom 10:9–10, "That if thou shalt confess with thy mouth the Lord Jesus, and shalt believe in thine heart that God hath raised him from the dead, thou shalt be saved. For with the heart man believeth unto righteousness, and with the mouth confession is made unto salvation."

1 Jn 1:9, "If we confess our sins, He is faithful and just to forgive us our sins, and to cleanse us from all unrighteousness."

Jn 5:24, Jesus said: "Verily, verily I say unto you, he that heareth my word, and believeth on him that sent me, hath everlasting life, and shall not come into condemnation, but is passed from death unto life."

Heb 4:12, "For the word of God is quick, and powerful, and sharper than any twoedged sword, piercing even to the dividing asunder of soul and spirit, and of the joints and marrow, and is a discerner of the thoughts and intents of the heart."

Jesus said in John 3:15–16, "That whosoever believeth in him should not perish, but have eternal life. For God so loved the world, that He gave his only begotten Son, that whosoever believeth in him should not perish, but have everlasting life."

Eph 1:13, "In whom ye also trusted, after ye heard the word of truth, the gospel of your salvation: in whom also after that ye believed, ye were sealed with that Holy Spirit of promise...."

Eph 4:30, "And grieve not the Holy Spirit of God, whereby ye are sealed unto the day of redemption."

Jn 11:25–26, "Jesus said unto her, I am the resurrection, and the life: he that believeth in me, though he were dead [spiritually], yet shall he live. And whosoever liveth and believeth in me shall never die [spiritually]. Believest thou this?"

2 Cor 5:17–19, "Therefore, if any man be in Christ, he is a new creature: old things are passed away; behold, all things are become new. And all things are of God, who has reconciled us to himself by Jesus Christ, and hath given to us the ministry of reconciliation; To wit, that God was in Christ, reconciling the world unto himself, not imputing their trespasses unto them; and hath committed unto us the word of reconciliation."

Jam 2:26, "For as the body without the spirit is dead, so faith without works is dead also."

Answers to my Two Faithless Eternal Salvation Concerns

The answer to my two faithless concerns was that my decision to accept Jesus' eternal salvation was mine alone to make; and the result would be that the I would never experience hell (1 Jn 5:10–13). Becoming spiritually born-again was the solution to finding and resolving the question of the "spiritual missing part." Additionally, knowing that I would spend eternity in heaven released many of the physical, mental, and spiritual shackles from my decision making (Rom 6; Rom 14:17).

I knew I could trust God to keep his promises because God's character is always holy, loving, and just. Therefore, he cannot lie! It took a Christian comedy video to bring me to an understanding that I needed to relate to God as God, not as a human being capable of lying. Exodus 2:13–14 says that, God is "I Am." This understanding helped me to realize once more that God is God, the creator of humans, not the product of creation. Therefore, I should never place my relationship, view, and understanding of God on a human level.

Understanding God's Word and Repetitions

As I studied the Bible, I asked myself why God frequently repeats his messages throughout the Bible? Is he just emphasizing important spiritual truths, or do I need to hear the same message from different perspectives many times before I understand the meaning? Repetition is an established training method to improve effective learning and performance proficiency. God wants me to develop and improve my personal skills, talents, and capabilities in developing my body, mind, and soul. This helps me to become a more productive individual. Why wouldn't God use the same repeating methodology to help me to grow spiritually in my Bible study and faith actions[5]?

God's love for me is never ending. It is comprehensive and inexhaustible (*New Believers Bible, New Testament*, Laurie, 2019). I have confirmed in my life experiences that the repetition of my faith-actions is the only way to exercise, increase, and employ God's knowledge, understanding, wisdom, and effectiveness of my efforts to emulate and share God's love (Prov 3:5–21; Prov 2:6; Eph 4).

Seeking God's Messages in His Creation

As I studied, I questioned why God designed single earth days to go from darkness to light. God's day starts at 6PM and ends at the next day's 6PM for a full day (Gen 1). I also considered that God's creation of spring, summer, fall, and winter follows a similar life-aging pattern, as does his single day sequence. This seems to emphasize similar time patterns applicable to the spiritual importance of my life's beginning and ending on earth. In short, what is God's spiritual timing message relative to my earthly life and my spiritual life, if not to emphasize that I need to seriously consider my life's purpose, meaning, and fulfillment right here and now? I came into the world with my soul, spirit, and body (1 Thess 5:23); and I will leave with the same entities. Therefore, during my life on earth I must address my salvation decision.[6]

Titus 2:11 states, "For the grace of God that bringeth salvation hath appeared to all men." I concluded that a God of pure love would certainly provide many various life signs and repeated messages in his Word out of love. Whether through creation, life roles, education, life experiences, as well as pagan, moralist, and legalist ideologies, God desires to encourage me to seek him and to make my decision concerning my eternal salvation.[7]

The Meaning of Death in the Bible

During my studies, I confirmed that the Bible states that our earthly bodies will die. However, we will receive a new spiritual body after our earthly body expires.[8] Based on this statement and the Bible references to heaven and hell, I concluded again that my soul and spirit would never spiritually die, because God intended me to live forever.[9] The Biblical definition for death often refers to spiritual separation between God's Holy Spirit and my spirit (Jn 3:3, 5–8; James 2:26). This led me back to my previous question about my eternal destination. What did I need to do to resolve this question and my spiritually dead state?

Chapter Five
SCRIPTURE REFERENCES

1. Rom 10:17; Josh 1:8; Prov 2:1–6; Prov 3:1–23; 2 Tim 1:7; 2 Tim 3:16–17
2. Gen 1:26; Gen 2:7; James 2:27; 1 Thess 5:23
3. Rom 3:10, 23; Jn 3:36; Jn 3:3, 5; 1 Jn 3:4; Matt 22:37–40; 1 Tim 1:5
4. Rom 13:10; 1 Tim 1:5; Prov 17:17; Jer 31:3; 1 Jn 4:7–8, 16
5. Jn 3:15–16; Rom 10:9–10; Jn 3:36; Jn 5:24; Deut 31:6; Heb 13:5; 1 Jn 4:13–16
6. James 4:14; 1 Jn 2:15–17; Heb 9:27; Prov 25:2
7. 2 Tim 3:15–17; Rom 1:19–20; Rom 2:2, 6, 11, 16; Rom 10:9–10; Jn 3:36; Jn 5:24
8. Luke 20:34–38; 2 Cor 5:1–8; 1 Thess 5:23; Gen 1:26
9. Prov 20:27; John 4:23–24; 1 Thess 5:23; Jn 11:26; 1 Cor 2:9–16; Jn 3:15–16

Chapter Six

Finding My "Spiritual Missing Part"

(Jn Ch 3; Rom 10:9–10; Eph 1:13)

After more in-depth research of God's concept of love, as defined in the Bible, my conclusion that God's love will always be pure, holy, and just, whatever the circumstances, was continually reaffirmed. This is completely different from our human concept of love that focuses on "what is in it for me" or "what good or bad consequences will I receive from my decisions?"

God's Love Standard

God's love standard is holy, pure, and just. It is this absolute standard that he wants me to strive toward daily. As a result, he can bless me and help me to grow spiritually in tune with his mindset and attitude through my life choices. Spiritual growth through life's experiences is similar to the way a stone becomes smoother as it travels down a waterway.

I confirmed many times in my Bible studies that my transgression of God's love standard is sin. In other words, having non-loving thoughts, words, or actions. Transgression of God's love standard comes out of a mindset that is selfish, inconsiderate, and disrespectful (1 Jn 2:15–17; Luke 4:1–13). I also discovered that God is not as interested in the number of our sins as he is in our mindset being holy, loving, and just. James 2:10 says, "For whosoever shall keep the whole law, and yet offend in one point, he is guilty of all."

God's Holy Spirit Cannot be Connected to Sin

The Bible says that God's Holy Spirit cannot be associated with sin (Rom 3:10, 23; Jer 17:7–10; Rom 5:8). In addition, I learned that if I choose to accept Jesus into my life, my sins' consequences will be forgiven, redeemed by Jesus' love sacrifice on the cross (1 Jn 1:8–10). Therefore, my soul and spirit can now be re-united with the Holy Spirit forever.[1]

Jesus' Hell Experience on the Cross

God created me in his image. I have a soul, spirit, and body just like him (Gen 1:26; 1 Thess 5:23). Therefore, God made me a personal, rationale, and a responsible person, not a puppet. God also provided me with the Bible to advise me of his knowledge, understanding, and wisdom so that I can understand his purpose and meaning for creation, his created living beings, and for my life. In particular, God presented his concept of true love in the Bible. This turned out to be the essential key for my wife and me to unlock our "spiritual missing part." Our lives were missing Jesus' Holy Spirit. The absence of this spiritual connection meant that we could not effectively communicate or relate with God the Father, who is a Spirit, and can only be contacted through a spiritual connection. John 4:24, "God is a Spirit: and they that worship him must worship him in spirit, and in truth."

When Jesus hung on the cross during those three hours of darkness over the earth, he suffered the most horrifying and excruciating sacrifice possible. In that time, he was separated from his Father's love for the first and last time. This sacrifice of separation from his Father's love was so excruciating for Jesus that it became the atonement for the sins of all mankind. It was his "spiritual death" reality atonement sacrifice for all mankind (i.e. Jesus' "hell" period (Ps Chs 22–24)).

Before He was arrested and taken away from the garden of Gethsemane to be crucified, Jesus prayed so fervently that his sweat contained great drops of blood falling to the ground (Luke 22:39–46). The blood and sweat he experienced as he prayed in the garden show the ultimate degree of love sacrifice that Jesus was willing to suffer. He covered the sin consequences for all people of all time in order to show his unlimited and unconditional love for us. Jesus made it possible for everyone to choose to become born-again. We have no excuse! His love for us is truly unlimited and unconditional; we are of great value to him, so much so he chose to give us a free will and not to restrict our decisions and consequences.

"You Reap What You Sow"

God's offer of reconciliation does not require me to suffer such an excruciating sacrifice. Rather, God provided me with a simple, fair, and faithful Love Concept to help me understand and accept his love for me: "we reap what we sow" (Gal 6:7–8). For every action, there is an equal reaction. This is similar to the "golden rule" and is reiterated in Matthew 7:2. The Bible states that Jesus' love sacrifice during his death on the cross for me covered the consequences of all of my sins: past, present, and future. In essence, Jesus' love sacrifice during those three dark hours on the cross was the ultimate example of God's great love for me. In addition the veil in the Temple split at the moment Jesus said, "It is finished," (John 19:30). People could now have access to God. We could finally wake up to the positive blessings of God's Love Concept (2 Cor 3:6–18).

God wants us to trust him and his Love Concept. He wants us to strive to be more loving and to grow spiritually by exercising his Love Concept in our lives. When we do, God can bless us directly, as related to our faith action decisions. God provided his knowledge, understanding, and wisdom in the Bible regarding Jesus' purpose on earth and eternal salvation so that we can make an informed decision. However, we must be willing to seek out his wisdom; only then will we reap its benefits (Prov 25:2; Jn 3:1–12; Jn 14:26).

God's Love Concept rationale of "you reap what you sow" is the fundamental concept that God employs in his plan of reconciliation between himself and all humanity (Jer 17:5–10; Prov 17:17). God wants us to become mature Christians and to make good life decisions that receive fair blessings.

A successful relationship must be founded upon both parties being unselfish, caring, and respectful of one another to have a successful relationship (1 Jn Ch 4). There are always consequences to the actions of both parties in a relationship (both good and bad). How each party handles those consequences shows the level of respect each has for the other. Reaping what I sow is not always negative. Decision-making consequences can be good or bad depending on my decisions and how I learn from the consequences. I should grow wiser in my decision-making depending on my commitment to my life's purpose, Jesus' love for me, and my awareness of the great blessings God wishes to bestow upon me.[2.]

God Wants a Personal Relationship with Me

According to my Bible studies, I am responsible for my choices. This is in concert with God's Love Concept. A good relationship is validated if I am allowed to receive the benefits and consequences of my choices. "For with what judgment ye judge, ye shall be judged: and with what measure ye mete, it shall be measured to you again" (Matt 7:2). The Bible repeatedly states that God wants a direct, reciprocal, mutual, loving, eternal relationship with me because he wants to bless me based upon my own faith-based personal decisions, continuing spiritual growth, and daily striving to execute his loving spiritual plan for my life.[3] In turn, God will be blessed. He wants me to execute his Love Concept daily in my life in order for me to be the best Christian worker possible. God alone can see the best plan for my life. Why would I try to implement my imperfect plans instead of seeking his perfect plan for my life (Prov 3)?

Revelation that My Past Spiritual Education was Faulty

At this point in my journey, it became evident that a majority of what I had learned or absorbed in my first 27 years of life concerning my life, death, purpose, meaning, and God's Love Concept, prior to studying the Bible, was in error. Jesus himself rebuked the Jewish religious leaders of his day for their lack of understanding the spiritual truth of his words, parables, and actions (Jn 3:11–12). It became obvious to me that I needed to continue to learn, appreciate, and absorb God's definitions of love and everlasting life. I needed to decide now, while I am alive on this earth, if I wanted to spent my eternity in heaven or hell. How could I ever consider making the right life choice for myself if I didn't understand God's love standard and how it applied to me (Prov 3:5–7)?

Basis of God's Love Concept

My understanding of God's Love Concept and his mindset became even clearer to me when I read Matt 22:36–40: "Master, which is the great commandment in the law? Jesus said unto him, Thou shalt love the Lord thy God with all thy heart, and with all thy soul, and with all thy mind. This is the first and great commandment. And the second is like unto it, Thou shalt love thy neighbour as thyself. On these two commandments hang all the law and prophets." (See also Josh 1:8; 1 Tim 1:5). God's love, his laws, Jesus' sacrifice, and the Holy Spirit's mindset are all based upon the same standard of true unselfishness, consideration, and love. Complying with God's standard means I must live out his concept of love of being holy, loving, and just through my choices and actions. This is opposed to complying with the devil's standard of selfishness, inconsideration, and disrespect: SIN. The more I decide to live in God's love, the more God blesses me and helps me to grow spiritually (2 Cor 12:10–11). In other words, obeying God's commands helps me to become a more mature, effective Christian who can encourage others. This does not mean I relinquish my decision-making control to God, resulting in me becoming merely a puppet (Eph 4).

My Eternal Salvation Decision and Prayer

On October 16, 1970, while walking my dog and praying, I finally acknowledged and confessed my sins and my sin nature. I repented of my worldly, sinful mindset, accepted Jesus' love sacrifice for all my sins' consequences, and invited him into my soul and spirit. I thanked Jesus and his Holy Spirit for re-uniting with my soul and spirit at that moment. I was spiritually born-again, a Christian forever according to Jesus' promise.[4]

I prayed, "Dear Lord Jesus, I confess that I am a sinner and unable to keep your standard of being holy, loving, and just. I am sorry for all my sin choices, which caused you, others, and me to suffer greatly and needlessly. I accept your love sacrifice on the cross that paid for the consequences of all my sin choices, and I ask you to come into my life and unite my spirit with your Holy Spirit right now. Help me to closely follow your will and plan for my life. I thank you for coming into my life right now, forgiving all my sins right now, and re-uniting my spirit with your Holy Spirit right now. Thank you for eternal life according to your Word. I pray in Jesus' name, eternally grateful for what you have just now done for me. Amen."

No Longer A "Spiritually Missing Part"

This decision fulfilled my "spiritual missing part." I needed to be connected and reconciled with God's love forever through his Holy Spirit, bringing me out of my state of spiritual death (Jn 3:3–7). I have never experienced a "spiritual missing part" in my life since that day! I avoided spiritual death with my spirit's love connection to Jesus' Holy Spirit.

My quest now was to grow spiritually from being a spiritual baby into a spiritually mature adult. As I grew, I was able to encourage my Christian brothers and sisters, and other folks that I met in my life (Eph 4). In particular, my wife and I also realized we wanted to ensure that our immediate family, our children and their children, became spiritually born-again Christians, so that they could spend eternity in heaven too. I whole-heartily did not want to entertain the thought that anyone in my family might not spend eternity in heaven.

Bible Study Promotes Spiritual Faith Growth

My wife and I realized that our faith is an important spiritual attribute, and children have the greatest faith based upon our parental role experiences as mother and father of six children. We also realized that a child-like faith is usually eroded over time as the result of living in this world. Therefore, my wife and I decided that we would have weekly Bible studies with our children to increase their faith and to reduce or mitigate their faith's potential erosion in order to keep them closer to God's Love Concept. Romans 10:17 states, "So then, faith comes by hearing, and hearing by the word of God." We wanted them to find the "spiritual missing part" in their lives as soon as possible.

My Wife, the Evangelist's, Growth

My wife Janice was always a very personable and sociable person. She would talk to every person she encountered, no matter what the circumstances. Later in our marriage, as her bi-polar condition was mitigated and she began to grow spiritually, she would present God's eternal salvation plan to everyone she encountered.

We had a sign hanging in our kitchen that stated: "If Nana [my wife, Janice] can't be found, check Wal-Mart!" Janice would frequently shop at Wal-Mart and many consignment clothing stores for hours. Arriving home from her shopping trips, she would tell us how many folks she met in the stores, including their family history, work, religion, education, concerns, problems, clothes worn, dreams, disappointments, where they lived, what church they attended, likes, dislikes, etc. Then she would share about their eternal salvation conversation and include any plans for future meetings or Bible studies. The point I gained from Janice's social adventures is that, no matter what others' background, current circumstances, or expectations, many folks are also looking for their life's purpose, meaning, fulfillment, and "missing part" just as Janice and I had. I knew I needed to become an effective "missionary" where I am planted on this earth in order to receive many blessings and to be in concert with Jesus' missionary directions.

Mark 16:15, "And he said unto them, Go ye into all the world, and preach the gospel to every creature."

Matt 9:37, "Then saith he unto his disciples, the harvest truly is plenteous, but the labourers are few."

Ephesians chapter four delineates the walk and service of believers, to grow and produce fruit wherever they are planted.

Family Bible Studies Enhance our Children's Education

Besides supporting our children's faith, the Bible studies helped them to better understand, comprehend, and use God's word in their lives. Bible studies also helped our children to read, comprehend concepts, and express themselves, as evidenced by their good grades in school and by getting along with one another in our family setting. Hebrews 4:12, "For the word of God is quick (living), and powerful, and sharper than any twoedged sword, piercing even to the dividing asunder of soul and spirit, and of the joints and marrow, and is a discerner of the thoughts and intents of the heart."

Our children chose to become spiritually born-again Christians early in their lives. Because we studied the Bible together, they were able to resolve their life, love, death, and missing part questions early in their lives. During my younger years, my faith grew mainly from reading Bible verses on a day calendar that hung on my parents' kitchen wall. I did not realize that I was reading Bible verses from the day calendar until much later in my life. However, they made an impact on my young mind.

Benefits of Choosing to Become Born Again

Being born-again, spiritually, provided me with the answers to my life questions concerning my purpose, meaning, and fulfillment. First, my life's purpose (finding my "spiritual missing part") can only come from the reconciliation of my spiritual relationship with God, through Jesus' love sacrifice and the Holy Spirit[5] (*Changes That Heal*, Cloud 1992).

Secondly, my life's meaning and love can only come from understanding, accepting, and sharing Jesus' love sacrifice with others.[6]

Thirdly, my life's fulfillment comes from living in God's love through the Holy Spirit's leading. This happens through prayer, faith actions, grace living, and a humble, grateful attitude. Knowing that my soul and spirit will never die and will exist eternally in a new body in heaven is also a part of my life's fulfillment.[7]

Consideration of Future Spiritual Conflicts

Even after becoming spiritually born-again, I knew that I would have continuing spiritual battles here on earth between my new born-again nature, my old sin nature, and the world's sinful standards. These battles will happen until I go to heaven (Eph 6; Gal 5:16–26). I was a saved sinner, and not yet saint. I would continue to commit sins here on earth, but God's Holy Spirit would always be available inside of me to help me get back on the straight and narrow road of striving to employ God's Love Concept in my thoughts, words, and actions.

Accepting God's grace gift of spiritual rebirth not only saved my eternal soul and spirit from hell, but I was no longer held captive to my sin nature or the world's sinful standards. My decision-making was truly free from these shackles. I was still responsible for my decisions and their consequences as a saved sinner (Gal 6:7–8; Matt 7:2), and I realized that I would have a sin nature that would commit future sins until the day that my body expires. However, these sin consequences have been redeemed already by Jesus' love sacrifice. Now, because I was born again, I had the Holy Spirit's help to reduce my sinning. Being aware of my sin potential keeps me humble, more thankful to Jesus, aware of the devil's tricks. It also helps me become more selfless, considerate, and respectful of others and their need to become spiritually born-again.[8]

The Devil Does Not Love Me

The devil does not like me. He will continue to keep me involved in spiritual battles daily to keep me from sharing the simple plan of salvation with others. The devil and his demons, as well as other people, will create life distractions, diversions, and misinformation. However, Ephesians 6:11–12 states, "Put on the whole armour of God, that ye may be able to stand against the wiles of the devil. For we wrestle not against flesh and blood, but against principalities, against powers, against the rulers of the darkness of the world, against spiritual wickedness in high places."

The devil's greatest trick is to make us think that he does not exist and that he does not influence our choices and lives. When we ignore that possibility, he is free to use some of his chief corrupting tools: fear, guilt, hatred, anger, peer pressure, pride, the snare of gradualism, suicide, egotism, depression, drugs, alcohol, mindless

compliancy, control. His aim is to meld us into world conformity in order to divert us from our spiritual goals. I discovered in my life journey that the devil's three most concerned targets are:
1. Eroding our faith, so that we will trust God less as we grow older
2. Convincing us to rely on religion, worldly ideology, wealth, power, intelligence, physical capabilities, fame, fortune, etc. for our physical and emotional needs
3. Replacing relational reconciliation with God with egotistic ideology instead.[9] The devil and his evil spirits use these tools, because they do not want me to go directly to the Holy Spirit for daily guidance, spiritual knowledge, understanding, and wisdom (Prov 3:5–6; Prov 1:7).

Future Spiritual Growth Decisions

After I chose to become born again, my aim was to live in concert with God's Love Concept (i.e. his basic character of being holy, loving, and just). I wanted to lead a life that would help me become a mature and wise spiritual decision-maker in spite of the spiritual challenges I faced each day. My goal at this point was to grow more mature, spiritually, in my life's journey in order to receive blessings for myself and for those with whom I came in contact. I did not want to remain an unproductive and immature Christian.[10] In other words, since I was going to heaven for eternity and nothing could take that away from me according to Jesus, I wanted to share God's simple plan for obtaining eternal salvation in heaven through Jesus with everyone who was willing to listen to my testimony!

Chapter Six
SCRIPTURE REFERENCES

1. Rom 10:9–10, Eph 1:13–14; 1 Pet 1; 1 Jn 2:24–27
2. Heb 12:6–15; Jam 1:1 to 25; 1 Cor 2:9–16, Prov 25:2
3. Matt 22:39–40; Josh 1:8–9; 1 Tim 1:5; Mic 6:8; Gal 6:7–8
4. Jn 14:6; Heb 11:6; Rom 10:9–10; Eph 2:8–9; Jn 5:24; Eph 1:13; Rom 1:16; Eph 4:30; Titus 3:5
5. 2 Cor 5:17–19; Matt 6:31–33; Matt 22:37–40
6. 2 Cor 5:19; Matt 28:19; 1 Jn 3:23
7. Jn 3; Jn 11:25–26; Rom 8; Eph Ch 4; Mic 6:8; 1 Tim 1:5
8. Rom 8; 1 Jn 4; 1 Jn 5:10–15
9. Luke 4:1–13; 1 Jn 2:15–17
10. Mark 16:15–16; Eph Ch 4; Rom 10:17; Heb 11:6

Chapter Seven

How to Obtain Maximum Blessings Daily

(Ps 37:3–7; Jer 9:23–24; Gal 5:13–26; Prov 22:4)

I learned from my Bible study over and over again that the more I followed God's plan daily, the more blessings I could obtain and share with others.

God wants Maximum Blessings for Everyone

Because God sent his Son Jesus to cover my sins,[1] my Bible studies confirmed over and over again that God wanted me to receive and share as many blessings as possible.[2.] Further, any blessings that I receive must come from my faith actions and will be made possible by my decisions to exercise my faith in God. These daily faith actions include prayer, Bible study, loving thoughts, walking out my faith, and humble thanksgiving.[3.]

The Holy Spirit Provides the Lead for Blessings

Employing, exercising, and growing in my faith with fervor from the Holy Spirit's leading is the only way to receive blessings from God. My past and present personal plans did not consistently provide life successes without God's help. The following verses confirmed this belief.

Heb 11:6, "But without faith it is impossible to please him: for he that cometh to God must believe that he is, and that he is a rewarder of them that diligently seek him."

Matt 22:36–40, "Master, which is the great commandment in the law? Jesus said unto him, Thou shalt love the Lord thy God with all thy heart, and with all thy soul, and with all thy mind. This is the first and great commandment. And the second is like it, Thou shalt love thy neighbour as thyself. On these two commandments hang all the law and prophets."

Josh 1:8–9, "This book of the law shall not depart out of thy mouth; but thou shalt meditate therein day and night, that thou mayest observe to do according to all that is written therein: for then thou shalt make thy way prosperous, and then thou shalt have good success. Have not I commanded thee? Be strong and of a good courage; be not afraid, neither be thou dismayed: for the LORD thy God is with thee whithersoever thou goest."

Eph 4:11–13, "And he gave some, apostles; and some, prophets; and some, evangelists; and some, pastors and teachers; For the perfecting of the saints for the work of the ministry for the edifying of the body of Christ: Till we all come in the unity of the faith, and of the knowledge of the Son of God, unto a perfect man, unto the measure of the stature of the fullness of Christ."

2 Tim 3:16–17 "All scripture is given by inspiration of God, and is profitable for doctrine, for reproof, for correction, for instruction in righteousness: That the man of God may be perfect, thoroughly furnished unto all good works".

Jn 14:26, "But the Comforter, which is the Holy Ghost [Holy Spirit], whom the Father will send in my name, he shall teach you all things, and bring all things to your remembrance, whatever I have said unto you."

Mic 6:8, "He hath shewed thee, O man, what is good; and what doth the LORD require of thee, but to do justly, and to love mercy, and to walk humbly with thy God."

2 Cor 5:17–19, "Therefore, if any man be in Christ, he is a new creature: old things are passed away; behold, all things are become new. And all things are of God, who has reconciled us to himself by Jesus Christ, and hath given to us the ministry of reconciliation; To wit, that God was in Christ, reconciling the world unto himself, not imputing their trespasses unto them; and hath committed unto us the word of reconciliation."

1 Thess 5:16–18, "Rejoice evermore. Pray without ceasing. In every thing give thanks: for this is the will of God in Christ Jesus concerning you."

Ps 37:3–5, "Trust in the LORD, and do good; so shalt you dwell in the land, and verily thou shalt be fed. Delight thyself also in the LORD: and he shall give thee the desires of thine heart. Commit thy way unto the LORD; trust also in him; and he shall bring it to pass."

Prov 3:5–6, "Trust in the LORD with all thine heart; and lean not unto thine own understanding. In all thy ways acknowledge him, and he shall direct thy paths."

Isa 26:3–4, "Thou wilt keep him in perfect peace, whose mind is stayed on thee: because he trusteth in thee. Trust ye in the LORD forever; for in the LORD JEHOVAH is everlasting strength."

Phil 4:6–7 "Be careful for nothing; but in every thing by prayer and supplication with thanksgiving let your requests be made known unto God. And the peace of God, which passeth all understanding, shall keep your hearts and minds through Christ Jesus."

Prov 22:4, "By humility and fear [reverential trust] of the LORD are riches, and honour, and life."

Need for Daily Spiritual Nourishment

Practicing my various capabilities like spiritual knowledge, understanding, wisdom, and faith, coupled with God's Love Concept perspective has helped me to become more proficient in my spiritual endeavors. Accordingly, my soul and spirit need spiritual nourishment every day through prayer, Bible study, and faith actions. Spiritual nourishment helps me to become more aligned with God's Love Concept. As I grow, I receive blessing for myself and others whom I encounter in life. Like Daniel in the Bible who prayed three times a day, I needed to have a spiritual breakfast, lunch, and dinner at minimum each day, in order to strengthen and grow my faith in God.

One of the keys to keeping in contact with God's plan for my life daily is prayer. Prayer turns my mindset to God's mindset, which helps me to focus on God's spiritual fundamentals, priorities, and goals for my life. In short, I know that I will receive many blessings when I exercise these spiritual faith endeavors daily.[4]

Chapter Seven
SCRIPTURE REFERENCES

1. Rom 5:8; Rom 3:21–28; Rom 8:31–32
2. Luke 24:44–47; Mark 16:15–16; Matt 28:19–20; Jn 21:30–31; Ps 37:3–7; Josh 1:8–9
3. Matt 11:28; James 2:26; Mic 6:8; 1 Pet 2; Jer 3:23–24; Prov 3:5–6; Phil 4:4–9
4. 1 Jn 4; 1 Thess 5:16–18; Josh 1:8–9; Prov 3:5–6; 2 Tim 1:6–7

Chapter Eight

Adjusting My Life's Purpose Toward God's Love Concept

(Rom 12:1–2; 1 Jn Ch 4)

As I grew spiritually, I realized that I needed to keep my focus on God's Love Concept in all that I did. It would enable me to maintain a clearer picture of God's spiritual purpose for my life.

God's Love Concept and Relationships

Life experience has shown me that I need to be a friend in order to get a friend. People usually want their friendships to have beneficial experiences to express and share their care and concern (Prov 17:17). Maintaining a focus on God's Love Concept was key in helping me to develop and maintain good relationships with others and even with animals.

A good relationship needs to be founded on mutual, reciprocal, and consequential faith, trust, and actions. This is reflected in the following Bible verse: "But without faith it is impossible to please him [God], for he that cometh to God must believe that he is, and that he is a rewarder of them that diligently seek him" (Hebrews 11:6). In other words, all my choices and related actions require consequences to confirm the true relationship that I have with God and other people.

My research also revealed that the expression "Fear God" in the Bible would be better understood as "have reverential trust in God," which is more in concert with a God of love. Galatians 6:7 says, "Be not deceived, God is not mocked, for whatever a man soweth, that shall he also reap." How could I understand and comprehend Jesus' love sacrifice on the cross for my sins if it did not exonerate my sins' eternal consequences when I accepted Jesus' promise of eternal salvation?

Child-Like Faith is an Important Trust Element

Growing spiritually, I have been especially encouraged by verses that revealed that I need to have a child-like, pure, faith in Jesus. This child-like faith was essential in enabling me to recognize and employ God's knowledge, understanding, and wisdom from the Bible and in my daily walk more effectively.[1]

My faith was further strengthened by Bible verses that stated that my faith would grow through studying the Bible.

Rom 10:17, "So then faith cometh by hearing, and hearing by the word of God."

2 Tim 3:15–17, "And that from a child thou hast known the holy scriptures, which are able to make thee wise unto salvation through faith which is in Christ Jesus. All scripture is given by inspiration of God, and is profitable for doctrine, for reproof, for correction, for instruction in righteousness: That the man of God may be perfect [spiritually and relationally positioned], furnished unto all good works."

2 Pet 1:20–21, "Knowing this first, that no prophecy of the scripture is of any private interpretation. For the prophecy came

not in old time by the will of man: but holy men of God spake as they were moved by the Holy Spirit."

Benefits of Spiritual Growth

As I grew, protecting my faith in God became essential to my purpose, spiritual growth, and blessings.[2.] I also learned from experience that the devil's greatest passion is to destroy, or erode, my faith in God. Faith requires my decision to trust and accept, with childlike faith, Jesus' earthly living purpose and love sacrifice on the cross for me, in order to practice my faith actions daily (Prov 22:4).

God's Love Concept is founded upon "You Reap What You Sow" Principle

Through my studies, I realized I needed to better understand and employ "God's Love Concept." This is found in Galatians 6:7, "Be not deceived, God is not mocked, for whatever a man sows, that shall he reap." This includes blessings for each decision (Matt 7:2). My love capability, strength, and benefits needed to extend to all people, even my adversaries, if I wanted my love to be pure, unfailing, and beneficial. It also became obvious, through my life experiences as a born-again Christian, that my spiritual growth was directly related to my continuing practice of loving God first and my neighbor as myself daily.[3.] My love for God and for my neighbor was especially strengthened when I prayed for my adversaries—people who were not loving toward to me.

Reconciliation with God by the Holy Spirit

I concluded from my Bible studies that my purpose in life, my meaning, fulfillment, and spiritual growth needed to be based on regularly following certain guidelines:

1. Continue to grow and increase my relational reconciliation between God's Holy Spirit and my spirit (2 Cor 5:17–19).

2. Maintain and grow in pure faith in Jesus (Rom 10:17).
3. Continue to study the Bible to increase in wisdom, knowledge, and understanding of God and his Love Concept (Prov 2).
4. Share Jesus' Gospel with everyone I come in contact with by following the Holy Spirit's leading with gratitude and humility.[4]

Chapter Eight
SCRIPTURE REFERENCES

1. Prov Ch 2; Mark 10:15; Prov 3:5–6; Psalm 37:7; Jn 14:26
2. Rom 12:1–2; Matt 16:24–28; Prov 3:5–6; Heb 11:6
3. Col 3:12–13; Rom 7:4; Rom 6:14; 2 Pet 1–10
4. Mark 16:15; Phil 4:4–7; Matt 11:28–30; 1 Thess 5:16–18

Chapter Nine

Adjusting Our Mindset to Follow God's Will

(Rom 5, 8, 12)

Seeking God's love and leading first, before I made decisions, provided greater peace, joy, and happiness to me (Prov 3:5–6; Phil 4:4–7). My conclusion was that my blessings would be more evident, beneficial, and enjoyable if my mindset, attitude, and associated actions were more in line with God's Love Concept. I also concluded that since Jesus had covered all my sins (i.e. past, present, and future sins), it would be better for me to have a humble, thankful attitude and spiritual mindset in order to continue receiving blessings for myself and those I encountered.[1.] Never take God's love and blessings for granted!

It became obvious that the more I followed the Holy Spirit's leading in all of my ways, the more I would relish and enjoy the Holy Spirit's virtues and blessings of spiritual power, love, and self-discipline.[2.] As an example, Proverbs 22:4 states, "By humility and the fear [reverential trust] of the LORD are riches, and honour, and life."

Encouraging, Edifying, and Uplifting Brothers and Sisters

Another aspect of God's Love Concept mindset is encouraging, or edifying, my Christian brothers and sisters (Eph Ch 4). In order to effectively uplift others, I needed daily spiritual nutrition. After all, if I don't use my skills, talents, and capabilities, my proficiencies in these areas degrade. So I perseveringly worked at having a spiritual breakfast, lunch, and dinner every day (Rom 5:3). My spiritual nourishment came from Bible study, prayer, faith actions, and remembering that I was going to heaven, and nothing could stop that from happening.

In addition, I knew that I should be fervently seeking to share the good news of God's eternal salvation with others as opportunities presented themselves through the Holy Spirit's divine appointments.[3.] I found that praying daily with thanksgiving for the Holy Spirit's leading helped me to keep my mindset closer to God's mindset. This enabled me to be more prepared to share the good news with whomever I encountered.[4] The following Bible verses nourished my soul and spirit, and encouraged daily use of God's spiritual fundamentals to strengthen my spiritual growth and sharing with others:

Heb 11:6, "But without faith it is impossible to please him: for he that cometh to God must believe that he is, and that he is a rewarder of them that diligently seek him."

Prov 3:5–6, "Trust in the LORD with all thine heart; and lean not unto thine own understanding. In all thy ways acknowledge him, and he shall direct thy paths."

Jam 2:26, "For as the body without the spirit is dead, so faith without works is dead also."

Jn 15:7, "If ye abide in me, and my words abide in you, ye shall ask what ye will, and it shall be done unto you."

Phil 4:6, "Be careful for nothing; but in every thing by prayer and supplication with thanksgiving let your requests be made known unto God."

Deut 31:6, "Be strong and of a good courage, fear not, nor be afraid of them: for the LORD thy God, he it is who doth go with thee; he will not fail thee, nor forsake thee."

Ps 37:3–5, "Trust in the LORD, and do good; so shalt thou dwell in the land, and verily thou shall be fed. Delight thyself also in the LORD, and he shall give thee the desires of thine heart. Commit thy way unto the LORD; trust also in him, and he shall bring it to pass."

Isa 26:3–4, "Thou wilt keep him in perfect peace, whose mind is stayed on thee: because he trusteth in thee. Trust ye in the LORD forever; for in the LORD JEHOVAH is everlasting strength."

Jn 14:26, "But the Comforter, which is the Holy Ghost [Holy Spirit], whom the Father will send in my name, he shall teach you all things, and bring all things to your remembrance, whatever I have said unto you."

2 Tim 3:16, "All scripture is given by inspiration of God, and is profitable for doctrine, for reproof, for correction, for instruction in righteousness."

Col 3:17, "And whatsoever ye do in word or deed, do all in the name of the Lord Jesus, giving thanks to God and the Father by him."

Enhanced Faith Strengthens Us to Grow Spiritually

Most of all I tried to remember that Jesus suffered for my sin consequences out of his love for me. I cannot duplicate this kind of love and sacrifice. Therefore, I reminded myself that I needed to do all things in Jesus' name so that I can practice my gratitude and thankfulness to Jesus and keep a humble mindset.[5] Memorizing Bible verses keeps my mind in tune with God's mindset and prepares me to share his Love Concept with others quickly. I desire to increase my faith daily in Jesus because my faith helps me to seek a spiritually pure heart, clean conscience, and a strong God-like love.[6] Sharing Bible verses with others eliminates a lot of adverse discussions, arguments, and conjectures concerning God's mindset or what he means. This also allows me to remind folks that if they have a question, if they're confused or disagree with what I relate, their concern is with God, not me.[7]

Practice Spiritual Growth Values

After much consideration and prayer, I became convinced that I needed to follow a strategy to assist me in my daily Christian mindset growth efforts (practice, practice, practice my spiritual fundamentals daily!).

1. Study God's mindset.[8]
2. Strive to grow in God's knowledge, understanding, and wisdom.[9]
3. Stay within God's mindset.[10]

Spiritual Value of My Life Skills, Talents, and Capabilities

God placed me where I needed to live so that I would be able to successfully develop and use my talents, skills, and spiritual perspective to be a more effective born-again Christian. God's Word states that I will never be in a situation that would not have a way to get out. Consequently, I can have effective confidence in my family, neighborhood, and life work because God has my back. It is important, however, that I express the proper spiritual mindset of joy, a strong prayer-life, and thankfulness for all blessings and learning situations I have encountered.[11]

God made me spiritually equal to others in his perspective. Each of us is highly valued by God. However, I am not necessarily equal to others' capabilities in relation to our talents, skills, and effectiveness. Each of us has been given unique abilities by God. Otherwise, we would not be unique individuals, which contradicts God's Love Concept.

Chapter Nine
SCRIPTURE REFERENCES

1. Jn 14:6; 1 Thess 5:16–18; Mic 6:8
2. Jn 14:26; 2 Tim 1:6–7; Gal 5:16–26
3. Matt 28:19–20; 1 Tim 2:1–4; Mark 16:15
4. Matt 28:19–20; Eph 4; 1 Thess 5:17; Eph 5:20
5. Matt 11:28–30; Eph 5:20; Phil 4:4–7; Mic 6:8
6. Rom 4:10; 1 Tim 1:5; Rom 10:17; Mic 6:8; Eph 4:2; Psalm 37:3–7
7. Deut Ch 6; Josh 1:8–9; Jn 14:6; Jn 14:26; Prov 3
8. Matt 22:36–40; Luke 18:16–17; Jn 5:39–40; Josh 1:8–9; Prov 3:5–6; Heb 11:6; Gal 6:7–9
9. Luke 24:25–27; Jn 14:26; Jn 5:39; 2 Tim 1:6–7
10. 1 Tim 1:5; Rom 12:1–2; James 1:22–25; Rom 2:28–29; Mic 6:8; 2 Cor 12:9–10; Deut 31:6
11. 1 Thess 5:16–18; Mic 6:8; Josh 1:8–9

Chapter Ten

Growing Daily into a Mature Spiritual Being

(Matt 22:37–40; 1 Thess 5:16–18; Mic 6:8)

In order to be a more fruitful Christian, share my learned lessons, and grow spiritually I needed to understand and explain God's Love Concept in simple terms.

Mature Spiritual Growth Simplified

I imagine God's Love Concept as a very large picture puzzle whose parts consist of the messages in the 66 books of the Bible, the Mosaic Law, and God's grace concept. God's grace concept consists of believing and accepting that Jesus' death on the cross that redeemed all of humanity's sin consequences for free. Jesus established a sinless, undeserved grace account for all humans in heaven. It requires people to confess their sin nature, repent, and to ask Jesus to come into their lives with thankfulness in order to receive their grace gift of eternal salvation in heaven.[1]

Foundation for God's Love Concept Versus the Mosaic Law

My concept of a spiritual picture puzzle helps me to better understand the purpose, meaning, and relationship between the Mosaic Law and the two most important royal commandments as stated by Jesus: love God first and love your neighbor as yourself (Matt 22:36–40). My overall puzzle's theme serves as a reflection of God's Love Concept. The puzzle pieces represent smaller "parts" of the overall picture, the various spiritual aspect of God's Love Concept. These smaller parts identify all of the total actions that I would have to comply with daily in order to not violate God's Love Concept and work my way into heaven (James 2:10). However, it was evident that if I could work my way to obtain eternal life in heaven, then Jesus would not have needed to come to earth in human form to accomplish his love sacrifice on the cross for me.[2] The puzzle picture concept helps me to effectively concentrate on the two commandments identified by Jesus as the basis of God's Love Concept instead of trying to comply every moment of everyday with all the requirements in the 66 Bible books and the Mosaic Law, which I can never do.[3]

All 66 Bible Books have a Spiritually Mature Central Theme

Each of the 66 Books in the Bible has an individual and specific theme to address specific human spiritual conditions (i.e. 66 different perspectives of addressing God's Love Concept, mindset, and plan of salvation). For example, the Book of Matthew views Jesus as King, the Book of Mark views Jesus as a Servant, the Book of Luke views Jesus as a Man, and the Book of John views Jesus as Deity. As a further note, I discovered that the Book of Romans is the one book that contains the majority of Christian truths.

Spiritual Growth Objectives

God wants me to exercise the following three management processes daily to grow spiritually and to keep my mindset focused on him (Rev 1; Thess 5:16–18).

1. Praying to the Holy Spirit daily keeps my mind, attitude, and faith actions focused on God's love and his purposes.[5]

2. Seeking God's lessons from all good and bad decisions and circumstances produces great spiritual training, growth, and blessing.[6]

3. Thanking God for all my circumstances, regardless of whether they are good or bad, provides the greatest knowledge, understanding, wisdom, rewards, spiritual growth (1 Thess 5:17–19). It also promotes the transformation of my mind, soul, and spirit to God's Love Concept.[7]

Chapter Ten
SCRIPTURE REFERENCES

1. Jn 14:6; Eph 2:8–9; Rom 1:16; Rom 10: 9–10; John 5:24; Eph 1:13; Titus 3:5; Rom 6:23
2. Rom 3:9–27; Eph 2:8–9; Jn 14:6; Heb 11:6; Rom 5:1–12
3. Rom 3:21–28; Jer 17:9–10
4. Matt 22:29–40; Luke 24:25–27; Jn 5:39–40; Jn 14:26
5. Prov 3:5–6; Ps 37:3–7; Matt 11:28–30; Rom 12:1–2; Jn 15:5; Deut 31:6; Mic 6:8; Isa 40:31; Matt 18:28–29; John 14:26; 2 Tim 3:16–17; Jn 14:6; John 15:7
6. Prov 22:4; 1 Cor 10:11–15; Prov 25:2; 2 Cor 12:9–10; Heb 12:1–15
7. Romans 12:1–2; Rom 8:31–39; Matt 7:1–2; Rom 1; Prov 25:2; Jn 3:11–12; 1 Thess 5:16–18; James 1

Chapter Eleven

Adjusting My Behavior to God's Love Concept in My Daily Life

(Col 3:12–13; Matt 1:26; Matt 11:28–30)

In order for me to adjust my behavior to employ God's Love Concept daily and have a closer walk with God, I need to adjust my behavior through the Holy Spirit's leading. Most importantly, I need to remember that God is holy, loving, and just—all the time, no matter what. I must remember to be grateful, humble, and thankful for Jesus' love and practice the following guidelines, which I obtained from my Bible studies.

Faith-Actions Daily Checklist

I have placed the following guidelines at various locations in my living space to remind me to practice, practice, practice my faith-actions frequently. They prompt me to remember God's love and blessings, and not take them for granted, and to keep a humble, thankful, and loving mindset.[1]

1. Be thankful for Jesus' love and his sacrifice that covered my sins' consequences. Continue to grow spiritually in wisdom, knowledge, and understanding of God's Love Concept and how it is essential in every aspect of life.[2]

2. I am a spiritually born-again Christian, a saved sinner who is going to be in heaven forever according to Jesus' promise; I will never die a spiritual death.[3]

3. Be a repentant, humble, grateful saved sinner, remembering Jesus' love sacrifice on the cross. He has helped me to understand and find the "spiritual missing part" in my life through the reunion of my spirit and his Holy Spirit.[4]

4. Remember that God's commandments, ordinances, and judgments (the intent of the Mosaic Law) are based on the big picture of loving God first and my neighbor as myself. Emulate God's Love Concept by being holy, loving, and just.[5]

5. God wants everybody to go to heaven and be with him for eternity, but he foreknew that not everybody will choose to live by his love standard of being holy, loving, and just (1 Tim 2:4–6; Romans 8:32; Romans 1). The Bible states that folks who do not choose to be spiritually born-again through Jesus are blotted out of God's Book of Life.[6] This infers that the names of all people were initially written into God's Book of Life. I need to follow the Holy Spirit's lead on whom I share God's simple plan for eternal salvation with, because I can't see into folks' souls and spirits.

6. All people are sinners, and their souls and spirits will live forever. Everyone needs to make a decision to accept Jesus and his love sacrifice to secure eternal salvation in heaven.[7]

7. All people have to decide by faith to accept Jesus' love sacrifice to cover their sins and be spiritually born-again, or to reject Jesus' love sacrifice and live under the Mosaic Law and its consequences.[8]

8. Pray daily for God's will and plan. This is a great practice of my faith and the best way to keep my mindset on God's spiritual mindset and plan for me.[9]

9. Follow the Holy Spirit's lead daily. I don't have all the answers for my life actions or for other humans I encounter in my divine appointments.[10]

10. Grow spiritually each day through prayer, Bible study, humble faith actions, and thankfulness.[11]

11. Use God's Word in all my divine appointments with others as Jesus did when he was encountered by the devil.[12]

12. Test the spirits of those I encounter to see if they are trying to live by God's love standard, which is holy, loving, and just, or are they living by the devil's non-loving standard, which is selfish and disrespectful.[13]

13. The tribulations in this life are the consequences of unwise human decisions, not God's desire, planning, or design, "Who will have all men to be saved, and to come unto the knowledge of the truth" (1 Tim 2:4). God, as the Creator, can take human lives by appropriate means whenever he wants, in order to reveal his pure Love Concept, and to provide opportunities for blessings to all who are willing to make wise decisions.[14]

14. Share the message of eternal salvation in heaven. It is a gift of grace (not works). I must share this truth with everyone I encounter so that they can decide to accept the gift now by their own free choice.[15]

15. Remember: all Christians are members of the same spiritual family and are filled with the same Holy Spirit.[16]

16. Participate in a Bible-believing and Bible-practicing church and small group Bible study to grow spiritually, encourage other believers, and to support the spiritual growth of other church members. The Church is composed of people; it is not the building.[17]

17. Research the faith doctrine statement of the church where I participate in order to ensure that the statement is in concert with the Bible.[18]

18. Love, encourage, uplift, edify everybody—though not their sinful actions. Striving to live in God's pure love daily will help me to be a fruitful and productive Christian. [19]

19. Rejoice always, especially about going to heaven. Pray without ceasing and give thanks in everything, for this is the will of God in Christ Jesus for me (1 Thess 5:16–18).

20. Thank God in Jesus' name for covering all the consequences of my past, present, and future sins through his love sacrifice on the cross, coming into my life forever, and by renewing my spirit with his Holy Spirit to confirm my eternal salvation in heaven forever.[20.]

21. I need to ensure that my communications and relationships are based upon God's spiritual common ground: Jesus is my Lord and my Savior, the Bible is God's Word, and the Holy Spirit will lead me in all of my decisions and activities, otherwise my activities will not produce blessings for me or for others.[21]

22. Trust that God, through Jesus' love sacrifice, and life examples will pour out blessings.

Embrace God's Love Concept and Receive Many Blessings

I trust that others will also decide to follow the Holy Spirit's leading daily and will be blessed using the knowledge, understanding, and wisdom that I've gained and documented in this guide based upon my Bible studies. [22] I hope that you will allow God to bless you and yours by making wise spiritual decisions in your life. [23] Remember that practice, practice; practice living and walking in the Holy Spirit. This will help you become a mature and effective spiritual person (Gal 5:16, 18, 22–26).

Many of the Bible verses and much of the information about God's Love Concept through this book because I feel that repetition is a good way to comprehend and learn basic fundamental Bible truths. I have also developed 48 Bible Lessons that will support your daily spiritual thoughts, walk, and talk. These Bible lessons can be found on my JC Power and Light Company Blog Site at https://ixoyecc.com/ (product two).

I pray that you discover your "spiritual missing part," and that you will make your eternal salvation decision to be spiritually born-again immediately to secure your place in heaven forever through Jesus' promise.[24]

I trust that you now know how to avoid spiritual death and hell by accepting God's pure love through Jesus' love sacrifice on the cross by faith. I trust also that you will be able to grow spiritually to receive many blessing for you and all whom you encounter (2 Tim 7).

Bible Verses to Support Spiritual Growth

I encourage you to research the following Bible verses for spiritual nourishment to your soul and spirit. Good spiritual nutrition will encourage your growth: Jn 5:39–40, Heb 4:12; 2 Tim 16–17; Prov 3; Gal 5:13–26; Jn 11:25–26; Jn 14:26; Eph 4; Mic 6:8; Jos 1:8; Gal 5:16; Col 2:8; 1 Tim 1:5; 2 Tim 3:15–17.

Bible Verses to Enhance Your Spiritual Walk with God

Jn 11:25–26, "Jesus said unto her, I am the resurrection, and the life: he that believeth in me, though he were dead, yet shall he live: And whosoever liveth and believeth in me shall never die. Believest thou this?"

1 Jn 1:9, "If we confess our sins, he is faithful and just to forgive us our sins, and to cleanse us from all unrighteousness."

Rom 10:9–10, "That if thou shalt confess with thy mouth the Lord Jesus, and shalt believe in thine heart that God hath raised him from the dead, thou shalt be saved. For with the heart man believeth unto righteousness; and with the mouth confession is made unto salvation."

1 Jn 5:14, "And this is the confidence that we have in him, that, if we ask any thing according to his will, he heareth us."

Ezek 36:26–27, "A new heart also will I give you, and a new spirit will I put within you: and I will take away the stony heart out of your flesh, and I will give you a heart of flesh, And I will put my spirit within you, and cause you to walk in my statues, and ye shall keep my judgements, and do them" (See also 2 Cor 5:17; 2 Cor 6:16).

Mic 6:8, "He hath shewed thee, O man, what is good; and what doth the Lord require of thee, but to do justly, and to love mercy, and to walk humbly with thy God."

Prov 3:5–6, "Trust in the Lord with all thine heart; and lean not unto thine own understanding. In all thy ways acknowledge him, and he shall direct thy paths."

2 Cor 5:17–19, "Therefore, if any man be in Christ, he is a new creature: old things are passed away; behold, all things are become new. And all things are of God, who has reconciled us to himself by Jesus Christ, and hath given to us the ministry of reconciliation; To wit, that God was in Christ, reconciling the world unto himself, not imputing their trespasses unto them; and hath committed unto us the word of reconciliation."

Looking Forward to Jesus' Return

I am trusting that this memoir's message will help you to support the Great Commission of seeking to help others to become spiritually born-again so that they can enjoy the many blessings you are enjoying. In addition, if you are looking forward to Jesus' return and future events in the seven years of tribulation, I recommend you read *New Believers Bible, New Testament*, by Greg Laurie (2019), and *Dispensational Truth of God's Plan and Purpose in the Ages* by Rev. Clarence Larkin (2011).

Dare to Choose to Accept God's Blessings

I hope that this book is helpful in promoting your spiritual growth. I pray many blessings for you, and I trust that you will grow spiritually where you are planted and that you will share your blessings with many (1 Pet 1:3–8). In Jesus' name I have prayed.

Chapter Eleven
SCRIPTURE REFERENCES

1. Matt 11:28–30; 1 Thess 5:16–18; 1 Tim 1:5; Mic 6:8; Deut 6:1–9; Josh 1:8–9
2. Matt 22:37–40; Prov 3:5–6; Rom 5:8; Eph 1:13; 2 Cor 5:17–19; Titus 3:5; Mic 6:8; 1 Thess 5:16–18
3. Rom 10:9–13; Rom 8:14–17; Col 2:6, 13
4. Rom 5:8; Jn 14:6; Jer 26:13; Jer 18:8
5. Ex 19–40; Leviticus; 1 Jn 3:23; Matt 22:37–40; Eph 3:16–19; 1 Tim 1:5; Gal 6:7–9
7. Jn 14:6; Ex 32:32–33; Rev 20:15; Rev 3:5
8. Jn 15:7; Jn 5:24; Rom 3:19–28; Rom 6:23; Rom 8:1–17
9. Jn 15:7; 1 Jn 4:7–16; 1 Jn 3:23–24; 1 Jn 2:15–17; Jam 2:10; Gal 3:10–12; Gal 2:16
10. 1 Thess 5:17; Gal 3:3; Prov 3:5–6; James 2:26
11. Rom Ch 8; 1 Tim 1:7; Gal 5:16
12. Heb 11:6; Rom 10:17; Josh 1:8–9; 1 Thess 5:17; Eph 4; 2 Tim 3:16–17; Prov 9:9–10; Prov 1:1–7; 2 Pet 1:20
13. Luke 4:1–13; Heb 4:12; 2 Tim 1:7; Col 3:17; 2 Tim 3:15–17; Phil 4:4–7; Prov 3:6–7; Psalm 37:4–8; Heb 4:12
14. Matt 22:37–40; 1 Jn 4; 1 Jn 2:15–17; Luke 4:1–13; 1 Jn 2:15–17; 1 Cor 15:33; 1 Cor 14:33; 1 Cor 3:16–17
15. Gal 3:10–12; Rom 3:19–28; Gal 6:7–9; Rom 1:16–32; 1 Jn 2:15–17; Deut 20; Heb 12:10–15; Jam 1:1–25
16. Luke 4:14–21; Mark 28:18; Eph 2:8–9; Rom 10:9–10
17. Eph 4:4–6; Prov 3:5–6; Deut 31:6
18. Heb 10:24–25; Eph 4:1–16; James 1:22–27; 1 Jn 4; Titus 2; 1 Pet 4:7–8

19. "Doctrinal Statement," Dallas Theological Seminary, Dallas, Texas; 2 Pet 1:20–21; Heb 4:12; 2 Tim 3:16–17

20. 1 Jn 4:1–10; Gal 6:7–9; Eph 4:11–16; James 2

21. Jn 5:24; Eph 1:13–14; Col 3:17; 1 Jn 5:10–14

22. 1 Jn 4:1–9; 1 Tim 6; 2 Tim 3:16–17; Rom 8:1–17; Jn 15:3–5

23. Prov 2:3–6; Prov 1:7; Isa 40:31

24. Prov 3:5–6; Josh 1:8–9; Deut 31:6

25. Jn 3:3, 5–7, 15–17, 36; Jn 5:24; Eph 2:8–9; Rom 10:9–10; Eph 1:13

Appendix 1:
References and Acknowledgements

1. Scofield, C. I. Scofield, *New Scofield Reference Bible*, New York: Oxford University Press, 1967.

2. Jeremiah, David, *The Jeremiah Study Bible*, Worthy Book Publishers, 2019.

3. Jeremiah, David, *God Loves You*, FaithWords, 2012.

4. Swindoll, Charles R., *The Owner's Manual for Christians*, Nashville, Tennessee: Thomas Nelson Publications, 2009.

5. Laurie, Greg *New Believer's Bible, New Testament*, Carol Stream, Illinois: Tyndale House Publishers, Inc., 2019.

6. Cloud, Henry, *Changes That Heal*, Clinical Psychology, Zondervan, 1992,

7. "Doctrinal Statement," Dallas Theological Seminary, Dallas, Texas.

8. LaHaye, Tim, *Spirit-Controlled Temperament*, Carol Stream, Illinois, Tyndale House Publishers, Inc., 1992.

9. Larkin, Clarence, *Dispensational Truth of God's Plan and Purpose in the Ages*, Manfield Centre, Connecticut: Martino Publishing, 2011.

Appendix 2:
Christian References and Organizations to Assist in your Spiritual Growth

---

"Turning Point", Dr. David Jeremiah, www.davidjeremiah.org/radio

"Insight for Living Ministries", Dr. Charles Swindoll, www.insight.org

"New Life Live!", Dr. Henry Cloud, www.newlife.com/broadcasts

Thru the Bible Radio, Dr. J. Vernon McGee, www.ttb.org

Family Institute, Dr. James Dobson, www.drjamesdobson.org

Author, Dr. Tim LaHaye, www.timlahaye.com

"Harvest Christian Fellowship," Greg Laurie, www.harvest.org

Dallas Theological Seminary, www.dts.edu

Child Evangelism Fellowship Ministries, www.cefonline.com/ministries

Campus Crusade for Christ Ministries, www.cru.org/us/en/about.html

Josh McDowell Ministries, www.cru.org

Narramore Christian Foundation, www.ncfliving.org

Appendix 3:
Abbreviations of Books of the Bible:

A list of abbreviations of the Books of the Bible according to *The SBL Handbook of Style*, 2d ed., 2014.

Old Testament

Gen	Genesis	Song	Song of Solomon
Ex	Exodus	Isa	Isaiah
Lev	Leviticus	Jer	Jeremiah
Num	Numbers	Lam	Lamentations
Deut	Deuteronomy	Ezek	Ezekiel
Josh	Joshua	Dan	Daniel
Judg	Judges	Hos	Hosea
Ruth	Ruth	Joel	Joel
1, 2 Sam	1, 2 Samuel	Amos	Amos
1, 2 Ki	1, 2 Kings	Obad	Obadiah
1, 2 Chr	1, 2 Chronicles	Jonah	Jonah
Ezra	Ezra	Mic	Micah
Neh	Nehemiah	Nah	Nahum
Esth	Esther	Hab	Habakkuk
Job	Job	Zeph	Zephaniah
Ps	Psalms	Hag	Haggai
Prov	Proverbs	Zech	Zechariah
Eccl	Ecclesiastes	Mal	Malachi

New Testament

Matt	Matthew	1, 2 Thess	1, 2 Thessalonians
Mark	Mark	1, 2 Tim	1, 2 Timothy
Luke	Luke	Titus	Titus
Jn	John	Phlm	Philemon
Acts	Acts	Heb	Hebrews
Rom	Romans	Jas	James
1, 2 Cor	Corinthians	1, 2 Pet	1, 2 Peter
Gal	Galatians	1, 2, 3 Jn	1, 2, 3 John
Eph	Ephesians	Jude	Jude
Phil	Philippians	Rev	Revelation
Col	Colossians		

Appendix 4:
Fundamental Bible Truths

Below are Bible references to the fundamental truths addressed in this book.

1 Jn 4 (God's Love Standard)
Heb 4:12 (God's Wisdom)
2 Tim 3:16 (God's Knowledge)
1 Tim 2:4–6 (God's Intent)
1 Cor 2:10–14 (God's Understanding)
Jn 4:24 (God is a Spirit)
Phil 4:4–8 (God's Peace)
Rom 14:17 (God's Joy)
Ps 46:10 (God's Deity)
Gen 2:7 (Man's Soul)
James 2:26 (Man's Spirit)
Matt 22:36–37 (God's Love Commandments)
Matt 27:45–53 (Jesus' Love Sacrifice)
Heb 11:6 (Faith)
Gal 6:7–8 (Life Choices)
Rom 3:3, 23 (Sin Nature)
James 2:10 (Transgression of the Law)
Eph 2:1–10 (Spiritual Death)
Jer 26:13 (Repentance)
Rom 3:3, 5–7 (Spiritual Birth)
Eph 2:8–9 (Salvation by Grace)
Titus 3:5 (Holy Spirit Renewal)
Rom 10:9–10 (Salvation is Our Choice)

1 Jn 5:10–14 (Salvation Confirmation)
1 Tim 1:5 (End of the Law by Love)
2 Cor 5:14–19 (Reconciliation)
1 Jn 4:16 (Dwell in Love)
Gal 5:16–26 (Walk in Holy Spirit)
Prov 3:5–6 (Trust)
Prov 25:2 (God's Delight)
Prov 2:6 (Wisdom)
Rev 20:10–15 (Blotted out of God's Book of Life)
1 Cor 13:4–8 (Pure Love)
Eph 1:13 (God's Promise)
Eph 4 (One Spirit, Family, Body)
Deut 31:6 (No Fear in Mature Love)
Mic 6:8 (Love, Mercy, Humility)
Heb 12 (Tribulation Lessons)
Rom 5:3–5 (Adversity Virtues)
1 Jn 2 (Spiritual Growth)
1 Pet 1:2 (Sanctification)
2 Pet 1 (Christian Virtues).

Appendix 5

48 Basic Bible Lessons Table of Contents
To assist to in your spiritual growth, I am including 48 proposed bible lessons. The titles of the bible lessons are:

1. Bible Teachers Perspective concerning God's Love, Dilemma, and Eternal Life
2. Searching for My "Spiritual Missing Part"
3. My Decision to Research the Bible
4. Conclusions from My Past Life
5. Bible Revelations and Verses
6. My Decision to Obtain Eternal Life
7. Understanding the Value of God's Love
8. How to Obtain Maximum Blessings Daily
9. Adjusting my Life's Purpose Toward God's Live Concept
10. Adjusting my Mind-Set to follow God's Will for Me
11. Growing daily into a Mature Spiritual Being
12. Adjusting my Behavior to God's Love Concept in my Daily Life
13. Spiritual Roles of God
14. God's Grace versus Mosaic Law
15. God's Love Defined
16. God's Simple Plan of Salvation Bible Verses
17. God's Holy Spirit Role vs Mosaic Law Mandates
18. God's Love, Responsibility, and Accountability
19. Our Childlike Trust is Essential to Our Spiritual Life
20. Jesus Pure Love Questions
21. Daily Priorities to Live By
22. Biblical Concepts I
23. Biblical Concepts II

24. Employing God's Plan for us provides Rescue, Redemption, and Better Choices
25. Spiritual Values, Morals, Ethics requires Jesus' Love
26. Key Bible Truths Revealed
27. Verses related to Predestination
28. Christian Doctrinal Statement Sample
29. Key Bible Questions
30. God's Use of Three in Bible Verses
31. Sample Love Letter to a Friend
33. Spiritual Growth requires Jesus' Love
32. God's Fundamentals for Living a Successful Christian Life
34. A Recommended Prayer for Eternal Salvation
35. A Salvation Testimony
36. God's Standard to be Holy, Loving, Just
37. Books of the Bible
38. God's Love Concept Perspective
39. Fundamental Bible Truths – Life's Purpose
40. Fundamental Bible Truths – Life's Meaning
41. Fundamental Bible Truths - Life's Fulfillment
42. Best Christmass Gift Ever Sample Letter
43. Bible Verses that support God's Love Concept
44. Free Will Choice versus Mosaic Law Mandates
45. Consideration regarding Heaven and Hell
46. An Easter Story Letter Sample
47. All Decisions have Consequences
48. Jesus' Love and Reconciliation Bible Verses

The 48 bible lessons follow:

Lesson 1: Teacher's Guide Perspective

God's Love, Dilemma, and Eternal Life Promise
(Ref Rom 5:8; Rom 3: 23; Jn 3: 3, 5: Jn 5: 24; Eph 1: 13)!

What is True Love? Does God Really Love Me? How Do I Know? Or, How is Spiritual Re-Birth Essential to Obtain Eternal Salvation and Love Now

"God's Love Concept" (i.e. *God wants everyone to be the best that they can be, to love as he does, to receive many blessings, and to spend eternity in heaven with him)* could possibly help me in my quest to understand my life's purpose, meaning, fulfillment, and "spiritual missing part" questions (Ref *Matt 22: 36 to 40; Gal 6: 7, 8; 1 Tim 2: 4 to 6;* Jn Ch 3: All; Rom 5: 8 to 11; Heb 11: 6; Rom 10: 9, 10; Jn 5: 24; Eph 2: 8, 9; Rom Ch 3: All; 1 Tim 1: 5; Rom 8: 1 to 16; Gal Ch 3: All; Eph 1: 13; Titus 3: 5).

I discovered later after in-depth bible study that God's Love Concept is based upon God sharing his love, blessings, and wisdom with me not because he wants to exert his control over me, exert a feeling of re-payment, or exert a price for his love; rather just for my free will return love. In other words, God wants me to obey his commandants and directions only from my own free will choices; so I can live with him forever in heaven as his family member, spiritually grow, and receive many appropriate holy, loving, and just blessings for my choices (Ref Rom 5: 8; John 3: 15, 16; John 3: 3, 5, 6, 7: Gal 6: 7, 8; James 2: 10; Rom 10: 9, 10; Rom 1: 16, 17; John 5: 24; Heb 11: 6; Titus 3: 4 to 7; Eph 2: 8, 9; 1 Tim 1: 5; Rom 3:

20; Luke 18: 15 – 17; Eph 1: 13; Eph 4: 30; 1 John 5: 9 – 13; Matt 22: 34 – 40; Heb 13: 5b; Rom Ch 8: All; (all NT bible references are in the Catholic and Protestant Bibles, and the same messages are in the OT prophets writings (Ref Jn 5: 39, 40; Luk 24: 25 to 27)).

God's Mind-Set is based upon Pure Love (1 John 4: 7 – 10), and God's wish is that everybody will choose to accept his simple plan of salvation and live in heaven with him for all eternity (Ref 1 Tim 2: 4 – "Who will have all men to be saved, and to come unto the knowledge of the truth").

Pure Love must allow free, unforced, and personal/accountable choices; otherwise we would be just puppets (i.e. and we would make forced, impersonal, and non-accountable choices which is not loving). A God of Love has to provide us with the ability to choose and to be accountable for our decisions (good or bad decisions) (Ref Gal 6: 7, 8).

Pure Love must be holy, loving, and just (i.e. righteous) all the time, and this is God's Mind-Set toward us (i.e. his mark-goal/target/standard for living). Transgression of God's standard is called sin (i.e. missing God's mark: making a decision that is not loving, and entering into a sin condition (i.e. non-loving Mind-Set reality-capability)). (Ref Rom 6: 23; 1 Jn 3: 4; 1 Jn 5: 17). The chief attributes of sin are to be Selfish, Inconsiderate, and Non-respectful (i.e. SIN – non-loving).

Because God loves us, we were created with our spirit and God's Holy Spirit joined together. When we reach the age of accountability and committed a non-loving act (i.e. sin), we enter into the sin Mind-Set condition (i.e. sin nature capable of committing sin) that causes God's Holy Spirit to separate from our spirit. Why? Cause God's Spirit cannot be a part of a sin Mind-Set (i.e. a non-loving Mind-Set) that would be capable of committing sin(s). We need to re-unite our spirit with God's Holy Spirit now while we are on earth in order to be spiritually re-born again (i.e. to become spiritually alive again in God's eyes); because when our body expires (i.e. physical death, not spiritual death), our spirit and soul are released into immediate eternal spiritual judgment (Ref Heb 9: 27). The re-uniting of our spirit and the Holy Spirit will provide us eternal salvation/life in heaven (i.e. being spiritually born again) with God per God's own words/promise, but only if we choose to accept Jesus' love sacrifice on the cross for all of our sin consequences (Ref John 3: 3 to 7; John 5: 24; Jn 14:6; Jn 3: 15 to 17; Rom 10: 9, 10; Titus 3: 4 to 7; Ephesians 1: 1 to 13; Eph 4: 30; Eph 2: 10 to 17; 1 John 5: 9 to 13; 1 Tim 1: 5; Heb 13: 5b; Heb 11: 6).

God's Dilemma:

God wants everybody to go to heaven with him for eternity; but he foreknew that everybody would not choose to be holy, loving, and just all the time based upon the erosion of our original faith from dealing with the world and our human shortcomings due to our sin nature. Nevertheless, God has to allow everybody to make their own life decisions and receive the consequences of their decisions, or He is not a God of Love (Ref Gal 6: 7, 8). Therefore, he had to provide a way (i.e. an option) for everybody to have their sin consequences covered/paid for by another means (i.e. only Jesus vicarious sacrifice could pay for all our sins (past, present and future) for us. However, we have to choose to accept this grace gift (i.e. free gift) by our own free will decision or not, which is in concert with God's Love Mind-Set toward us (Ref John 5: 24; Jer 17: 10; Heb 10: 10 to 18).

In other words, <u>God wants us to strive to have his Love Mind-Set, so we can receive many blessing.</u> In addition, if Jesus (i.e. God) had to cover our sin consequences, how could we ever think that we could do anything to equal his payment for all of our sin consequences?

Only Jesus could cover our sins consequences, because he had no sin nor could commit any sin (i.e. his purpose was totally driven by his pure love for us). <u>When Jesus was on the cross and the earth was dark for his last 3 hours, this was the first and only time that God the Father turned his back on his Son.</u> **Jesus experienced true hell (i.e. absence of God the Father's Love for the first and last time) for us.** This absence of God the Father's love for his Son was so horrible for Jesus that it covered all the consequences for everybody's sins (i.e. hell is absence of God's love). **Our soul and spirit will live forever with a new body (after our earthy body expires/dies.** Otherwise, why does the Bible continually assert that we will spend our eternal lives in either Heaven or Hell? (Ref Gal 6: 7. 8; Matt 7: 2; Rom 1: 16, 17; Rom 6: 23; Jer 17: 7 to 10; John 3: 36; John 5: 24). **We can however live in heaven with God forever, if we ask, accept, and thank Jesus with childlike faith/trust for his love sacrifice on the cross for our sins consequences** – Ref Rom 10: 9, 10; Jn 14: 6; Jn 3: 15, 16; Jn 3: 36; 1 Jn 5: 10 to 15). <u>Our new bodies will have no shortcomings, which is also in concert with God's Love Mind-Set.</u>

<u>We must decide (i.e. by personal free will choose) if we live forever in heaven or in hell for eternity according to the Bible.</u>

We must choose to accept Jesus' love sacrifice/gift in order to cover all of our past, present, and future sin consequences; and we must choose to accept our eternal life with him in heaven based upon his great sacrifice for us with thanksgiving (i.e. our exercised Faith/Belief/Trust in Jesus via our own words/action) (Ref Eph 2: 8. 9; Heb 11: 6; Romans 10: 9, 10). ☺☺☺

How do we become spiritually re-born: we must realize/admit we are sinners (i.e. we are capable of committing sin(s); accept Jesus' vicarious sacrifice for all our sins (past, present, and future); ask Jesus to re-unite our spirit with his Holy Spirit right now; and thank Jesus for his gift of eternal spiritual life with him which we have just now received by requesting/allowing/trusting/thanking him and his Holy Spirit for re-uniting our spirit with Jesus' Holy Spirit right now and forever! (Ref John 3: 3 to 7; Heb 11: 6; John 5: 24; Rom 10: 9, 10; Titus 3: 5; 1 Jn 5: 10 to 14; Eph 1: 13: Eph 4: 30; Heb 3: 5b)).

God's Love is not the same as Human Love (God's Love is always Holy, Loving, & Just all the time no matter what (i.e. it is never Selfish, Inconsiderate, & not-Respectful - Sin) (Ref 1Cor 13: All)).

Pure Love requires proof from our thoughts, talk, and life style actions (Ref Rom 5: 8; Rom 12: 1, 2).

Pure Love requires the consequences of our decisions (good or bad). We reap what we sow, because this is the consequences/fair receipt of our free, unforced, personal/accountable decisions that we make as non-puppets Ref Gal 6: 7, 8).

Heaven will be filled with God's Pure Love, and Hell will not have God's love of any kind of love in it (Ref 1 John 4: 8b; 2 Thess 1: 5 – 9; Rom Ch 8: All).

God allows us to experience trails and temptations to help us to make **good decisions,** to improve our **reconciliation** with God, to **grow** spiritually, and to **receiving** more blessings (Ref Heb 12: 11 – " Now no chastening for the present seems to be joyous, but grievous; nevertheless, afterward it yields the peaceful fruit of righteousness unto to them who are exercised by it" (Ref also Rom 5: 1 to 11; James 1: 2 - 4, 12, 13 – 15; and Deut 31: 6, 8). We get a new body in heaven that will be perfect, never have illnesses, sicknesses, shortcomings, handicaps, or deformities of any kind; and our new body will encase our undying soul and spirit for eternity!!! **Our soul and spirit never die, otherwise why are their many Bible verses (Jesus' words) and religions, which state that we will live eternally in either an eternal heaven or an eternal hell? (Ref John 3: 36; John 5: 24; Rev Ch 20: 10 to 15; Matt 23: 29 to 33).**

God's promises are realized by daily Bible study with Holy Spirit's teaching; because **God is pure Love (not a man) and can not lie** (Ref 1 John 5:11, 12 – "And this is the record that God has given to us eternal life, and this life is in **his Son.** He that has the Son has life; and he that has not the Son of God has not life") (Ref also 2 Pet 3: 9; Heb 4: 12; Prov 3: 5, 6; 2 Pet 1: 20, 21; John 5: 24; Ps 37: 3 – 5; 2 Tim 3: 15 – 17; Eph 4: 30; John 14: 6; Num 23: 19). Where will you spend eternity? How can you be sure? Shouldn't God's salvation plan be simple, **so all can** understand no matter what circumstances they exist within (Ref Gal 6: 7, 18)? If not,

God is not a God of pure love (i.e. all-ways holy, loving, and just)!!!

A recommended Prayer of Faith / Belief / Trust to request / accept / thank Jesus for your eternal salvation right now

Dear Lord Jesus I confess that I am a sinner and unable to always keep your standard of being Holy, Loving, and Just all the time (i.e. Loving all the time); and I am sorry for all my sin choices (past, present, and future) which caused you, others, and me to suffer greatly and needlessly. I accept your love sacrifice on the cross that paid for the consequences of all my sin choices (past, present, and future), and I ask you to come into my life and unite my spirit with your Holy Spirit again **right now** to help me to more closely follow your will/plan for my life. **I thank you** for coming into my life **right now, forgiving all my sin consequences right now**, and re-uniting my spirit with your Holy Spirit **right now; resulting in me receiving** eternal life with you **right now according to your word**. I pray in Jesus name to let you know that I am eternally grateful for what you have **just now** done for me and to remind me that I could not have been **spiritually re-born again** without your help. Amen. ☺☺☺

If you were sincere with above prayer, then at this moment you were re-united with Jesus' Holy Spirit. You became a child of God again, right now, and forever/unconditionally by your choice and Jesus promise (i.e. being spiritually born again back into God's Holy Spirit forever per Jesus' unconditional promise to us – i.e. I received my new spiritual nature that I can never, never lose again per Jesus promise) (Ref Romans 10: 9, 10; Ephesians 2: 8, 9; Titus 3: 4 to 7;

John 14: 6). God does not lie like humans, because it is against his love character, personality, and nature!!!

How can you be sure you are spiritually born again right now: God is not a man and cannot lie (i.e. God is always Holy, Loving, and Just)!!! He loves you, and He keeps his promises because He is GOD: not a man (Ref Ps 46: 10). Therefore, He always keeps his promises. In addition, God had to make sure that his eternal life plan was very simple, so that everyone could understand it no matter what their physical, mental, psychologically, social, cultural, moral, rational, and man's training/condition's, etc impacts are. Another example of God's true love!!! (Ref Rom 1: 16; Rom 1: 19, 20; Heb 11: 6; Gal 6: 7, 8; Rom 10: 9 – 13; Jer 17: 5 - 10; Eph 2: 8, 9; Isa 6: 3; 1 John 4; 8, 16). God will always keeps his promises!!! ☺☺☺

If you doubt the above Bible based truth, then do a diligent research of these above truths/Bible verses; and you will be convinced of their veracity and fact. After all, your eternal life's existence depends upon our making the correct, proper, and sincere choice concerning where our soul and spirit will exist for all eternity (Ref Bible Books of Romans; Ephesus; & Galatians).

If you are not concerned if you go to heaven or hell, what about your loved ones (i.e. spouse, partners, friends, children, associates?) They have to make their own decisions/chooses about being born again spiritually while they are on this earth. Are you content not to advise them how to be spiritually born again and live in heaven forever???
Do your research first in the New Testament Books until you understand the reality of the books before you study the Old

Testament Books; because the Old Testament Books are a little more difficult to understand as revealed by the Apostle Paul's Christian conversion and subsequent life (i.e. he wrote most of the new testament books after he became spiritually born again on his trip to Damascus to kill Christians). He subsequently received in-depth Christian instruction in the bible truths (i.e. truths in the Old Testament/Jewish Prophets writings (Ref Matt 22: 36 to 40; Books of Romans, Galatians, Ephesians, Hebrews: All; 1 Tim 1: 5) in Damascus by Christians, because he did not understand God's Love Concept and truths. Paul stopped killing Christians after his Damascus revelations.

Sincerely In Jesus' Love for you and even me,
Chuck, the grateful and thankful saved sinner.

Lesson 2: Searching for My Spiritual "Spiritual Missing Part" in My Life
(Ref Prov 25: 2; Prov 3: 5, 6; Gal 6: 7 to 9; John 3: 3 to 7)!

-- <u>God's standard is Pure Love (i.e. is Holy, Loving, and Just all the time)</u> **(Ref 1 John 4: 8, 13, 16); therefore, he wants everybody to decide to spend eternity in heaven with him (Ref 1 Tim 2: 4). A true love decision must come from the consent of the heart, not be forced!**

- <u>God's Law is based upon loving God first</u> with whole mind/heart/soul <u>and your neighbor as yourself</u> (Ref Matt 22: 36 to 40; Rom 8: All; 1 John Chs 4 and 5).

- <u>My first sin separated my spirit from God's Holy Spirit</u> (i.e. Spiritual Death in God's eyes (<u>i.e. reason for my "missing part"</u>)); <u>and therefore interrupted my spiritual relationship with God</u> and my understanding of true love (Ref Rom 3: All; Rom 3: 19 to 28; Jam 1: 10; Rom 10: 4; Jam 2: 26).

- <u>Sin is a non-loving thought/talk/walk action</u> (i.e. a transgression of God's standard (Ref Eph 2: 1 to 3; Jer 17: 5 to 10).

- Understand that all have sinned; and must repent, confess sin nature, ask/accept Jesus' Love sacrifice on the cross personally along with his Holy Spirit with thanksgiving to obtain eternal salvation (<u>i.e. become spiritually alive again and resolve my "missing part"</u>) (Ref Rom 3: 10; 23; 1 John 1: 9; Eph 2: 8, 9; Rom 10: 9, 10; Rom 6: 15 – 18; Jn 3: 3, 5).

- God created us to be personal, rationale, and moral beings that are responsible for our decisions; and <u>I will be judged</u>

according to the truth, my deeds, my knowledge, and the gospel (Ref Genesis 1: 26; Romans 2: 1 to 16; Matt 7: 2; 1 John 1: 9, 10; 1 John 2: 15 to 17 & 22 to 25; John 5: 24; 1 John 4: 13 to 16).

- A true, pure love relationship between God and me requires that all my decisions require consequences in order to validate the value, quality, and commitment degree of our relationship (Ref Gal 6: 7, 8; Romans 2: 1 to 16; Jer 17: 10; Matt 7: 2).

Romans 3 23 – "For all have sinned, and come short of the glory of God".

Romans 5:8 – "But God commended his love toward us in that, while we were sinners, Christ died for us".

1 Tim 2:4, 5 – "Who will have all men to be saved, and to come unto the knowledge of the truth. For there is one God, and one mediator between God and men, the man, Christ Jesus".

Romans 6: 23 – "For the wages of sin is death, but the gift of God is eternal life through Jesus Christ, our Lord".

John 11:25, 26 – "Jesus said unto her, I am the resurrection, and the life; he that believeth in me, though he were dead (i.e. spiritually dead), yet shall he live. And whosoever lives and believes in me shall never die (i.e. experience eternal spiritual death). Believe thou this"?

John 3:3 to 7 – "Jesus answered, and said unto him, Verily, verily, I say unto you, Except a man be born again, he cannot see the kingdom of God. Nicodemus said to him, How can a man be born when he is old? Can he enter the second time into his mother's womb, and be born? Jesus answered, Verily, verily, I say to you, Except a man be born of water and of the "Holy Spirit", he cannot enter in the kingdom of God. That which is born of the flesh is flesh; and that which is born of the "Holy Spirit" is spirit. Marvel not that I say unto you, you must be born again".

Colossians 2:13 – "And you, being dead in your sins (i.e. spiritually dead), and the uncircumcision of your flesh, has he made alive together with him, having forgiven you all trespasses".

Matthew 22:37 to 40 – "Master, which is the great commandment in the law? Jesus said unto him, Thou shall love the Lord, thy God, with all your heart, and with all your soul, and with all your mind. This is the first and great commandment. And the second is like it, Thou shall love your neighbor as your self. On these two commandments hang all the law and the prophets".

Romans 10:9, 10 – "That if you shall confess with your mouth the Lord Jesus, and shall believe in your heart that God has raised him from the dead, you shall be saved. For with the heart man believes unto righteousness, and with the mouth confession is made unto salvation".

John 3:15, 16 – "That whosoever believeth in him should not perish, but have eternal life. For God so loved the world that He gave his only begotten Son, that whosoever believes in Him should not perish, but have everlasting life".

Titus 3:5 – "Not by works of righteousness which we have done, but according to his mercy he saved us, by washing of regeneration, and renewing of the Holy Spirit".

Ephesians 1:13 – "In whom ye also trusted, after you heard the work of truth, the gospel of your salvation; and in whom also after you believed, you were sealed with the Holy Spirit of promise".

Lesson 3: My Decision to Research the Bible
(Ref 2 Tim 3: 15 to 17; John 3: 3, 5 to 7; John 3: 15, 16; Prov 22: 6; John 6: 40)!

-- My past life and my associated past life's research for answers concerning my life, love, and death were not provided by my worldly education, religion, relationships, and career pursuits (Ref Ecclesiastes 12: 8 to 14; Col 2: 8 to 23).

- Many world activities (i.e. songs, stories, poems, movies, religions, etc.) focused on the concepts of life, love, and death, but don't seem to provide good life, love, and death answers (Ref Proverbs 1:1 to 7; Prov 22: 6; Rom 1: 16 to 32; Matt 11: 28 to 30).

- The bible states that God is a God of Love, and presents that only Jesus has come back from death to provide life, love, and death answers (Ref 1 Jn 4: 8, 16; Jn 14: 6; 2 Tim 3:15 to 17).

-What evidence is there that God really cares about me and loves me (Ref Rom 5:8 to 11; Jn 11: 25, 26; Jn 15: 13)?

- If Jesus, God's Son, had to endure a love sacrifice for my sins, then I obviously could not have accomplished anything greater than God's Son to cover my sins' consequences (Ref John 14: 6; Rom 6: 14 to 23; Ps 46: 10)?

- What proof do I have that God will keep his promises? (i.e. healings, miracles, rising people from death, walking on water, rising Jesus from death, calming a storm, walking on water, answering prayers, fulfilling over 200+ prophecies from creation to his love sacrifice on the cross) (Ref Jn 5: 39, 40; Luke 24:25 to 27; 1 John 5: 10 to 14).

- The bible states that my life's purpose needs to come from a relational reconciliation with God's Holy Spirit and my spirit (i.e. become "spiritually alive again" by being "spiritually born again") (Ref 2 Cor 5: 17 to 19; James 2: 26; Jn 11: 25, 26; Eph 1: 13; Rom Ch 8: All).

- The bible states that my life's purpose, and meaning comes from understanding, requesting, and accepting (i.e. by my sincere child-like faith) Jesus' Love-Sacrifice on the cross for all my sins' consequences and my personal eternal salvation gift from Jesus (Ref Matt 16: 26; Jn 14: 6; Rom 10: 9, 10; Jn 5: 24).

- The bible states that my life's self-fulfillment comes from being spiritually born again and my subsequent spiritual growth by exercising God's Love daily with gratefulness, humbleness, and thanksgiving to Jesus (Ref Prov 3: 5, 6; Josh 1: 8, 9).

> Rom 3:20 to 25 – "<u>Therefore, buy the deeds of the law (i.e. Mosaic Law) there shall no flesh be justified in his sight; for by the Mosaic Law is the knowledge of sin (i.e. law of sin and death)</u>. But now the righteousness of God apart from the law is manifested, being witnessed by the law and the prophets, <u>Even the righteousness of God which is by faith of Jesus Christ unto all and upon all them that believe; for there is no difference.</u> **For all have sinned and come short of the glory of God**; and only being justified freely by his grace through the redemption that is in Christ Jesus, whom God has set forth to be a propitiation

through faith in his blood, to declare his righteousness for the remission of sins that are past, through the forbearance of God".

Acts 4:12 – "Neither is there salvation in any other; for there is no other name under heaven given among men, whereby we must be saved".

John 14:6 – "Jesus said unto him, I am the way, the truth, and the life; no man comes to the Father, but by me".

Heb 4:12 – "For the word of God is living, and powerful, and sharper than any two-edged sword, piercing even to the dividing asunder of soul and spirit, and of the joints a marrow, and is a discerner of the thoughts and intent of the heart".

2 Tim 3:15 to 17 – "And that from a child thou has known the holy scriptures, which are able to make thee wise unto salvation through faith which is in Christ Jesus. All scripture is given by inspiration of God, and it profitable for doctrine, for reproof, for correction, for instruction in righteousness, that the man of God may be perfect, thoroughly furnished unto all good works".

Hebrews 11:6 – "But without faith it is impossible to please him; for he that comes to God must believe that he is, and that he is a rewarder of them that diligently seek him".

Rom 8:2 – "**For the law of the Spirit of Life in Christ Jesus** has made me free from the **law of sin and death**" (Ref Rom Ch 8: All vs Mosaic Law respectively – i.e.

Mosaic Law refers to 10 commandments, and 600+ worship ordinances and social judgments spelled out in the bible books of Exodus, Leviticus, Numbers, and repeated in the book of Deuteronomy). (Note: Use of the word Law refers to teachings/instruction (Ref Ps 19; 7; Ps 119: All).

Ephesians 2:8, 9 – "For by grace are you saved through faith; and that not of yourselves, it is the gift of God – not of works, lest any man should boast (i.e. God's grace means a free, undeserved gift!)".

Matthew 18:3 to 5 – "Jesus said, Verily I say unto you, except you be converted, and become as little children (i.e. in your faith/belief/trust toward and in Jesus Christ), you shall not enter into the kingdom of heaven. Whosoever, therefore, shall humble himself as this little child, the same is greatest in the kingdom of heaven. And whosoever shall receive one such little child in my name receives me".

John 5:24 – "Verily, verily, I say unto you, He that hears my word, and believes on him that sent me, has everlasting life, and shall not come into judgment, but is passed from death unto life".

Proverbs 3 5, 6 – "Trust in the Lord with all your heart, and lean not to your understanding. In all things acknowledge Him, and He will direct your paths."

Ezekiel 36:26, 27 – " A new heart also will I give you and a new spirit will I put within you; and I will take away the stony heart out of your flesh, and I will give you a heart of flesh. And I will put my Spirit within you, and cause you to walk in my statues, and you shall keep mine ordinances, and do them" (Ref 2 Cor 5: 17; 2 Cor 6: 16).

John 6:63 -- "It is the spirit that gives life; the flesh profits nothing. The words that I speak unto you, they are spirit, and they are life".

2 Cor 5:17 to 19 – "Therefore, if any man be in Christ, he is a new creation; old things are passed away; behold, all things are become new. And all things are of God, who has reconciles us to himself by Jesus Christ, and has given to us the ministry of reconciliation."

Ephesians 1:13 – "In whom ye also trusted, after you heard the work of truth, the gospel of your salvation; and in whom also after you believed, you were sealed with the Holy Spirit of promise".

Lesson 4: Conclusions from my Past Life
(Ref Bible Book of Romans: All Chapters)!

--Searching for answers to my life questions about life, love, death, and my "missing part" (i.e. re-uniting my spirit with God's Holy Spirit) in my past life resulted in little success (Ref John Ch 3: All; Romans Ch 1: All; Romans Ch 3: All).

-Sin is to do a non-loving thought, word, or action (i.e. transgression of God's Love Concept Standard – i.e. always being Holy, Loving, and Just (Ref 1 Jn 3: 4; Matt 26: 36 to 40).

-My first sin (i.e. non-loving thought, word, action) separated my spirit from God's Holy Spirit and interrupted our relationship (Ref John 3: 3, 5, 6; Romans 3: 10, 23; Col 2: 13).

-Neither religion, grade school, high school, sports, girl friend, world travel, military service, family, or college helped me to find my "missing part" (Ref Matt 16: 26, 27).

-Joining a bible study opened my eyes that my "missing part" was caused by my spirit's separation from the Holy Spirit that made me spiritually dead in God's eyes (Ref 2 Tim 3: 15 to 17; John Ch 3: All; Jn 3: 3, 5; Rom Ch 8: All).

1 Jn 3: 4 – "Whosoever commits sin transgresses the law; for sin is the transgression of the law".

Rom 3: 23 – "For all have sinned, and come short of the glory of God".

Matthew 16: 26 – "For what is a man profited, if he shall gain the whole world, and lose his own soul? Or what shall a man give in exchange for his soul?"

Colossians 2: 13 – "And you, being dead (i.e. spiritually dead) in your sins, and the uncircumcision of your flesh, has he made alive together with him, having forgiven you all trespasses".

John 5: 24 – "Verily, verily, I say unto you, He that hears my word, and believes on him that sent me, has everlasting life, and shall not come into judgment, but is passed from death (i.e. spiritual death) unto life (i.e. spiritual life)".

Ezekiel 36: 26, 27 – " A new heart also will I give you and a new spirit will I put within you; and I will take away the stony heart out of your flesh, and I will give you a heart of flesh. And I will put my Holy Spirit within you, and cause you to walk in my statues, and you shall keep mine ordinances, and do them" (Ref also 2 Cor 5: 17; 2 Cor 6: 16).

John 6: 63 -- "It is the spirit that gives life; the flesh profits nothing. The words that I speak unto you, they are spirit, and they are life".

2 Cor 5: 17 to 19 – "Therefore, if any man be in Christ, he is a new creation; old things are passed away; behold, all things are become new. And all things are of God, who has reconciles us to himself by Jesus Christ, and has given to us the ministry of reconciliation).

Ephesians 1: 13 – "In whom ye also trusted, after you heard the work of truth, the gospel of your salvation; and in whom also after you believed, you were sealed with the Holy Spirit of promise".

1 John 5: 11 to 13 – "And this is the record, that God has given to us eternal life, and this life is in his Son. He that has the Son has life; and he that has not the Son of God has not life. These things have I written unto you that believe on the name of the Son of God, that you may know that you have eternal life, and that you may believe on the name of the Son of God".

Titus 3: 5 – "Not by works of righteousness which we have done, but according to his mercy he saved us, by washing of regeneration, and renewing of the Holy Spirit".

Romans 8: 16 – "The Holy Spirit himself bears witness with our spirit, that we are the children of God".

Lesson 5: Bible Revelations and Verses
(Ref John 5: 39; Luke 24: 25 to 27; Eph 1: 12 to 14; Matt 7: 2; Eph 6: 11, 12)!

-- God wants to reconcile with me (Ref 2 Cor 5: 17 - 19; Jam 2: 26; Rom 8: 11; Rom 8: 14-17).

- God's Love and Grace (free gift) provides a sinless Jesus' love sacrifice to cover all of my sins and free me from the law of sin and death (Ref Rom 5: 8; Heb 10: 10 to 18; Eph 2: 8, 9; Rom 2: 28; Rom Ch 8: All; Eph 4: 30; Eph 1: 13; Col 2: 13).

- **For the law of the Spirit of Life in Christ Jesus** has made me free from the **law of sin and death**" (i.e. Mosaic Law). (Note: Use of the word Law refers to teachings/instruction) (Ref Rom 8: 2; Ps 19; 7; Ps 119: All; 1 Tim 1: 5).

- The law of sin and death refers to the Mosaic Law respectively (i.e. Mosaic Law refers to 10 commandments, and 600+ worship ordinances and social judgments spelled out in the bible books of Exodus, Leviticus, Numbers, and repeated in the book of Deuteronomy).

- The law of the Spirit of Life in Christ Jesus refers to God's Standard of being Holy, Loving, and Just that is based upon God's Pure Love Concept (Ref Matt 22: 36 to 40).

- My first sin (i.e. first non-loving thought, word, action) separated my spirit from God's Holy Spirit, and interrupted our spiritual relationship (Ref 1 Jn 3: 4; Romans 3: 10, 23; John 3: 3, 5; Romans 10: 9, 10; Titus 3: 5).

- Transgression of God's Love Standard's (i.e. being Holy, Loving, and Just all the time) is based upon having a mindset of being Selfish, Inconsiderate, and Not-respectful (i.e. SIN) (Ref 1 John 2: 15 to 17; Luke 4: 1 to 13).

- God's Holy Spirit cannot be connected to my sinful spirit, because God's Holy Spirit can never be associated with sin (i.e. non-loving thought/word/action) (Ref Romans 3: 10, 23; Jer 17: 7 to 10; Romans 5: 8).

- Jesus covered all my' sin consequences when his Father turned his love from his Son for the first and last time during Jesus' last 3 hours on the cross (i.e. hell for Jesus in my place) when the earth was covered by darkness and the Temple Veil split at the end of the darkness (Ref Matt 27: All; Titus 2: 11; 1 Jn 1: 8 to 10).

- According to the bible, I must choose (i.e. not just believe) to repent/confess my sin nature, believe/trust/ask/accept Jesus Love sacrifice for us, and thank Jesus to become spiritually born again into God's Holy Spirit for eternity (i.e. become a child of God forever); cause I am not a puppet – John 5: 24; John 3: All; Rom 10: 4, 9 to 13; Rom 2: 28, 29; Matt 11: 28 to 30; John 3: 15, 16; Eph 1: 12 to 14.

- Some of the devil's chief tools that he uses to erode or destroy our faith are: fear, guilt, hatred, anger, peer pressure, pride, snare of gradualism, wealth, fame, suicide, chemical imbalances (e.g. bi-polar, obsessive-compulsive, PTSD, etc.) (Ref Matt 22: 37, 40; 1 John 4: All; 1 John 2: 15 to 17; Luke 4: 1 to 13; 1 John 2: 15 to 17; 1 Cor 15: 33; 1 Cor 14: 33; 1 Cor 3: 16, 17).

- All decisions require consequences to verify its value, quality, and commitment degree of relational love/caring between two parties; and tribulations place me in many situations that provide opportunities to test my character, temperament, and wisdom to make good decisions and receive many blessings, or not (Ref Prov 3: 5, 6, Rom 12: 1, 2; Gal 5: 13 to 26; Gal 6: 7, 8; 2 Cor 12: 7 to 10; Matt 11: 28 to 30; Micah 6: 8).

Rev 3: 5 – "He that overcometh, the same shall be clothed in white raiment; <u>and I will not blot his name out of the book of life</u>, but I will confess his name before my Father, and before his angels."

Rev 20: 15 – "And whosoever was not found <u>written in the book of life</u> was cast into the lake of fire".

Rom 3: 20 to 25 – "<u>Therefore, buy the deeds of the law (i.e. Mosaic Law) there shall no flesh be justified in his sight; for by the Mosaic Law is the knowledge of sin (i.e. law of sin and death)</u>. But now the righteousness of God apart from the law is manifested, being witnessed by the law and the prophets, <u>Even the righteousness of God which is by faith of Jesus Christ unto all and upon all them that believe; for there is no difference.</u> **For all have sinned and come short of the glory of God**; and only being justified freely by his grace through the redemption that is in Christ Jesus, whom God has set forth to be a propitiation through faith in his blood, to declare his righteousness for the remission of sins that are past, through the forbearance of God".

John 3: 5 – "Jesus answered, Verily, verily I say unto you, except a man be born of water and of the "Holy Spirit", he cannot enter into the kingdom of God".

John 14: 6 – " Jesus said, I am the way, the truth, and the life; and no one comes to the Father except by me".

John 3: 15, 16, 17 – "That whosoever believeth in him (i.e. Jesus Christ) should not perish, but have eternal life. For God so loved the world that He gave his only begotten Son, that whosoever believes in Him should not perish, but have everlasting life" (note: Jesus Christ translated is "God Saved his Anointed One). For God sent not his Son into the world to condemn the world, but that the world through him might be saved" (i.e. a true love relationship requires both parties to have a faith, trust, and reciprocal holy, loving, and just attitude/thoughts/actions toward one another based upon their own free will decisions, not because of forced decisions).

Romans 10: 9, 10 – "That if you shall confess with your mouth the Lord Jesus, and shall believe in your heart that God has raised him from the dead, you shall be saved. For with the heart man believes unto righteousness, and with the mouth confession is made unto salvation".

Isa 56: 15 – "For thus says the high and lofty One who inhabits eternity, whose name is Holy: I dwell in the high and the holy place, with him also who is of a contrite and humble spirit, to revive the spirit of the humble, and to revive the heart of the contrite ones".

2 Cor 7: 10 – "For the kind of sorrow God wants us to experience leads us away from sin and results in salvation (i.e. contrite heart). There's no regret for that kind of sorrow. But worldly sorrow, which lacks repentance, results in spiritual death".

Heb 11: 6 – " But without faith it is impossible to please Him; for he that comes to God must believe that He is, and that He is a rewarder of them that diligently seek Him".

Luke 18: 16 – "Verily I say unto you, Whosoever shall not receive the kingdom of God like a little child shall in no way enter it".

Ephesians 1: 13 – "In whom ye also trusted, after you heard the work of truth, the gospel of your salvation; and in whom also after you believed, you were sealed with the Holy Spirit of promise".

Titus 3: 5 –" Not by works of righteousness which we have done, but according to his mercy he saved us, by washing of regeneration, and renewing of the Holy Spirit".

Ephesians 2: 8, 9 --"For by grace are you saved through faith; and that not of yourselves, it is the gift of God – not of works, lest any man should boast".

Ephesians 4: 30 – "And grieve not the Holy Spirit of God, by whom you are sealed unto the day of redemption".

Romans 10: 17 – "For faith comes by hearing, and hearing from the word of God".

Hebrews 4: 12 – "For the word of God is living, and powerful, and sharper than any two-edged sword, piercing even to the dividing asunder of soul and spirit, and of the joints and marrow, and is a discerner of the thoughts and intents of the heart".

Jer 17: 10 – "I, the LORD, search the heart. I test the conscience, even to give every man according to his ways, and according to the fruit of his doings".

Eph 6: 11, 12 – "Put on the whole armor of God, that you may be able to stand against the wiles of the devil. For we wrestle not against flesh and blood but against principalities, against powers, against the rulers of the darkness of the world, against spiritual wickedness in high places".

2 Cor 5: 17 to 19 – "Therefore, if any man be in Christ, he is a new creation; old things are passed away; behold, all things are become new. And all things are of God, who has reconciles us to himself by Jesus Christ, and has given to us the ministry of reconciliation".

1 Thess 5: 16 to 18 -- "Rejoice evermore, pray without ceasing, in everything give thanks; for this is the will of God, in Christ Jesus concerning you".

Psalms 37: 3 to 5 – "Trust in the LORD, and do good; so shall you dwell in the land, and verily you shall be fed. Delight yourself also in the LORD, and he shall give you the desires of your heart. Commit your way unto the LORD; trust also in him, and he shall bring it to pass".

Prov 3: 5, 6 – "Trust in the LORD with all your heart, and lean not unto your own understanding. In all your ways knowledge him, and he shall direct your paths".

John 14: 26 – "But the Comforter, who is the Holy Spirit, whom the Father will send in my name, he shall teach you all things, and being all things to your remembrance, whatever I have said unto you".

Eph 4: 11 to 13 – "And he gave some, apostles; and some, prophets; and some, evangelists; and some, pastors and teachers; For the perfecting of the saints for the work of the ministry for the edifying of the body of Christ, Till we all come in the unity of the faith, and of the knowledge of the Son of God, unto a perfect man, unto the measure of the stature of the fullness of Christ".

Mark 16: 15 – "And he said unto them, Go you into the world and preach the gospel to every creature".

Isaiah 26: 3, 4 – "Thou will keep him in perfect peace, whose mind is stayed on thee, because he trusted in thee. Trust you in the LORD forever; for in the LORD God is everlasting strength".

Prov 22: 4 – "By humility and reverential trust of the LORD are riches, and honor, and life".

Lesson 6: My Decision to Obtain Eternal Life
(Ref John Ch 3: All; Romans 10: 9, 10; Eph 1: 13; Eph 4: 30)!

-- Bible study provided answers concerning my life questions about life, love, death, and "missing part" (Ref Gen 1: 26; Romans 5: 8; Romans 5 12; Col 2: 4 to 23; John 5: 24).

- Jesus' love sacrifice on the cross covered all my sins' consequences (i.e. past, present, and future) (Ref Heb 10: 10 to 18).

- My bible study showed that God's Pure Love was the key for answering my life, love, death, and "spiritual missing part" life questions (i.e. I was spiritually dead in God's view, because my spirit was separated from his Holy Spirit when I committed my first sin) (Ref Col 2: 13).

- I determined from my bible studies that re-uniting my spirit with Jesus' Holy Spirit is required in order to be "spiritually born again", and re-uniting my relationship with God by re-uniting my spirit with God's Holy Spirit (John 3: 3, 5, 6; Eph 1: 13).

John 3:3 – "Verily, verily I say unto you, except a man be "spiritually" born again, he cannot see the kingdom of God".

Matthew 16:26 – "For what is a man profited, if he shall gain the whole world, and lose his own soul? Or what shall a man give in exchange for his soul?"

Romans 3:23 – "For all have sinned, and come short of the glory of God".

John 3:5 – "Jesus answered, Verily, verily I say unto you, except a man be born of water and of the "Holy Spirit', he cannot enter into the kingdom of God".

Gal 3:10 to 12 – "For as many as are of the works of the law are under the curse; for it is written, Cursed is everyone that continues not in all things which are written in the book of the law, to do them. But that no man is justified by the law in the sight of God, it is evident; for the just shall live by faith. And the law is not of faith, but the man that does them (i.e. try to comply with the Law – the 10 commandments, social judgments, worship ordnances) shall live in them (i.e. Law's consequences)".

Rom 3:20 to 25 – "Therefore, buy the deeds of the law (i.e. Mosaic Law) there shall no flesh be justified in his sight; for by the Mosaic Law is the knowledge of sin (i.e. law of sin and death). But now the righteousness of God apart from the law is manifested, being witnessed by the law and the prophets, Even the righteousness of God which is by faith of Jesus Christ unto all and upon all them that believe; for there is no difference. **For all have sinned and come short of the glory of God**; and only being justified freely by his grace through the redemption that is in Christ Jesus, whom God has set forth to be a propitiation through faith in his blood, to declare his righteousness for the remission of sins that are past, through the forbearance of God".

John 14:6 – " Jesus said, I am the way, the truth, and the life; and no one comes to the Father except by me".

Heb 11:6 – " <u>But without faith it is impossible to please Him</u>; for he that comes to God must believe that He is, and that He is a rewarder of them that diligently seek Him".

Romans 10:9, 10 – "That if you shall <u>confess with your mouth</u> the Lord Jesus, and shall <u>believe in your heart</u> that God has raised him from the dead, you shall be saved. For <u>with the heart man believes unto righteousness</u>, and with the mouth <u>confession is made</u> unto salvation." **(i.e. trust by concent of my mind, act of my heart, and by my will) not just believe, to personally accept his free love gift** (i.e. free undeserved grace gift) **in order to live in heaven with him with my new body forever).**

Jn 5:24 – "<u>I tell you the truth, whosoever hears my word, and believes (i.e. choose by your own free will and faith (i.e. trust by concent of my mind, act of my heart, and by my will with thanks (i.e. not just believe) to personally ask/accept his free love gift (i.e. free undeserved grace gift) of eternal salvation in order to live in heaven (i.e. a place with God's eternal love) with him with my new body forever; or choose to reject his free gift and live in a place devoid of God's love forever with my new body (Ref also Heb 11: 6; Rom 3: 23; Rom 10: 9, 10; Jn 14: 6; Jn 3: 15, 16; Eph 2: 8, 9; Eph 1: 13; Titus 3: 5; Eph 4: 30)</u> him who sent me has eternal life and will not be condemned; **he has crossed over from "death" to life**")).

Heb 10:10 – "<u>By which will we are sanctified (i.e. being spiritually born again) through the offering of the body of Jesus Christ once for all</u>".

Heb 10:12 – "But after Jesus had offered one sacrifice for sins forever, sat down on the right hand of God".

Luke 24:25 to 27 – "Then Jesus said unto them O foolish ones, and slow of heart to believe all that the prophets have spoken! Ought not Christ to have suffered these things, and to enter into his glory? And beginning at Moses and all the prophets, he expounded unto them, in all the scriptures, the things concerning himself."

Ephesians 1:13 – "In whom ye also trusted, after you heard the work of truth, the gospel of your salvation; and in whom also after you believed, you were sealed with the Holy Spirit of promise".

Titus 3:5 –" Not by works of righteousness which we have done, but according to his mercy he saved us, by washing of regeneration, and renewing of the Holy Spirit".

Ephesians 4:30 – "And grieve not the Holy Spirit of God, by whom you are sealed unto the day of redemption".

Luke 18:16 – "Verily I say unto you, Whosoever shall not receive the kingdom of God like a little child shall in no way enter it".

John 6:63 -- "It is the spirit that gives life; the flesh profits nothing. The words that I speak unto you, they are spirit, and they are life".

2 Cor 5:17 to 19 – "Therefore, if any man be in Christ, he is a new creation; old things are passed away; behold, all things are become new. And all things are of God, who

has reconciles us to himself by Jesus Christ, and has given to us the ministry of reconciliation".

Lesson 7: Understanding the Value of God's Love
(Ref Rom 5: 8; Rom 8: 32; John 11: 25, 26; 1 Tim 1: 5; Romans 8: 32)!

-- God loves me so much that He sent his Son (i.e. Jesus) to sacrifice "hell" (i.e. a condition/place without any love) for me on the cross (i.e. the absence of God the Father's Love from Jesus for the 3 dark hours while Jesus was on the cross) that covered all of my past, present, and future sins and redeemed my soul and spirit for all eternity, <u>but only if I choose to accept this free, grace, unforced, love sacrifice by my faith-action decision</u> (Ref Rom 5: 8; Rom 8: 32; Jn 11: 25, 26; Rom Ch 8: All; Jn 5: 24; Jn 3: 15, 16; Rom 10, 9, 10; Eph 1: 13; Titus 3: 5).

- Living via God's Love Concept promotes spiritual growth; direct personal relationship with God; access to God's knowledge, understanding, and wisdom from the Holy Spirit; membership in God's family forever; eternal salvation in heaven; and abundant holy, loving, and just blessings (Ref Jn 14: 26; 2 Tim 3: 16, 17; Jn 11: 25, 26; Jn 15: 1 to 17; Prov 3: 5, 6; Prov 9: 10; Gal 5: 16; Gal 6: 7 to 9; Eph Ch 4: All; Matt 11: 28 to 30; Micah 6: 8; Josh 1: 8, 9; 1 Jn Ch 3: All; Jer 9: 23, 24; Deut 31: 6; 2 Tim 1: 7; Ps 46: 10).

- God's Love consists of allowing me free decisions and associated consequences, as well as, allowing me opportunities of confessing of my sins/sin nature; believing/trusting Jesus' love sacrifice covered all of my sins consequences; asking/accepting Jesus' and his Holy Spirit into my life/spirit; thanking Holy Spirit for returning into my life and sealing my eternal salvation now; and sharing God's above simple faith plan of salvation. Otherwise, I am just puppet; and God is not a God of Pure Love (Ref Rom 5:8; John 3: 15, 16; John 5: 24; Rom 10: 9, 10; 1 John 5: 11 to 13; Titus 3: 4 to 7; Titus 2: 11; John 4: 24; Heb 11:6; John 14: 6; Eph 3: 14 to 19).

- I can only connect to God/Eternal Salvation/Heaven through Jesus' Holy Spirit (Ref Eph 2: 8, 9; Rom 8: 14 to 17; Titus 2: 11; Col 1: 19-22; Jam 2: 26; Rom 8: 11; Jn 11: 25, 26; Jn 4: 24).

- Understand that my faith/trust in God's Love is strengthened by studying the bible (i.e. God Talking to us) (Ref Rom 10: 17; 2 Pet 1: 20, 21; Heb 4: 12; Heb 11: 6; 2 Tim 3: 15 – 17).

- Comprehend that God's Law (i.e. 10 Commandants and 600+ Social Judgments and Worship Ordinances), reveal that I have a sin nature, and I cannot obtain eternal salvation by my actions (Ref Rom 3: 20; Rom 8: 1 to 4).

- Personally accepting God's Grace gift of Salvation releases me from the shackles of my sinning past, sin nature, and world's sin standards, if I choose; so I can now live with proper faith decisions daily in God's grace, joy, peace, love, wisdom, humility, gratefulness, trusting prayer, thankfulness, mature spiritual growth, and successful living for me which is the ultimate blessing (Ref 1 Thess 5: 16 to 18; Prov 3: 5, 6; Prov 1: 7; Romans Ch 8; Eph Chs 4 & 6; Matt 11: 28 to 30; Gal 6: 7, 8; Ps 37: 3 to 7).

- Heaven is a place full of God's Love that is the ultimate reward from re-uniting my spirit with God's Holy Spirit (Ref Romans 14: 17; Ecc 5: 2; John 5: 24; John 3: 3, 5;

John 14: 2, 3; 1 Pet 1: 3 to 5).

- My soul/spirit will exist forever in heaven with a new spiritual body by my faith choice of asking/accepting Jesus into my life with thanksgiving (Ref Eph 1: 13; Titus 3: 4 to 7)!

Romans 5:8 -- "But God commended his love toward us in that, while we were yet sinners, Christ died for us".

Eph 3:14 to 19 –"For this cause I bow my knees unto the Father of our Lord Jesus Christ, of whom the whole family in heaven and earth is named, that he would grant you, according to the riches of his glory, to be strengthened with might by his Spirit in the inner man; that Christ may dwell in your hearts by faith that you being rooted and grounded in love, may be able to comprehend, with all saints, what is the breath, and length, and depth, and height, and to know the love of Christ, which passes knowledge, that you might be filled with all the fullness of God".

John 15:13 – "Greater love has no man than this, that a man lay down his life for his friend".

John 3:3 to 7 – "Jesus answered, and said unto him, Verily, verily, I say unto you, Except a man be born again, he cannot see the kingdom of God. Nicodemus said to him, How can a man be born when he is old? Can he enter the second time into his mother's womb, and be born? Jesus answered, Verily, verily, I say to you, Except a man be born of water and of the "Holy Spirit", he cannot enter in the kingdom of God. That which is born of the flesh is flesh; and that which is born of the "Holy Spirit" is spirit. Marvel not that I say unto you, you must be born again".

John 11:25, 26 –"Jesus said unto her, I am the resurrection, and the life; he that believeth in me, though he were dead (i.e. spiritually dead), yet shall he live (i.e. spiritually alive). And whosoever lives and believes in me shall never die (i.e. spiritually die). Believe thou this"?

Jn 14:6 – "Jesus said, I am the way, the truth, and the life; no man come to the Father but by me (i.e. we must re-unite our spirit with Jesus' Holy Spirit to be spiritually born again and become a child of God **again** forever)".

John 3: 15,16 – "That whosoever believeth in him should not perish, but have eternal life. For God so loved the world that He gave his only begotten Son, that whosoever believes in Him should not perish, but have everlasting life".

Romans 10:9, 10 – "That if you shall confess with your mouth the Lord Jesus, and shall believe in your heart that God has raised him from the dead, you shall be saved. For with the heart man believes unto righteousness, and with the mouth confession is made unto salvation".

Ephesians 1:13 – "In whom ye also trusted, after you heard the work of truth, the gospel of your salvation; and in whom also after you believed, you were sealed with the Holy Spirit of promise".

Romans 8:32 – "He that spared not his own Son, but delivered him up for us all, how shall he not with him also freely give us all things"?

1 Cor 13:4 to 7 – "Love is patient. Love is kind. It does not envy. It does not boast. It is not proud. It is not rude. It is not easily angered. It keeps no records of wrongs. Love does not delight in evil, but rejoices with the truth. It always protects, always trusts, always hopes, and always perseveres. Love never fails".

Romans 10 4 – "For Christ is the end of the law for righteousness to every one that believes".

1 Tim 1:5 – "Now the end of the commandment is love out of a pure heart, and of a good conscience, and of faith unwavering".

Romans 14:17 – "For the kingdom of God is not food and drink, but righteousness, and peace, and joy in the Holy Spirit".

1 Peter 1:3, 4 – "Blessed be the God and Father of our Lord Jesus Christ, who, according to his abundant mercy, has begotten us again unto a living hope by the resurrection of Jesus Christ from the dead, to an inheritance incorruptible, and undefiled, and that fades not away, reserved in heaven for you".

Lesson 8: How to obtain Maximum Blessings Daily
(Ref Jer 9: 23, 24; Gal 5: 13 to 26; Prov 22: 4)!

-- Employing God's Knowledge, Understanding, and Wisdom should be my daily spiritual goal (Ref Psalm 37: 3 to 5; 1 Pet 1: 20, 21; Prov 1: 7; Prov 2: 1 - 6; Prov 3: 1 - 35; 1 John 2: 15 – 17).

- Realize that God's Standard/Law/Mark is based upon loving God first and my neighbor as our self (Ref Matt 22: 37 to 40; 1 John: 4 All; 1 John 3: 11 to 24; John 11: 25, 26).

- God wants me to have maximum blessings, because He loves me and wants me to make wise decisions, not as a puppet, to receive maximum blessings (Ref Gal 6: 7, 8).

-Understand that my good / bad choices / actions / experiences, with God's help, are meant to help me adjust my attitude/actions/thoughts, so I can receive many blessings for me and others (Ref Gal 6: 7, 8; Heb 12: 6 to 15; Heb 11: 6 (i.e. I receive blessings for all our faith actions (e.g. prayer, bible study; thanking, rejoicing, sharing, listening, serving, growing)).

- Pursue God's goal that I try to get closer to God's Love Concept by loving all humans, even myself; but not our non-loving actions (Ref Eph Ch 4; Josh 1: 8, 9; Deut 31: 6; Col 3: 12, 13; 2 Cor 12: 9, 10).

- Being aware that Human's philosophy "What's In It For Me" stems from Selfishness, Inconsideration, and Non-respect (i.e. Sin) (Ref Rom 3: 23; Rom 12: 1, 2; John 5: 39).

Proverbs 3:5, 6 – "Trust in the Lord with all your heart, and lean not to your understanding. In all things acknowledge Him, and He will direct your paths."

Psalms 37:3 to 5 – "Trust in the LORD, and do good; so shall you dwell in the land, and verily you shall be fed. Delight yourself also in the LORD, and he shall give you the desires of your heart. Commit your way unto the LORD; trust also in him, and he shall bring it to pass."

Matt 6:33 – "But seek ye first the kingdom of God, and his righteousness, and all these things (i.e. life's spiritual and basic needs) shall be added unto you".

1 Cor 2:9, 10 – "But as it is written, Eye has not seen, nor eye heard, neither have entered into the heart of man, the things which God has prepared for them that love him (e.g. God's ever faithful, unending, unwavering Love; assured eternal salvation now; re-uniting with God's Holy Spirit now; and the eternal joys of heaven now). But God has revealed them unto us by his Holy Spirit; for the Holy Spirit searches all things, yea, the deep things of God".

Matt 11:28 to 30 – "Come unto me all ye that labor, and are heavy burden, and I will give you rest. Take my yoke upon you, and learn of me; for I am meek and lowly in heart, and ye shall find rest unto your souls. For my yoke is easy, and my burden is light".

James 2:26 – "For as the body without the spirit is dead, so faith without works is dead also".

2 Tim 3:16 -- "All scripture is given by the inspiration of God, and is profitable for doctrine, for reproof, for correction, for instruction in righteousness".

John 6:63 -- "It is the spirit that gives life; the flesh profits nothing. The words that I speak unto you, they are spirit, and they are life".

John 4:24 -- "God is a Spirit, and they that worship him must worship him in spirit and in truth".

John 14:26 -- "But the Comforter, who is the Holy Spirit, whom the Father will send in my name, he shall teach you all things, and bring all things to your remembrance, what I have said unto you".

Rom 8:32 - " <u>He that spared not his own Son, but delivered him up for us all</u>, how shall he not with him also freely give us all things"?

2 Tim 1:7 – "For God has not given us the spirit of fear, but of power, and of love, and a sound mind".

1 Tim 1:5 – "Now the end of the commandment is love out of a pure heart, and of a good conscience, and of faith unwavering".

Eph 4:11 to 13 – "And <u>he gave some, apostles; and some, prophets; and some, evangelists; and some, pastors and teachers;</u> <u>For the perfecting of the saints</u> for the <u>work of the ministry</u> for the <u>edifying of the body of Christ,</u> <u>Till we all come in the unity of the faith</u>, and of the knowledge of the Son of God, unto a perfect man, unto the measure of the stature of the fullness of Christ".

Micah 6:8 – "He has shown you, O Man, what is good; and what does the LORD require of you, but to do justly, and to love mercy, and to walk humbly with your God."

Lesson 9: Adjusting my Life's Purpose toward God's Love Concept
(Ref 1 Tim 1: 5; Eph 5: All; 1 Jn 4: All; Rom 12: 1, 2)!

-- My Bible study stated that my life's purpose was to reconcile with God through Jesus, grow spiritually through the Holy Spirit, and share my eternal life news with others via Holy Spirit's divine appointments (Ref 2 Cor 5: 17 to 19; John 14: 16; Mark 16: 15; 1 John 1 to 4; Eph 4: Ch 4: All).

- Faith actions provide blessings/consequences/spiritual growth (Ref Heb 11: 6; Phil 4: 4 to 9; Prov 25: 2; 2 Tim 3: 16, 17 (i.e. all choices/actions require consequences).

- Trusting God with the faith of a child is key to real faith/trust/belief in God, and our faith strength comes from understanding how God's Love is essential for our eternal life salvation (Ref Mark 10: 15; Prov 3: 5, 6; Psalm 37: 3 to 7; John 14: 26).

- Protection/growth of our faith in God is essential to receiving blessings as opposed to not receiving blessings from employing our sinful past, our sin nature, and the world's standards (Ref Rom 12: 1, 2; Matt 16: 24 to 28; Prov 3: 5,6; Heb 11: 6).

- Understand/employ God's Love equation (i.e. "You Reap What You Sow") which is the foundation of God's love; because it requires an overall trust, minimum 50/50% love relationship, and loving God first and our neighbor as our self (Ref Col 3: 12, 13; Rom 7: 4; Rom 6: 14; 2 Pet 1 to 10 (e.g. for every action, there is an equal reaction/consequence)).

Eph 4: 0 -- "And grieve not the Holy Spirit, by whom you are sealed unto the day of redemption".

Micah 6:8 – "He has shown you, O Man, what is good; and what does the LORD require of you, but to do justly, and to love mercy, and to walk humbly with your God".

2 Cor 5:17 to 19 – "Therefore, if any man be in Christ, he is a new creation; old things are passed away; behold, all things are become new. And all things are of God, who has reconciles us to himself by Jesus Christ, and has given to us the ministry of reconciliation."

1 Thess 5:16 to 18 -- "Rejoice evermore, pray without ceasing, in everything give thanks; for this is the will of God, in Christ Jesus concerning you".

Psalms 37:3 to 5 – "Trust in the LORD, and do good; so shall you dwell in the land, and verily you shall be fed. Delight yourself also in the LORD, and he shall give you the desires of your heart. Commit your way unto the LORD; trust also in him, and he shall bring it to pass".

Prov 3:5, 6 – "Trust in the LORD with all your heart, and lean not unto your own understanding. In all your ways knowledge him, and he shall direct your paths".

2 Tim 3:15 to 17 – "And that from a child thou has known the holy scriptures, which are able to make thee wise unto salvation through faith which is in Christ Jesus. All scripture is given by inspiration of God, and it profitable for doctrine, for reproof, for correction, for instruction in

righteousness, that the man of God may be perfect, thoroughly furnished unto all good works".

Isaiah 26:3, 4 – "Thou will keep him in perfect peace, whose mind is stayed on thee, because he trusted in thee. Trust you in the LORD forever; for in the LORD God is everlasting strength".

Prov 22:4 – "By humility and reverential trust of the LORD are riches, and honor, and life".

Rom 12:1, 2 – "I beseech you therefore, brethren, by the mercies of God, that you present your bodies a living sacrifice, holy, acceptable unto God, which is your reasonable service. And be not conformed to this world, but be ye transformed by the renewing of your mind, that ye may prove what is that good, and acceptable, and perfect, will of God".

Gal 5:16 – "This I say then, Walk in the Spirit, and ye shall not fulfill the lust of the flesh".

Lesson 10: Adjusting my Mind-Set to follow God's Will for Me
(Ref Rom Chs 12, 5, 8: All; Josh 1: 8, 9; Micah 6: 8; 1 Thess 5: 16 to 18)!

-- Seeking God's love and lead in all of my decisions provides peace/joy/happiness (Ref Prov 3: 5, 6; 1 John 3: 23; 1 John Chs 4, 5 All; 1 John 4: 16).

- Since Jesus had to cover my sins, why would I think that I could do better than God's Son (Ref John 14: 6; Gal 2: 16; Gal 5: 13 to 18; Rom 12: 1, 2).

- Follow Holy Spirit's leading in all of my thoughts/decisions/actions is my only true source of power, love, and self-discipline (Ref John 14: 26; 2 Tim 1: 7; Gal 5: 16 to 26).

- Realize that I should be seeking to share eternal salvation/heaven with everybody when the opportunities occur per Holy Spirit's divine appointments with other humans to help us share God's Love (Ref Matt 28: 19. 20; 1 Tim 2: 1 to 40).

- Praying daily with thanksgiving for Holy Spirit to set up divine appointments for me with others (Ref Matt 28: 19, 20 (i.e. Great Commission Direction); Eph Ch 4 All).

- Good spiritual mind-set comes from studying God's word, trusting him, sharing his love; a pure heart, good conscience, strong faith, and most of all praying often in order to keep your mind-set on God's will for your life and in order to block the devil from planting sinful thoughts in your mind-set

(Ref Romans 12: 1, 2; 1 Thess 5: 16 to 18; Romans 4: 10; 1 Tim 1: 5; Rom 10: 17; Micah 6: 8; Eph 4: 2; Psalm 37: 3 to 7).

Prov 3: 5, 6 – "Trust in the LORD with all your heart, and lean not unto your own understanding. In all your ways knowledge him, and he shall direct your paths".

Hebrews 11, 6 - "But without faith, it is impossible to please Him; for he that comes to God must believe that He is, and that He is a rewarder of them that diligently seek Him".

James 2: 26 – "For as the body without the Holy Spirit is "dead", so faith without works is dead also".

John 15: 7 – "If you abide in me, and my words abide in you, you shall ask what you will, and it shall be done unto you".

Philippians 4: 6, 7 – "Be anxious for nothing, but in everything, by prayer and supplication with thanksgiving, let your requests be made known unto God. And the peace of God, which passes all understanding, shall keep your hearts and minds through Christ Jesus".

Deuteronomy 31: 6 – "Be strong and of good courage, fear not, nor be afraid of them; for the LORD thy God, he it is who does go with thee; he will not fail thee, nor forsake thee".

Gal 5: 16 – "This I say then, Walk in the Spirit, and ye shall not fulfill the lust of the flesh".

2 Tim 1:7 – "for God has not given us the spirit of fear, but of power, and of love, and of a sound mind".

Psalms 37: 3 to 5 – "Trust in the LORD, and do good; so shall you dwell in the land, and verily you shall be fed. Delight yourself also in the LORD, and he shall give you the desires of your heart. Commit your way unto the LORD; trust also in him, and he shall bring it to pass".

Isaiah 26: 3, 4 – "Thou will keep him in perfect peace, whose mind is stayed on thee, because he trusted in thee. Trust you in the LORD forever; for in the LORD God is everlasting strength".

1 Thess 5: 16 to 18 – " Rejoice evermore. **Pray without ceasing. In everything give thanks; for this is the will of God in Christ Jesus concerning you**".

Eph 4: 11 to 13 – "And he gave some, apostles; and some, prophets; and some, evangelists; and some, pastors and teachers; For the perfecting of the saints for the work of the ministry for the edifying of the body of Christ, Till we all come in the unity of the faith, and of the knowledge of the Son of God, unto a perfect man, unto the measure of the stature of the fullness of Christ".

Col 3: 17 – "And whatsoever you do in word or deed, do all in the name of the Lord Jesus, giving thanks to God and the Father by him".

Micah 6: 8 - "He has shown thee; O man, what is good; and what does the LORD require of thee, but to do justly, and to love mercy, and to walk humbly with your God".

Isa 40: 31 – "But they that wait upon the LORD shall renew their strength; they shall mount up with wings like eagles; they shall run, and not be weary; and they shall walk, and not faint".

Lesson 11: Growing daily into a Mature Spiritual Being
(Ref Matt 22: 37 to 40; 1 Thess 5: 16 to 18; Micah 6: 8)!

-- Seeking God's lessons from all good and bad decisions/circumstances produces my greatest spiritual training/growth/blessings (Ref Heb 12: 1 to 15; Proverbs 22: 4; 1 Cor 10: 11 to 15; Prov 25: 2; 2 Cor 12: 9/10).

- Thanking God for all my circumstances, regardless if they are good or bad, provides greatest knowledge / understanding / wisdom / rewards / spiritual adult growth (Ref 1 Thess 5: 17 to 19); as well as provides best transformation of my mind, soul, and spirit to God's Love concept (Ref Rom 12: 1, 2; Rom 8: 31 to 39; Matt 7: 1, 2; Rom 1 All; Prov 25: 2; John 3: 11, 12; 1 Thess 5: 16 to 18; James Ch 1: All).

- Seek God's lessons from all good and bad decisions / circumstances produces my greatest spiritual training / growth / blessings (Ref Proverbs 22: 4; 1 Cor 10: 11 to 15; Prov 25: 2; 2 Cor 12: 9, 10; Heb 12: 1 to 15).

- Pray to Holy Spirit first daily to keep my mind, attitude, and faith actions focused on God's Love and purposes; so I can perform my best faith based actions in order to provide the greatest blessings for me, my love ones, and other humans (Ref Prov 3: 5, 6; Ps 37: 3 to 7; Matt 11: 28 to 30; Rom 12: 1, 2; John 15: 5; Deut 31: 6; Micah 6: 8; Isa 40: 31; Matt 18: 28, 29; John 14: 26; 2 Tim 3: 16, 17; John 14: 6; John 15: 7).

1 Thess 5: 16 to 22 – "Rejoice evermore. Pray without ceasing. In everything give thanks; for this is the will of God in Christ Jesus concerning you. Quench not the Holy

Spirit. Despise not prophesying. Prove all things. Abstain from all appearance of evil".

2 Tim 3: 15 to 17 – "And that from a child thou has known the holy scriptures, which are able to make thee wise unto salvation through faith which is in Christ Jesus. All scripture is given by inspiration of God, and it profitable for doctrine, for reproof, for correction, for instruction in righteousness, that the man of God may be perfect, thoroughly furnished unto all good works".

1 Tim 1: 5 – "Now the end of the commandment is love out of a pure heart, and of a good conscience, and of faith unwavering".

Matthew 22: 37 to 40 – "Master, which is the great commandment in the law? Jesus said unto him, Thou shall love the Lord, thy God, with all your heart, and with all your soul, and with all your mind. This is the first and great commandment. And the second is like it, Thou shall love your neighbor as your self. On these two commandments hang all the law (i.e. Mosaic Law) and the prophets (i.e. bible's Old Testament)".

Proverbs 3: 5, 6 – "Trust in the Lord with all your heart, and lean not to your understanding. In all things acknowledge Him, and He will direct your paths."

Gal 5: 16 – "This I say then, Walk in the Spirit, and ye shall not fulfill the lust of the flesh".

Eph 4: 11 to 13 – "And he gave some, apostles; and some, prophets; and some, evangelists; and some, pastors and teachers; For the perfecting of the saints for the work of the ministry for the edifying of the body of Christ, Till we all come in the unity of the faith, and of the knowledge of the Son of God, unto a perfect man, unto the measure of the stature of the fullness of Christ".

Ephesians 1: 13 – " In whom you also trusted, after you heard the word of truth, the gospel of your salvation; in whom also, after you believed, you were sealed with that Holy Spirit of promise".

2 Cor 5: 17 to 19 – "Therefore, if any man be in Christ, he is a new creation; old things are passed away; behold, all things are become new. And all things are of God, who has reconciles us to himself by Jesus Christ, and has given to us the ministry of reconciliation".

James 2: 26 – "For as the body without the Holy Spirit is "dead", so faith without works is dead also".

Mark 16: 15 – "And he said unto them, Go you into all the world, and preach the gospel to every creature".

1 John 3: 23 –"And this is the commandment, that we should believe on the name of his Son, Jesus Christ, and love one another, as he gave us commandment".

John 5: 24 – Jesus said: "Verily, verily I say unto you, he that hears my word, and believes on Him that sent me, has everlasting life, and shall not come into judgment, but is passed from death unto life".

John 6: 63 -- "It is the spirit that gives life; the flesh profits nothing. The words that I speak unto you, they are spirit, and they are life".

Isaiah 26: 3, 4 – "Thou will keep him in perfect peace, whose mind is stayed on thee, because he trusted in thee. Trust you in the LORD forever; for in the LORD God is everlasting strength".

Prov 22: 4 – "By humility and reverential trust of the LORD are riches, and honor, and life."

Lesson 12: Adjusting my Behavior to God's Love Concept in my daily life
(Ref Col 3: 12, 13; Matt 16: 26; Matt 11: 28 to 30)!

-- Remember daily that God's commandments, ordinances, and judgments are based on loving God first and my neighbor as myself, and I should try to emulate God's Love Concept (Ref Exodus Chs 19 to 40; Leviticus All; 1 John 3: 23; Matt 22: 37 to 40).

- Loving/Encouraging/Uplifting everybody, but not their sinful actions, should be my primary life goal/attitude (Ref 1 John 4: 1 to 10; Gal 6: 7 to 9; Eph 4: 12).

- Praying daily for God's will/ plan for me is a great act of faith (Ref 1 Thess 5: 17; Gal 3: 3).

- Using God's Word in all my encounters (i.e. divine appointments) with others (Ref Heb 4: 12/2 /Tim 1: 7/Col 3: 17; 2 Tim 3: 15 to 17; Phil 4: 4 to 7; Prov 3: 6, 7; Psalm 37: 4 to 8).

- Striving to increase my faith/belief/trust in God daily by bible study, prayers, thoughts, actions, gratefulness, and thanksgiving (Ref Heb 11: 6; Rom 10: 17; Josh 1: 8, 9; 1 Thess 5: 16 to 18; Eph Ch 4: All).

- In order for me to adjust my behavior to employ God's Love Concept daily and have a closer walk with God, I try to remember to be thankful for Jesus' Love and practice the following guidelines obtained from my bible studies as much as possible. In addition, I have placed below guidelines at various locations in my living spaces to remind me to practice, practice, practice my faith-actions daily and frequently (Ref Deut 6: 1 to 9):

(1) That I will be thankful daily for Jesus' Love and sin consequences' sacrifice for me by the absence of God the Father's Love toward Him for the 3 dark hours on the cross; and I will continue to spiritually grow based upon my increasing my knowledge, understanding, and wisdom of God's Love Concept and how it is essential in every aspect of my life (Ref Matt 22: 37 to 40; Prov 3: 5, 6; Romans 5: 8; Eph 1: 13; 2 Cor 5: 17 to 19; Titus 3: 5; Micah 6: 8; 1 Thess 5: 16 to 18).

(2) That I am a spiritually born again Christian (i.e. saved sinner) who is going to be in heaven forever per Jesus' promise, and my soul and spirit will never "die" a spiritual death (Ref Romans 10: 9 to 13; Romans 8: 14 to 17).

(3) That I should be a repentant, humble, grateful, and thankful saved sinner to Jesus daily for his love sacrifice on the cross for my sins consequences that helped me to understand and find the "missing part" in my life via his Holy Spirit and my spirit's reunion (Ref Romans 5: 8; John 14: 6; Jer 26: 13; Jer 18: 8).

(4) That I am to remember daily that God's commandments, ordinances, and judgments are based on the big picture of loving God first and my neighbor as myself; and I should try to emulate God's Love Concept (i.e. being Holy, Loving, and Just) as much as possible (Ref Exodus Chs 19 to 40; Leviticus All; 1 John 3: 23; Matt 22: 37 to 40; Ephesians 3: 16 to 19; 1 Tim 1: 5; Gal 6: 7 to 9).

(5) That I remember that all humans are sinners and their souls and spirits will live forever; and all humans need to make a decision to accept Jesus and his love sacrifice by faith action to secure eternal salvation in heaven or decide to reject Jesus and his love sacrifice and not spend eternity in heaven (Ref John 15: 7; John 5: 24; Romans 3: 19 to 28; Romans 6: 23; Romans 8: 1 to 17).

(6) That I remember that all humans have to decide to accept Jesus' love sacrifice by faith (i.e. belief/trust) to cover their sins and be spiritually born again, or humans have to decide to reject Jesus' love sacrifice and live under the Mosaic Law and its consequences (Ref John 15: 7; 1 John 4: 7 to 15; 1 John 3: 23, 24; 1 John 2: 15 to 17; James 2: 10; Gal 3: 10 to 12; Gal 2: 16).

(7) That I am to Pray often daily for God's will and plan for me that is a great practice of my faith and best way to keep my mind-set on God's spiritual mind-set and plan for me (Ref: 1 Thess 5: 17; Gal 3: 3; Prov 3: 5, 6; James 2: 26).

(8) That I am to follow the Holy Spirit's lead in my life daily, because I don't have all the answers for my life actions and of the issues of other humans that I encounter in my divine appointments (Ref Romans Cp 8: All; 1 Tim 1: 7; Gal 5: 16).

(9) That I am to strive to grow spiritually daily by prayer, bible study, humble gratitude, faith actions, and thanks (Ref Heb 11: 6; Rom 10: 17; Josh 1: 8, 9; 1 Thess 5: 17; Eph Ch 4: All; 2 Tim 3: 16, 17; Prov 9: 9, 10; Prov 1: 1 to 7; 2 Peter 1: 20).

(10) That I am to use God's Word in all my encounters (i.e. divine appointments) with others as much as possible like Jesus did when He was encountered by the Devil (Ref Luke 4: 1 to 13; Heb 4: 12; 2 Tim 1: 7; Col 3: 17; 2 Tim 3: 15 to 17; Phil 4: 4 to 7; Prov 3: 6, 7; Psalm 37: 4 to 8; Heb 4: 12).

(11) That I will test all the spirits of the humans that I encounter to see if they are trying to live by God's Love Standard (i.e. Holy, Loving, and Just); or are they living by the Devil's Non-Loving Standard (i.e. selfish, inconsiderate, and not-respectful) (Ref Matt 22: 37, 40; 1 John 4: All; 1 John 2: 15 to 17; Luke 4: 1 to 13; 1 John 2: 15 to 17; 1 Cor 15: 33; 1 Cor 14: 33; 1 Cor 3: 16, 17).

(12) That I remember that if anyone decides to live their life in accordance only by the Mosaic Law (i.e. 10 commandments, social judgments, and worship ordinances) or no Law instead of faith in Jesus; then they shall receive the appropriate consequences of the Law or no Law from their own decisions (e.g. the tribulations of humans in this life is the consequences of unwise human decisions, not God's desire, planning, or design; and God as the creator of humans can take human lives by his appropriate means whenever He wants in order to reveal his pure love concept) (Ref Gal 3: 10 to 12; Romans 3: 19 to 28; Gal 6: 7 to 9; Romans 1: 16 to 32; 1 John 2: 15 to 17; Deut Ch 20: All).

(13) That I am to share the message of eternal salvation in heaven is a free gift of grace (not works) with all that I encounter, so they can decide to accept the gift now by

their own free choice (Ref Luke 4: 14 to 21; Mark 28: 18; Eph 2: 8, 9; Romans 10: 9, 10).

(14) That all Christians are members of the same spiritual family, and are part of the same Holy Spirit (Ref Eph 4: 4 to 6; Prov 3: 5, 6; Deut 31: 6).

(15) That I am to attend and participate in a bible believing and bible practicing church and small group bible study in order to spiritually grow, encourage other believers, and support the spiritual growth of the church members (i.e. the church is composed of the members, not the building (Ref Heb 10: 24, 25; Eph 4: 1 to 16; James 1: 22 to 27; 1 John Ch 4: All; Titus Ch 2: All; 1 Pet 4: 7, 8)).

(16) That I will research the Faith Doctrine Statement of the church that I participate to ensure the statement is in concert with the bible scriptures (Ref 2 Peter 1: 20, 21; Heb 4: 12; 2 Tim 3: 16, 17).

(17) That I am to love, encourage, uplift, edify everybody (but not their sinful actions); because striving to live in God's Pure Love daily will help me to be a fruitful and productive christian (Ref 1 John 4: 1 to 10; Gal 6: 7 to 9; Eph 4: 11 to 16; James Ch 2: All).

(18) That I am to rejoice evermore (especially about going to heaven forever), pray without ceasing as much as possible, and give thanks in everything for this is the will of God in Christ Jesus for me (Ref 1 Thess 5: 16 to 18).

(19) That I am to thank God in Jesus Name daily for covering all the consequences of my past, present, and

future sins by his love sacrifice on the cross, by accepting my request to come into my life forever, and by renewing my spirit with his Holy Spirit to confirm my eternal salvation in heaven forever (Ref John 5: 24; Eph 1: 13, 14; Col 3: 17; 1 John 5: 10 to 14).

(20) That I also need to remember that humans are sinners (i.e. including myself); and I need to ensure that my communications, relationships, and working with other humans need to be based upon "God's Spiritual common ground" (i.e. Jesus is my Lord and my Savior; the Bible is God's Word; and the Holy Spirit needs to lead me in all of my decisions and activities), otherwise my activities will not produce blessings for me and others) (Ref 1 John 4: 1 to 9; 1 Tim 6: All; 2 Tim 3: 16, 17; Rom 8: 1 to 17; John 15: 3 to 5).

(21) That I trust that God through Jesus' love sacrifice and life examples will bless you as He has blessed me. I trust also that you will decide to follow the Holy Spirit's leading daily in your life to enable you to will receive many blessings for you and your relations with other humans by using the knowledge, understanding, and wisdom that I gained and documented in this guide based upon my bible studies (Ref Prov 2: 3 to 6; Prov 1: 7; Isa 40: 31).

Lesson 13: 3 Spiritual Roles/Manifestations of God
(Ref Gen 1: 26; Matt 3: 16, 17; Rev 4: 8; 1 Pet 1: 15, 16; Micah 6: 8)!

-- God is Love

    (i.e. his Love is graciously free; respectful; fair; unending; comprehensive; without restrictions, preconditions, or payment/re-payment; allows us to make own decisions without force/coercing; and is worthy/deserving of benefits/consequences of our decisions. (God's Love is not Selfish, Inconsiderate, nor Not-respectful – i.e. SIN based).

- God's is Holy, Loving, and Just all the time in all situations: (i.e.

    God is concerned with our Spiritual Mind Set-Thoughts; Spiritual Eternal Relationship / Life / Blessings / Morals / Values / Ethics; and Our relationship /communication with him through his Holy Spirit. (Ref Rom 7: 12; Rom 5: 8; Gal 6: 7-10; Rom 12: 1, 2; John 5: 24; 1 John: Chs 4 & 5; Eph 1:14 & 4: 30; Titus 3: 5; Heb 11: 6; John 4: 24).

- Jesus is fulfillment of God's Word/Salvation/His Promises: (i.e.

    Jesus is concerned with our Daily Spiritual Walk-Journey on Earth; Salvation from sin/hell, our sin nature, and world's sinful influence; reveals God's Knowledge, Understanding, Wisdom in Bible.

    (Ref II Tim 3: 6, 7; Heb 4: 12; John 14: 6, 15, 21, 26; Col 1: 9 to 11; Jer 9: 23, 24; John 15: 4, 5; Luke 18:

16, 17; Luke 24: 25 to 27; Matt 16: 24 to 27; Prov 3: 5, 6; Prov Ch 3; Prov 1: 7; Prov 2: 1 to 6).

- Holy Spirit is our eternal seal/trainer to know God's Will for us: (i.e. Holy Spirit provides God's love, power, and self control; Use of God's Knowledge, Understanding, and Wisdom; and is concerned with our spiritual growth/reconciliation to God (Ref; II Tim 3: 16, 17; II Tim 1: 7; Col 1: 9 to 11; John 14: 26; Prov 25: 2: Matt 11: 28 to 30; Heb 12: 11; Col 1: 19 to 23; Isa 11: 2; John 15:5; 2 Cor 5: 17 to 19).

In summary; **God wants us to be reconciled with him** thru **our humble- repentant decision;** so we can be immediately re-born again spiritually by our own choice; **Grow spiritually** to live a more righteous life in concert with his love for us; **foster more righteous life changes in others** in earth's mission fields; so we can receive more blessings from our choices.

Extra: Prov 25:2 – God uses his creation/nature, Godly institutions, and Faith rewards to help us better understand him (e.g. conscience, sun, moon, science, atoms, our body/brain, friendships, marriage, church, Bible, childlike faith, prayer, tribulations, repentance, forgiveness, thanksgiving, life, death etc).

Titus 3: 5 –**Not by the works of justice**, which we have done, but according to his mercy, he saved us, by the laver (i.e. spiritual washing) of **regeneration**, and **reuniting** of the Holy Spirit with our spirit*.

- How to Get Spiritually Saved (i.e. Spiritually Born Again): ☺☺☺

In sincere prayer to Jesus right now **in childlike faith** (Mark 10:15): admit that you can't work your way into heaven (**repenting**); acknowledge/confess your sin nature to yourself and to Jesus right now (i.e. **confession**); **accept** Jesus' cross love sacrifice for you right now which covers all of your sins and their consequences (i.e. exercising your faith in Jesus); and **thank him for removing all of your past, present, and future sin consequences** (i.e. trusting Jesus is our greatest faith action) and thank Jesus for reuniting with your spirit right now via **your decision**/request (i.e. eternal life hope realized). **Welcome back to the family of God!!!** Enjoy. **Now go splash your eternal blessings on others around you**, after sincere prayer for God's will for you, **with your new attitude, walk, and talk in daily humble thankfulness.** Remember **you are a saved sinner,** and your will not be a saint until you arrive in heaven. ☺☺☺

- A recommended/suggested salvation prayer:
Dear Lord Jesus I confess that I am a sinner and unable to keep your standard of being Holy, Loving, and Just all the time, and I am sorry for all my sins which caused you and others to suffer greatly for me. I accept your love sacrifice on the cross to pay for the consequences of all my sins, and I ask you to come into my life and unite my spirit with your Holy Spirit again to help me to more closely follow your plan for my life. **Thanks you for coming into my life and re-uniting my spirit with your Holy Spirit now to provide me eternal life with you in heaven per your promise and love sacrifice.** I pray in Jesus name to let you know that I am eternally

grateful for what you have just eternally done for me. Amen. ☺☺☺

If you were sincere with above prayer, then at this instance you were re-united with Jesus' Holy Spirit, and **you become children of God again, right now, and forever unconditionally** (i.e. being spiritually re-born again instantly **back into God's Holy Spirit forever per Jesus' unconditional promise to us** -- which you can never, **never lose again**) (Romans 10: 9, 10; Ephesians 2: 8, 9; Titus 3: 4 to 7). **How can you be sure you are spiritually born again right now, because Jesus cannot lie** (i.e. God is forever Holy, Loving, and Just)!!! He loves you, and He keeps his promises because **He is GOD: not a man**. Therefore, He always does what he says. God is Love; and Love is 1Cor 13: 4 to 8, especially verse 8. ☺☺☺

Lesson 14: God's Grace versus Mosaic Law
(Ref Josh 1: 8, 9; Rom 3: 20; Rom 1: 16; Rom Ch 5: All; Rom Ch 6: All; Rom Ch 8: All)!

-- Gal 3:10 to 12 – "For as many as are of the works of the law (i.e. Mosaic Law) are under the curse; for it is written, Cursed is everyone that continues not in all things which are written in the book of the law, to do them. But that no man is justified by the law in the sight of God, it is evident; for the just shall live by faith. And the law is not of faith, but the man that does them" (i.e. try to comply with the Mosaic Law – the 10 commandments, social judgments, worship ordnances) shall live in them (i.e. Law's consequences)".

-- Eph 2:8, 9 - "For by grace are you saved through faith; and that not of yourselves, it is the gift of God – not of works (i.e. trying to comply with the Mosaic Law within our sin nature), lest any man should boast (i.e. **God's grace means a free, undeserved gift!**)".

- Rom 3:20 - "Therefore by the deeds of the law there shall no flesh be justified in his sight; for by the Mosaic Law is the knowledge of sin".

- James 2:10 - "For whosoever shall keep the whole law, and yet offend in one point, he is guilty of all" (i.e. we cannot comply with the Mosaic Law with our sin nature, because our mind-set is not capable of having a pure love mind-set all the time without Jesus' help).

- Rom 8:1 to 4 – "There is, therefore, now no condemnation to them who are in Christ Jesus, who walk not after the flesh, but after the Spirit. **For the law of the Spirit of life in Christ**

Jesus (Ref Matt 22: 36 to 40) has made me free from the law of sin and death (i.e. Mosaic Law). For what the Mosaic Law could not do, in that it was weak through the flesh, God sending his own Son, in the likeness of sinful flesh and for sin, condemned sin in the flesh. That the righteousness of the law (i.e. Law of the Spirit of Life in Christ Jesus) might be fulfilled in us, who walk not after the flesh, but after the Holy Spirit".

- John 3:3 to 7 – "Jesus answered, and said unto him, Verily, verily, I say unto you, Except a man be born again (i.e. spiritually born again), he cannot see the kingdom of God. Nicodemus said to him, How can a man be born when he is old? Can he enter the second time into his mother's womb, and be born? Jesus answered, Verily, verily, I say to you, Except a man be born of water and of the "Holy Spirit", he cannot enter in the kingdom of God. That which is born of the flesh is flesh; and that which is born of the "Holy Spirit" is spirit. Marvel not that I say unto you, you must be born again".

- Matt 22:36 to 40- "Master, which is the great commandment in the law? Jesus said unto him, Thou shall love the Lord, thy God, with all your heart, and with all your soul, and with all your mind. This is the first and great commandment. And the second is like it, Thou shall love your neighbor as your self. **On these two commandments hang all the law and the prophets**" (i.e. we cannot comply with the Mosaic Law with our sin nature, because our mind-set is not capable of having a pure love mind-set all the time without the Holy Spirit's help. In other words, the Mosaic Law and God's above pure love requirements are in concert from God's Love Concept that requires humans to have a holy, loving, and just mind-set like God's mind-set in order to live with a pure love mind-set. In summary, God presents the Mosaic Law and his Love Concept to help to provide different perspectives to consider, understand, and comprehend God's pure love).

- Rom 10:4 – "For Christ is the end of the law for righteousness to every one that believes".

- John 14:6 – "Jesus said unto him, I am the way, the truth, and the life; no man comes to the Father, but by me".

- Luke 18:16 – "Verily I say unto you, Whosoever shall not receive the kingdom of God like a little child (i.e. with the pure faith of a child) shall in no way enter it".

- John 3:15, 16, 17 – "That whosoever believeth in him (i.e. Jesus Christ) should not perish, but have eternal life. For God so loved the world that He gave his only begotten Son, that whosoever believes in Him should not perish, but have everlasting life (note: Jesus Christ translated is "God Saved his Anointed One"). For God sent not his Son into the world to condemn the world, but that the world through him might be saved" (i.e. a true love relationship requires both parties to have a faith, trust, and reciprocal holy, loving, and just attitude/thoughts/actions toward one another based upon their own free will decisions, not because of forced decisions).

- Romans 10:9, 10 – "That if you shall confess with your mouth the Lord Jesus, and shall believe in your heart that God has raised him from the dead, you shall be saved. For with the heart man believes unto righteousness, and with the mouth confession is made unto salvation".

Basic Bible Lessons

- Heb 11:6 – " But without faith it is impossible to please Him; for he that comes to God must believe that He is, and that He is a rewarder of them that diligently seek Him".

- 1 Tim 1:5 – "Now the end of the commandment is love out of a pure heart, and a good conscience, and faith unwavering".

- Titus 3:5 – "Not by works of righteousness which we have done, but according to his mercy he saved us, by washing of regeneration, and renewing of the Holy Spirit".

- Ephesians 1:13 – "In whom ye also trusted, after you heard the work of truth, the gospel of your salvation; and in whom also after you believed, you were sealed with the Holy Spirit of promise".

- Ephesians 4:4 to 6 – "There is one body, **and one Spirit "(i.e. Holy Spirit)"**, even as you are called in one hope of your calling: One Lord, one faith, one baptism, One God and Father of all, who is above all, **and through all and in you all**." (**Note**: all spiritually born again Christians' spirits are re-united into God's Holy Spirit forever, and the Holy Spirit will live forever and never be rejected from living in heaven for all eternity).

Lessson 15: God's Love Defined (i.e. Love is Holy, Loving, and Just)
(God is Love: 1 John 4:8b; 1 Cor 13: 4 to 8; Rom 5: 8)!

Pure Godly Love requires us to be independent, loving, and accountable beings who have the capability to make our own personal decisions and have the right to receive the consequences of our decisions. God allows us to experience the consequences of our good and bad decisions, so we can make subsequential decisions which will help us to grow spiritually in order to receive greater blessings that will benefit us and those affected by our decisions. Finally, God will/must provide the consequences to both saved and unsaved people based upon their own decisions.

God covered the consequences of all of our sins with Jesus' love sacrifice on the cross (i.e. absence of the Father's Love to Jesus during the 3 dark hours on the cross), so we can better understand how great his love is for us. In addition, He allows us to experience the consequences of our decisions with the Godly hope that we will grow spiritually to better understand his holiness and righteousness and make decisions more in concert with his will for us to lead more holy, loving, and just (i.e. righteous) lives; so we can receive/share maximum blessings for us and our fellow human beings here on earth and in heaven.

God's will for us encompasses:

Love and Purpose of Life on Earth (Matt 22: 36 to 40; Matt 11: 28 - 30; Eph Ch 4: All) -

> Obtain personal salvation, reduce personal sin nature, reduce personal world influence, know God's Love daily, radiate inner peace, joy, and happiness, share

our love with others, and receive many blessings (Ref 1 Cor 2: 9 to 13).

Love Standard (Matt 22: 36 - 40; 1 Jn Ch 4: All; Jn 14: 6) -

Use God's standard in all facets of our life to guide our journey.

Love and Decision Making (Prov 3: 5, 6; Gal 6: 7, 8; Rom 12: 1, 2) -

> Realize that all decisions have consequences, so we should pray for God's plan for us daily.

Love and Applications in Life (Micah 6: 8; I Tim 1: 5; Deut 31: 6) -

Employ God's standard in all our thoughts, walk, and actions.

Love and Benefits (Ps 37 All; Gal 5: 18 to 26; Phil Ch 4 All) -

> Store all blessings in heaven by obeying God's commands to love him and our neighbor as yourself.
>
> Love and Problem Solving (Josh 1: 8, 9; Gal 6: 16; 1 Thess 5: 16 to 24; Rom 12: 1, 2) -
>
> Employ greater use of God's standard with frequent Bible Study, frequent prayer, and thanksgiving in all our decisions, thoughts, and actions; so we can maintain our focus on God's spiritual mind-set more often.
>
> Gal 5:16 – "This I say, Walk in the Spirit, and you shall not fulfill the lust of the flesh".

Eph 6 18 – "Praying always with all prayer and supplication in the Holy Spirit, and watching therefore with all perserverance and supplication for all saints."

Eph 5:20 – "Giving thanks always for all things unto God and the Father in the name of our Lord Jesus Christ".

Basic Bible Lessons

Lesson 16: God's Plan for Eternal Salvation Verses
(Ref 2 Tim 3: 15 to 17; 1 Pet 1: 20, 21)!

Romans 5:8 -- "But God commended his love toward us in that, while we were yet sinners, Christ died for us."

Romans 3:3:10 – "As it is written, there is none righteous, no, not one". (All humans Sin – sin is a non-loving thought, word, or action toward another i.e. a transgression of God's love standard).

Romans 6:23 – "For the wages of sin is death, but the gift of God is eternal life through Jesus Christ, our Lord" (John 14: 6 – Jesus is the way, truth, life: only way into heaven).

Sin state is generated by missing God's mark of being holy, loving, and just all the time no matter what; and our first sin (**i.e. first non-loving thought, word, or action) resulted in our spirit and God's Holy Spirit separating which placed us in a spiritually dead condition in God's eyes**.) (i.e. the Holy Spirit cannot be connected to a sinful spirit!).

John 3:5 – "Jesus answered, Verily, verily, I say unto thee, Except a man be born of water and of the Holy Spirit, he cannot enter into the kingdom of God". (Ask Jesus in your life, and his Holy Spirit will also come into your life to make you spiritually born again forever) (i.e. **we have to choose with thankfulness and gratitude, not just believe, to personally request accept his free love gift** (i.e. **free undeserved grace gift) to live in heaven with him forever).**

Romans 3:20 – "Therefore, by the deeds of the law there shall no flesh be justified in his sight; for by the Mosaic law is the knowledge of sin". (Only sinless Jesus' sacrifice can cover our sins).

Hebrews 11:6 – "But without faith it is impossible to please him; for he that comes to God must believe that he is, and that he is a rewarder of them that diligently seek him."

Matthew 18:3 to 5 – "Jesus said, Verily I say unto you, except you be converted, and become as little children (i.e. in your faith/belief/trust toward and in Jesus Christ), you shall not enter into the kingdom of heaven. Whosoever, therefore, shall humble himself as this little child, the same is greatest in the kingdom of heaven. And whosoever shall receive one such little child in my name receives me."

John 3:11, 12 – Jesus said, "Verily, verily, I say unto you, We speak that which we do know, and testify to that which we seen; and you receive not our witness. If I have told you earthly things, and you believe not, how shall you believe, if I tell you heavenly things?" (The priests and Jews of Jesus day did not understand that his words, parables, messages had spiritual meanings; because they were seeking selfish earthly meanings, treasures, and understandings).

Ephesians 2:8, 9 – "For by grace are you saved through faith; and that not of yourselves, it is the gift of God – not of works, lest any man should boast (i.e. God's grace means a free, undeserved gift!)."

Titus 3:5 – "Not by works of righteousness which we have done, <u>but according to his mercy he saved us</u>, by the washing of regeneration, and the renewing of the Holy Spirit".

Romans 10:9, 10 – "<u>If you confess</u> with your mouth the Lord Jesus, and <u>believe in your heart</u> that God raised him from the dead, you shall be saved. For with the heart man believes unto righteousness; and with the mouth confession is made unto salvation". (i.e. <u>believe /ask/accept/thank Jesus for our receiving his Holy Spirit again and being re-born spiritually for all eternity at that moment per Jesus promise</u>).

<u>God cannot lie</u>, so He keeps all of his promises forever (i.e. a very long time!).

Ezekiel 36: 26, 27 – " <u>A new heart also will I give you and a new spirit will I put within you</u>; and I will take away the stony heart out of your flesh, and I will give you a heart of flesh. <u>And I will put my Spirit within you</u>, and cause you to walk in my statues, and you shall keep mine ordinances, and do them" (Ref also 2 Cor 5: 17; 2 Cor 6: 16).

1 Thessalonians 5:16 to 18 – "Rejoice evermore. Pray without ceasing. <u>In everything give thanks;</u> for this is the will of God in Christ Jesus concerning you".

Hebrews 12:6 & 11 – "<u>For whom the Lord loves he disciplines</u>, and tests every son whom he receives". "Now no discipline for the present seems to be joyous, but grievous; nevertheless, afterward it yields the peaceful fruit of righteousness unto them who are exercised by it".

Proverbs 3:5, 6 – "<u>Trust in the Lord with all your heart and lean not on your own understanding</u>; in all your ways acknowledge him and he will make your path straight".

Proverbs 1:7 – "<u>The reverential trust of the Lord</u> is the beginning of knowledge, but fools despise wisdom and discipline".

James 4:6b – "God resists the proud, but <u>gives grace to the humble</u>".

A **recommended Prayer of Faith/Belief/Trust** to request/accept/thank Jesus **for your eternal salvation right now** (Sin means to miss God's mark of being holy, loving, just all the time no matter what):

Dear Lord Jesus, I confess that I am a sinner and unable to always keep your standard of being Holy, Loving, and Just all the time (i.e. Loving all the time); and I am sorry for all my sin choices (past, present, and future) which caused you, others, and me to suffer greatly and needlessly. I accept your love sacrifice on the cross that paid for the consequences of all my sin choices, and I ask you to come into my life and unite my spirit with your Holy Spirit again **right now** to help me to more closely follow your will/plan for my life. **I thank you** for coming into my life **right now**, forgiving all my sin consequences **right now**, and re-uniting my spirit with your Holy Spirit **right now; resulting in me receiving** eternal life with you **right now according to your word**. I pray in Jesus name to let you know that I am eternally grateful for what you have **just now** done for me and to remind me that I could not have been **spiritually re-born again** without your help. Amen. ☺☺☺

If you were sincere with above prayer, then at this moment you were re-united with Jesus' Holy Spirit. You became a child of God again, right now, and forever / unconditionally by your choice and Jesus promise (i.e. being spiritually born again back into God's Holy Spirit forever per Jesus' unconditional promise to us -- which we can never, never lose again per Jesus promise) (Romans 10: 9, 10; Ephesians 2: 8, 9; Titus 3: 4 to 7; John 14: 6). God does not lie like humans, because it is against his love nature!!! Rejoice daily with thanksgiving your eternal life with Jesus in heaven per Jesus promise.

How can you be sure you are spiritually born again right now: God is not a man and cannot lie (i.e. God is always Holy, Loving, and Just)!!! He loves you, and He keeps his promises because He is GOD: not a man. Therefore, He always keeps his promises. In addition, God had to make sure that his eternal life plan was very simple, so that everyone could understand it no matter what their physical, mental, psychologically, social, cultural, moral, rational, and man's training/condition's, etc impacts are. Another example of God's true love!!! (Rom 1: 16; Rom 1: 19, 20; Heb 11: 6; Gal 6: 7, 8; Rom 10: 9 – 13; Jer 17: 5 - 10; Eph 2: 8, 9; Isa 6: 3; 1 John 4; 8, 16). God keeps his promises!!! ☺☺☺

If you doubt the above Bible based truth, then do a diligent research of these above truths/Bible verses; and you will be convinced of their veracity and fact. After all, your eternal life's existence depends upon you making the correct, proper, and sincere choice concerning where your soul and spirit will exist for all eternity. Ref Bible Books of Romans; Ephesus; & Galatians.

If you are not concerned if you go to heaven or hell, what about your loved ones (i.e. spouse, partners, friends, children, associates?) They have to make their own decisions/chooses about being born again spiritually while they are on this earth. Are you content not to advise them how to be spiritually born again and live in heaven forever???

Do your research first in the New Testament Books until you understand the reality of the books before you study the Old Testament Books; because the Old Testament Books are a little more difficult to understand as witnessed by the Apostle Paul (who wrote most of the new testament books after he received further in-depth instruction in the bible truths within the old testament books concerning God's Love Concept which stopped him from continuing to kill Christians – 1 Tim 1: 5; Romans 5:8; John 15: 13; 1 John 3: 23; 1 John Ch 4: All; Eph Ch 4: All).

Lesson 17: God's Holy Spirit released me from Mosaic Law Mandates
(Ref Rom 3: 20 to 25; Eph 1: 13; Titus 3: 5; Rom 8: 2)!

These below bible verses support that living via God's Love Concept promotes spiritual growth; direct personal relationship with God; access to God's knowledge, understanding, and wisdom from the Holy Spirit; membership in God's family forever; eternal salvation in heaven; and receiving abundant holy, loving, and just blessings:

Jn 3: 5 to 7 – "Jesus answered, Verily, verily, I say unto thee, except a man be born of water and of the Spirit (i.e. Holy Spirit), he cannot enter into the kingdom of God. That which is born of the flesh is flesh; and that which is born of the Spirit is spirit. Marvel not that I said unto thee, you must be (i.e. spiritually) born again".

Rom 3: 20 to 25 – "Therefore, buy the deeds of the law (i.e. Mosaic Law) there shall no flesh be justified in his sight; for by the **Mosaic Law is the knowledge of sin (i.e. law of sin and death)**. But now the righteousness of God apart from the law is manifested, being witnessed by the law and the prophets, Even the righteousness of God which is by faith of Jesus Christ unto all and upon all them that believe; for there is no difference. **For all have sinned and come short of the glory of God**; and only being justified freely by his grace through the redemption that is in Christ Jesus, whom God has set forth to be a propitiation through faith in his blood, to declare his righteousness for the remission of sins that are past, through the forbearance of God".

Jam 2: 26 -"For as the body without the Holy Spirit is dead, so faith without works is dead also".

Ephesians 1: 13 – "In whom ye also trusted, after you heard the work of truth, the gospel of your salvation; and in whom also after you believed, you were sealed with the Holy Spirit of promise".

Jn 5: 24 – "Verily, verily, I say unto you, He that hears my word, and believes on him that sent me, has everlasting life, and shall not come into judgment, but is passed from death (i.e. spiritual death) unto life (i.e. spiritual life)".

1 Jn 5: 14 – "And this is the confidence that we have in him, that if we ask anything **according to his will**, he heads us".

Titus 3: 5 –" Not by works of righteousness which we have done, but according to his mercy he saved us, by washing of regeneration, and renewing of the Holy Spirit" (i.e. our first sin separates our spirit from the Holy Spirit, and we need to re-unite with the Holy Spirit to become spiritually alive again in God's eyes).

Rom 8: 2 – "**For the law of the Spirit of Life in Christ Jesus has made me free from the law of sin and death**" (Ref Rom Ch 8: All vs Mosaic Law respectively (i.e. Mosaic Law refers to 10 commandments, and 600+ worship ordinances and social judgments spelled out in the bible books of Exodus, Leviticus, Numbers, and repeated in the book of Deuteronomy). (Note: Use of the word Law in the bible refers to teachings/instruction (Ref Ps 19; 7; Ps 119: All).

Jn 14: 26 – "But the Comforter who is the Holy Spirit, by whom the Father will send in my name, he shall teach you all things, and bring all things to your remembrance, whatever I have said unto you".

Ephesians 4: 4 to 6 – "There is one body, **and one Spirit "(i.e. Holy Spirit)"**, even as you are called in one hope of your calling: One Lord, one faith, one baptism, One God and Father of all, who is above all, **and through all and in you all**." (**Note**: all spiritually born again christians' spirits are re-united into God's Holy Spirit forever, and the Holy Spirit will live forever and never be rejected from living in heaven for all eternity).

Rom 8: 14 – "For as many as are led by the Spirit of God, they are the sons of God".

1 Cor 3: 16 – "Know you not that you are the temple of God, and that the Spirit of God dwells in you"?

2 Tim 1: 7 – "For God has not given us the spirit of fear, but of power, and of love, and a sound mind".

1 Thess 4: 16 to 19 – "Rejoice evermore. Pray without ceasing. In everything give thanks; for this is the will of God in Christ Jesus concerning you. Quench not the Holy Spirit".

1 Cor 13: 13 – "And now abides faith, hope, and love; but the greatest of these is love".

1 Jn 4: 8b, 16b – "… God is love…".

1 Cor 13: 4 to 7 – "Love is patient. Love is kind. It does not envy. It does not boast. It is not proud. It is not rude. It is not easily angered. It keeps no records of wrongs. Love does not delight in evil, but rejoices with the truth. It always protects, always trusts, always hopes, and always perseveres. Love never fails".

Ps 46: 10 – "Be still, and know that I am God".

Lesson 18: God's Love, Responsibility, and Accountability
(Ref Gal 6: 7,8; Jn 6: 63; Micah 6: 8; 1 Jn Ch 4: All)!

God's Love is founded upon the spiritually balanced equation that ..."we reap what we sow" (Ref Gal 6: 7 to 10) (Note: in other words: apply the golden rule to treat others as you would have them treat you; or remember that for every decision there is an appropriate consequence: good decisions reap good blessings, and bad decisions do not real good blessings)!

In other words, our lives need to adhere to God's Mind-Set in our thoughts, words, and actions in all our life endeavors to receive our maximum blessings; and this can be accomplished by keeping all our choices close to God's standard of Being Holy, Loving, and Just frequently (Ref Heb 11:6; Proverbs 3 5, 6; John 5: 24; Matt 11: 28 to 30; 1 Thess 5: 16 to 24; Micah 6: 8).

Believe/Trust God always (i.e. accept his Holy Spirit by choice; be thankful for his sacrifice to cover all our sins; thank him for uniting our spirit with his Holy Spirit forever; thank him for our free choice and consequences daily; be humble daily and share your heavenly gift information with others through divine appointments; and maintain God's Mind-Set often via prayer).

Love, Responsibility, and Accountability must compliment and be reciprocal to each other to be true/real/beneficial (Ref Matt 22: 36 to 40 & John 15: 1 to 14).

God's Knowledge, Understanding, and Wisdom come from being humble, just, and righteous (Ref Proverbs 1: 7 & Proverbs Chs 2 and 3 & Isa 57: 15).

The Holy Spirit of God's teachings should be our guidance and source of our Spiritual Life/Walk/Growth (Ref John 6: 63).

Pure Love (God's Love) demands Childlike Trust as well as God's Mindset in all of our Faith Actions/Thoughts/Words (Ref Matt 18: 1 to 6 & Matt 19: 14).

Spiritual-Soul choices/decisions is the difference between us and God's other creations (Ref Romans Ch 12: All).

Judgments should always be based upon God's Love Standard: Holy/Loving/Just (Ref Matt 7: 2 & Matt 22: 36 to 40).

Love choices/decisions help us to grow spiritually, receive many blessings for others, and help us and to grow spiritually in God's Knowledge, Understanding, and Wisdom (Ref Matt 16: 24 to 27 & John 14: 26).

Love must be a mutual understanding between beings to be hopeful, evident, and trustworthy (Ref Luke 16: 10).

Love is direct opposite to being a puppet: love consequences need to be allowed (Ref John 11:25, 26).

God's Love and Jesus Sacrifice is the end of the Law for us and its consequences, if we accept it personally with thanksgiving (Ref 1 Tim 1: 5, 9; Matt 22: 36 to 40; John 5: 24).

Lesson 19: Our Childlike Trust is Essential to Our Spiritual Life (Ref Matt 18: 1 to 6; Rom 8: All)!

-- When Jesus was on the cross and the earth was dark for 3 hours, this was the first and only time that God the Father turned his back on his Son. This absence of God the Father's love for his Son was so horrible for Jesus that it covered all the consequences for everybody's sins. But we must choose to accept Jesus' sacrifice/gift in order to cover all of our past, present, and future sin consequences; and we must also choose to accept our eternal life with him based upon his great sacrifice for us with thanksgiving. ☺☺☺

- Matt 16: 26 – "What does it profit a man, if he gains the whole world and loses his soul. Or what shall a man exchange for his soul?" (i.e. Eternal life in heaven exceeds short time earthly gains which we cannot take with us after our short lived life on earth).

- Romans 1: 16 – "For I am not ashamed of the gospel of Christ; for it is the power of God unto salvation to everyone that believes; to the Jew first, and also to the Gentile. For it is the righteousness of God revealed from faith to faith; as it is written, the just shall live by faith" (God will loves us, provides eternal salvation, blesses us; if we trust Him completely with a humble soul and spiritual attitude and try to do his will for us daily).

- Ephesians 2: 8, 9 – "For by grace are you saved through faith; and that not of yourselves, it is the gift of God, Not by works, lest any man should boast" (i.e. True love can only come from our free choice, because God will not force us to choose him).

-- Pure Love requires the consequences of our choices.

> - Gal 6: 7, 8 – "We reap what we sow" (i.e. God covered our consequences by Jesus' suffering, but only if we accept his Son by faith/trust).

-- How does child-like faith lead us to become spiritually born again:

> - Luke 18: 16, 17 –"But Jesus called to him, and said, Let little children to come to me, and forbid them not, for of such is the kingdom of God. Verily, Verily I say to you, whosoever shall not receive the kingdom of God like a little child shall in no way enter it" (i.e. believe, trust, accept Jesus' word, actions, and faithfulness with a child's faith).
>
> - Heb 11: 6 – "Without (child-like pure) faith it is impossible to please him. Because you must believe that He exists, and He will reward them who diligently seek him".
>
> - John 1: 9 – "If we confess our sins, he is faithful and just to forgive us our sins, and to cleanse us from all righteousness" (i.e. God cannot lie (it is not-loving to lie) (Ref Matt 11: 28-30).

-- What does Spiritually Re-Born Again Mean; or how do we become a part of the "Christ Mass Spiritually again?" (i.e. re-joined to God's Holy Spirit forever).

- John 3: 3 to 7 – "Jesus answered, and said unto him, Verily, Verily, I say unto you, Except a man be born again, he cannot see the Kingdom of God. Nicodemus said to him, how can a man be born when he is old? Can he enter the second time into his mother womb, and be born? Jesus answered, Verily, Verily, I say to you, Except a man be born of water and of the Holy Spirit, he cannot enter into the kingdom of God. That which is born of the flesh is flesh, and that which is born of the Holy Spirit is spirit. Marvel not that I said to you that you must be born again". (i.e. Our first sin separates our spirit from God's Holy Spirit, because God cannot be joined to a non-loving Spirit).

- John 14: 6 – "Jesus said, I am the Way, the Truth, and the life; no man comes to the Father but by me."

- Romans 10: 9, 10 – "If you shall confess with your mouth the Lord Jesus, and shall believe in your heart that God has raised him for the dead, you shall be saved. For with the heart man believes unto righteousness, and with the mouth confession is made unto salvation" (i.e. a child trust their parents, and a true friend trusts his friend).

- Ephesians 1: 13 – "In whom you also trusted, after you heard of the word of truth, the gospel of your salvation; in whom also after you believed, you were sealed with the Holy Spirit of promise"(i.e. born again spiritually to God's Holy Spirit by choice and trust).

- Romans 8: 11 – "But if the Spirit of him that raised up Jesus from the dead dwell in you, he that raised up Christ from the dead shall also give life to your mortal bodies by his Spirit that dwells in you" (our non-dying Soul and Spirit receives a new spiritual body).

- Titus 3: 5 – "Not by works of righteousness which we have done, but according to his mercy he saved us, by the washing of regeneration, and renewing of the Holy Spirit".

-- Heaven will be filled with Pure Love, and Hell will have no love in it.

- 1 John 4: 8b; 2 Thess 1: 5 – 9; Rom Ch 8: All (i.e. Jesus did not know his Father's Love during the 3 hours of darkness while on the cross that covered the sins of all humans, that was his hell experience for us).

-- **God allows us to experience trails and temptations** to help us to make **good decisions for** improving **reconciliation** with God, **growing** spiritually, and **receiving** more blessings.

- Heb 12: 11 – " Now no chastening for the present seems to be joyous, but grievous; nevertheless, afterward it yields the peaceful fruit of righteousness unto to them who are exercised by it" (Ref also James 1: 2 - 4, 12, 13 – 15; and Deut 31: 6, 8). We get a new body in heaven that will be perfect, never have illnesses, sickness, or shortcomings; and our new body will encase our undying soul and spirit for eternity,!!! **Our soul and spirit never die, otherwise why is there a heaven and hell?**

A **recommended Prayer of Faith/Belief/Trust** to request / accept / thank Jesus **for your eternal salvation right now** (Sin means to miss God's mark of being holy, loving, just):

Dear Lord Jesus I confess that I am a sinner and unable to always keep your standard of being Holy, Loving, and Just all the time (i.e. Loving all the time); and I am sorry for all my sin choices which caused you, others, and me to suffer greatly and needlessly. I accept your love sacrifice on the cross, which paid for the consequences of all my sin choices, and I ask you to come into my life and unite my spirit with your Holy Spirit again **right now** to help me to more closely follow your will/plan for my life. **I thank you for coming into my life right now, forgiving all my sin consequences right now, and re-uniting my spirit with your Holy Spirit right now, resulting in me receiving eternal life with you right now according to your word**. I pray in Jesus name to let you know that I am eternally grateful for what you have **just now** done for me and to remind me that I could not have been **spiritually re-born again** without your help. Amen. ☺☺☺

If you were sincere with above prayer, then at this moment you were re-united with Jesus' Holy Spirit, and you became a child of God again, right now, and forever unconditionally by your choice and Jesus promise (i.e. being spiritually born again back into God's Holy Spirit forever per Jesus' unconditional promise to us when we trust his word and actions and thank him for his eternal faithfulness)!!! ☺☺☺

If you don't believe, trust, and accept the above Spiritual Truths from God's Bible and confirmed from Jesus Life, please do try to disprove it. The results will convince you otherwise, if you do a diligent, persevering, and humble research!!! ☺☺☺

After all, if God is a God of True Love (not of man's short sighted, inadequate, and unsatisfying love), wouldn't He make sure that his plan of eternal salvation was understood by all humans no matter what their handicaps are??? So if you don't want to believe a God of Heavenly Love, should you also deprive your loves ones of this love message and leave them in the eternal consequences of their own poor spiritual choices? ☺

Lesson 20: Jesus Pure Love Questions
(Ref Rom 3: 10, 23; Rom 5: 8; John 3: 15, 16)!

If God is Holy (i.e. cannot commit any sins), Loving (i.e. shows his caring concerns for us in all of his thoughts, talk, and actions), and Just/Righteous (i.e. ensure we receive the consequences of our decisions); wouldn't He require that we receive the benefits/consequences/results of our decisions as part of his pure love concept? (Ref Gal 6: 7, 8; Rom 6: 23; John 3: 3, 5, 36; Rom 10: 9, 10).

Is God's definition of "perfect" means that He cannot make any non-loving decisions, what kind of faith, love, and hope would he expect of us? (Ref 1 Cor Ch 13: All; Matt 22: 36 to 40; I John 4: 7 – 10; 1 Tim 1: 5).

If we could save ourselves (i.e. obtain our own salvation by our works); why did God (i.e. Jesus) have to pay for our sin consequences? (Ref Eph 2: 8, 9; Heb 11: 6; Titus 3: 4 to 7; John 3: 3, 5; John 14: 6; Rom 10: 9, 10; John 5: 24).

Why does God refer to us of being "spiritually dead", when we will live forever in either heaven or hell by our own choice? (Ref Rom 6: 23; John 3; 15, 16; John 11: 25, 26; Gal 6: 7, 8). Or in other words, doesn't it make more sense that a God of Love would have created us to live forever by our own choice, not by a forced choice?

How could the concepts of pre-existence rights and predetermined predestination possibly be in concert with God's Pure Love Concept, if our eternal salvation choice depends upon our personal decision to accept the love sacrifice of his Son Jesus for ours sins consequences? (Ref John 14: 6; Acts 4: 12; Rom 1: 16 to 20).

If God is a God of Pure Love, as opposed to humans' love (which is not totally pure all the time), wouldn't God ensure that everyone one who lives would have the adequate number of opportunities to make their own free, independent, and un-coerced decision that determines their own ultimate eternal fate? (Ref Titus 2: 11 – 14).

How do we know that Jesus is God (e.g. because he performed many healing miracles, raised people from dead; walked on water; 200+ prophecies fulfilled concerning his first coming; 200+ prophecies concerning his second coming filled and being filled; 30+ prophecies filled the day he was on the cross; and during his baptism God the Father acknowledged his Son by his voice from heaven while Jesus was being baptized, and Holy Spirit came down from heaven in form of a dove on Jesus (Ref Luke 3: 21, 23)? What other person has done or could claim any, or all, of performing these above extraordinary feats?

If God is not our creator, how do you explain the creation/function/energy of our brain, our heart, our body, the Universe, animals, fish, plants, trees, sunshine, stars, bacteria, air we breathe, our emotions, our nerve system, thinking, memory, senses, etc, without a single creator; and how do you explain how all this works together in relative harmony?

A recommended/suggested salvation prayer:
Dear Lord Jesus I confess that I am a sinner and unable to keep your standard of being Holy, Loving, and Just all the

time, and I am sorry for all my sins which caused you and others to suffer greatly for me. I accept your love sacrifice on the cross to pay for the consequences of all my sins, and I ask you to come into my life and unite my spirit with your Holy Spirit again to help me to more closely follow your plan for my life. **Thanks you for coming into my life and re-uniting my spirit with your Holy Spirit now to provide me eternal life with you in heaven per your promise and love sacrifice.** I pray in Jesus name to let you know that I am eternally grateful for what you have just eternally done for me. Amen. ☺☺☺

If you were sincere in above prayer, then at this instance you were re-united with Jesus' Holy Spirit, and **you become children of God again, right now, and forever unconditionally** (i.e. being spiritually re-born again instantly **back into God's Holy Spirit forever per Jesus' unconditional promise to us** -- which you can never, **never lose again**) (Ref Romans 10: 9, 10; Ephesians 2: 8, 9; Titus 3: 4 to 7). **How can you be sure you are spiritually born again right now, because Jesus cannot lie** (i.e. God is forever Holy, Loving, and Just)!!! He loves you, and He keeps his promises because **He is GOD: not a man**. Therefore, He always does what he says. ☺☺☺

Simple Guidelines for Christian Growth:
Study God's Mind-Set: (Ref Matt 22: 36 – 40; Luke 18: 16, 17; John 5: 39, 40).

Grow in God's Knowledge, Understanding, and Wisdom: (Ref Luke 24: 25 – 27; John 14: 26; John 5: 39; Prov 3: 5, 6).

Live within God's Mind-Set: (Ref 1 Tim 1: 5; Rom 12: 1, 2; James 1: 22 – 25; Rom 2: 28, 29).

Lesson 21: Daily Priorities to Live By:
(Ref Prov 3: 5, 6; Rom 12: 1, 2; Eph Ch 4: All)!

-- **Reminders** that God is Love (Daily Bible, Prayer, Thanks in Jesus' Name for blessings and trails for growth) (Ref Prov 3: 5, 6; Rom 5: 8; Prov 25: 2; 2 Pet 1:20, 21; Eph 6: 18 - 20; Jam 1: 2 - 12).

-- **Concentration** that God's Love is Patient, kind, protective, hopeful, trusts, perseveres, and never fails (Ref I Cor 13: 4 - 8; Rom 8:32; Gal 6: 7; 2 Tim 1: 7; Rom 12: 2).

-- **Thankfulness** daily for Jesus' love sacrifice for our eternal life opportunity and adventures of spiritual growth discipline (Ref 1 Thess 5:16 - 18; Prov 22: 4; 2 Tim 1: 7; 1 John 5: 7 - 15).

-- **Wisdom,** Knowledge, Understanding of God/God's Plans for us (Ref Heb 12: 2 to 15; Heb 4: 12; Rom 10: 17; Prov 2: 1 - 12; Ch 3 all).

-- **God's Standard focus**: Being Holy, Loving, and Just always (Ref 1 Tim 1: 5; 2 Cor 5: 17 - 19; Matt 22: 37 - 40; 1 John 4: 7; Rom 14: 17).

-- **Spiritual Growth in Humility**
(Ref Matt 11: 29; Heb 11: 6; Luke 16: 10; John 15: 5, 6; John 3: 3).

-- **Welfare** and Spiritual Growth for self and family members (Ref 1 John 4: 7 - 21; Phil 4: 4 to 9: Rom 1: 16, 17; Deut 6: 31).

-- **Christian Mission** of Saving Souls
(Ref Titus 3: 4 to 7; Eph 4: 29 to 32; Titus 2: 11; James 2: 26).

-- **Growing** Spiritually, Mentally, and Physically daily
(Ref Matt 11: 28 to 30; Col 1: 19 - 22; 1 Cor 1: 30; Jer 17: 5 - 10).

-- **Prudence** employment in economics, relations, living, and ethics (Ref 2 Pet 1: 1 - 10; 1 John 3: 18 - 24; Prov 3: 5, 6).

-- **Awareness** of Human Beings' 4 Major Temperaments:
Sanguine (extrovert, inspiring, not dependable),
Choleric (extrovert, demanding, not considerate),
Melancholy (introvert, sensitive, not secure),
Phlegmatic (introvert, persevering, not compromising)

-- **Awareness** of Devil's Chief Tools (e.g. Guilt, Fear, Anger, Hatred, Peer Pressure, Suicide, Depression, Snare of Gradualism, Compulsive-Obsessive, Bi-Polar, drugs, alcohol, money, pride, fame, etc).

-- **Spiritual Warfare** amour, tactics, strategy (Ref Eph 6: 1 – 17).

Lesson 22: Biblical Concepts I
(Ref 2 Tim 3: 16 to 17; Luke 13: 3; Luke 24: 25 to 27; Jn 5: 39; 1 Jn 4: 15, 16)!

God is perfect Love. God is always holy, loving, and just (Ref 1 John 4: 7 to 10).
Sin is selfish, inconsiderate, and not-respectful (i.e. non-loving/preview of hell) (Ref Rom Ch 1: All).

God with his foreknowledge was able to create a world and place us in his world to ensure we could make unforced, free, independent, responsible choices, and receive the just consequences/benefits of our choices (Ref Rom 10: 9, 10).
God's plan to make his will known to everybody has to be simple enough for all to understand (Ref Titus 2: 11; Jer 17: 5 to 10).

What is God's Commandment/Will for you?
(Ref 1 John 3: 18 to 24; Luke 10: 27; 2 Tim 3: 16, 17; Matt 22: 37 to 40; Rom 10: 9 to 13; Jer 9: 23, 24; Prov 5: 6, 7).
What is the difference between Grace and Mosaic Law?
(Ref Eph 1: 1 to 14; John 6: 63; John 1: 17; Gal 2: 16; 3: 10 to 12; Rom 3:20 to 28; 1 Tim 1: 5 to 11; Titus 2: All (note verse 11)).

How do you explain your Spiritual Position vs Spiritual Relationship with God?
(Ref John 3: 3 to 6; John 3: 15 to 21; 1 John 4: 23, 24; Titus 3: 4 to 7; Matt 11: 28 to 30).

Does God honor our Decisions (e.g. Love's correlation to Faith Choices not Predestination)?
(Ref Gal; 6: 7 to 9; Eph 1: 13, 14; John 1: 12; Rom 10: 9, 10).

What is Sanctification from Sin/Hell; sin nature; world's sin nature influence?
(Ref Eph 1: All; Gal 5, 6; 1 Thess 1:2, 3; 1 Thess 5: 16 to 18; 2 Tim 3: 16,17; Heb 4: 12).

What should be our Christian Work: i.e. supporting the ministry, spiritual growth of saved sinners, God's Wisdom?
(Ref John 4: 34 to 36; John 5: 24, 39 to 40; 3: 36; 6: 47; John 11: 25, 26; John 14: 26, 45; John 16: 12, 13).

How many major categories of Types of Temptations/Sin are there (i.e. Lust of Flesh, Lust of Eyes; Pride of Life)?
(Ref Luke 4: 1 to 13; 1 John 1: 15 to 17).

What are the Christian Benefits of being spiritually born again (i.e. Eternal Life/Love via God's Knowledge, Understanding, and Wisdom).
(Ref 1 John 4, 5; John 5:24; Titus 3: 4 to 7; John 3: 15, 16, 36; 2 Tim 1: 7; Prov 5 6, 7).

Does God want to give us blessings by allowing us to work through problems (i.e. grow spiritually): (Ref 1 Peter 1: 3 to 9; Hebrews 12: 1 to 15; Romans 5: 3; 1 Cor 10: 13).

Lesson 23: Biblical Concepts II
(Ref Prov 25: 2, Heb 4: 12, John 5: 16, John 14: 6; 2 Tim 3: 16 to 17; Luke 13: 3; Luke 24: 25 to 27; Jn 5: 39; 1 Jn 4: 15, 16)!

Jesus Christ translates to "God saved his anointed one"
(Ref Heb 11: 6; Eph 2: 8 – 10; Rom 5: 8; John 5:24; I John 5: 7 – 15; 1 Cor 1: 30).

Christ translates to "his anointed one"
(Ref Pet 1: 20, 21; Heb 4: 12; Prov 3: 5, 6; 2 Pet 3: 9; 1 John 3: 23).

God's Agapa Love is totally holy, loving, and just all the time
(Ref Titus 2: 11, 12; 1 John 4: 7 – 10; Jer 17: 7 – 10).

Sin translates to non-loving thought, word, action that is selfish, inconsiderate, not respectful (i.e. missing the Love Mark of God results in SIN).
(Ref Matt 22: 37 – 40; Gal 6: 7; John 1: 17; Gal 2: 16, Rom 3: 20 – 28).

Spiritually Born Again means to re-unite our spirit with God's Holy Spirit by our choice
(Ref Eph 1: 11 – 14; Eph 4: 30; John 3: 3, 5; Jam 2: 26; Rom 1: 16, 17; Rom 10: 9, 10).

Sanctification means to grow spiritually in God's Love through daily biblical practice
(Ref Prov 25: 2; Prov 3: 5, 6; Eph 4: 2 – 32; Eph 6: 18 – 20; Eph 6: 1 – 17).

Repent means to change/transform/renew our mind set, attitude, and lives
(Ref Rom 12: 2; Prov 22: 4; 2 Cor 7: 10; 1 John 1: 8 – 10; Luke 16: 10).

Death in the bible generally refers to spiritual death (i.e. separation from God's Love)
(Ref 1 Tim 1: 8 – 11; Jam 2: 26; Rom 8: 1 – 17; John 11: 25, 26; Matt 8: 22; Eph 2: 1. 5).

God wants us to have a **loving mind** set to receive more blessings, truth, and his love
(Ref 1 Tim 1: 5: Phil 4: 4 – 7; Eph 5: 10, 20, 22 – 33; John 15: 5; Prov Ch 1 & Ch 3).

God's most sincere desire is to be **reconciled** with us, and us with our spiritual family
(Ref Col 1: 19 – 22; 2 Pet 1: 1 – 10; 1 Col 1: 19 – 22).

God allows **adverse situations** to help us to grow spiritually stronger & receive rewards
(Ref Jam 1: 2 – 4, 12; Rom 5: 1-11; Heb 12: 2 – 15; John 14: 26).

God will not allow us to be in a temptation that does not have a **way to escape**
(Ref Rom 8: 26 – 28; 1 John 4: 4; 1 Cor 10: 13; 2 Tim 1: 7).

Heaven is more wonderful than we can imagine: and there is no sin, sin consequences, diseases, and our new eternal bodies will be perfect forever
(Ref Rom 14: 17; John 17: 24; 1 Pet 1: 4; 1 Cor 2:9; 13: 12; Rev 4).

Hell is a place without any love
(Ref Isa 6: 1; Isa 66: Matt 25:41; Matt 7: 21; Luke 13:27; Gal 5: 21; 1 Cor 2: 9; Rev 21: 8).

Words have meanings: **Jerusalem** (God's Peace), **Soul** (Real you), **Eternity** (Forever), **Church** (People), **Religion** (Service to others), **Consequences** (rewards of choices), **Distractions** (Devil's misdirection tools), **Saved Sinner** (Spiritually Born

Again Christian), **Saint** (Christian in Heaven), **Gradualism** (Devil's World Standard tool), **Trust** (Belief, Faith, Acceptance), **Good Person** (Devil's biggest lie).

Lesson 24: Employing God's Plan provides Rescue, Redemption, and Better Choices
(Ref Prov 3: 5, 6; Gal 6: 7, 8; 1 Jn 4: 10; 1 Tim 1: 5)!

A. **Life's Choices**: Gal 6: 7 "You reap what you sow" (Ref John 14:6; Mark 10:15; John 3: 3, 5; Rom 1: 16, 17; Gal 2: 16; Rom 3: 20; 1 Tim 1: 5; Eph 1: 13).

God's Mark/Goal/Standard is God's Pure Love all the time

God's Love (i.e. his Mark/Goal/Standard) is always: Holy, Loving, and Just/Righteous as opposed to sin's attributes (i.e. being Selfish, Inconsiderate, and Not-respectful)

B. **God's Message**:
Love vs Law: James 2: 10 vs 1 John 4:12;
Grace vs Works: 1 John 4: 10 vs Titus 3: 5 to 7
Choice & Results: Gal 6: 7, 8; Eph 1: 13; John 3:36

C. **Poor choice** leads to spiritual death (i.e. separation from God) (Ref Romans 3: 21 to 23).

D. **Good choice - Salvation from spiritual death is by trust in God's plan** (Ref Gal 2:16; Gal 3: 10; John 3:3; Eph 2: 8. 9; Rom 1:16; John 5: 24, Rom 10: 9, 10).

E. **God's Mind Set (i.e. being Holy, Loving, Just all the time)** should be our living goal (Ref Colossians 3: 7 to 10 and 12 to 14; Col 3: 1 to 17; I Tim 1:5, Col 3: 14).

E. **First Reconciliation** to God, then our spiritual growth begins from sin/penalty, habit, world's paths (Ref 2 Cor 5: 17 to 19; Matt 6: 31 to 33; John 14: 26; Rom 10: 17; Rom 10: 4).

F. **Salvation from self** and world's standards is by using God's Love; Trust/Faith; Bible Study; Prayer; Christian Life Living, Practice, Time
(Ref Matthew 5: 21 to 26; Rom 12: 1, 2).

G. **God's Word/Authority** (Ref 2 Pet 1: 20, 21; 2 Tim 3: 15; John 14: 26; Rom 10: 17; Matt 22: 36 to 40).

H. **God's Spiritual Knowledge, Understanding, Wisdom, and Rewards (Prov 25: 2)**:
(Ref Proverbs 1: 7; Proverbs 9: 10; Proverbs 22: 4; Joshua 1: 9; Deut 31: 6; Isa 40: 31),

God's Tools: (Grace vs Law)
Trust/Faithfulness- Hebrews 11: 6
Humbleness - 1 Pet 5:5;
Confession - 1 John 1:9;
Forgiveness - Romans 10: 9, 10;

J. **Devil's Tools**: (Law vs Grace) Distractions, Diversions, Mis-Directions, Guilt, Anger, Fear, Hatred, Peer Pressure, Feelings vs God's Promises, half truths, lies, Works vs Grace, Peer Pressure, Depression, Suicide, Obsession, Snare of Gradualism etc.

A recommended/suggested salvation prayer:
Dear Lord Jesus I confess that I am a sinner and unable to keep your standard of being Holy, Loving, and Just all the time, and I am sorry for all my sins which caused you and others to suffer greatly for me. I accept your love sacrifice on the cross to pay for the consequences of all my sins, and I ask you to come into my life and unite my spirit with your Holy Spirit again to help me to more closely follow your plan for my life. **Thanks you for coming into my life and re-uniting my spirit with your Holy Spirit now to provide me eternal life with you in heaven per your promise and love sacrifice.** I pray in Jesus name to let you know that I am eternally grateful for what you have just eternally done for me. Amen. ☺☺☺

If you were sincere in above prayer, then at this instance you were re-united with Jesus' Holy Spirit, and **you become children of God again, right now, and forever unconditionally** (i.e. being spiritually re-born again instantly **back into God's Holy Spirit forever per Jesus' unconditional promise to us** -- which you can never, **never lose again**) (Romans 10: 9, 10; Ephesians 2: 8, 9; Titus 3: 4 to 7). **How can you be sure you are spiritually born again right now, because Jesus cannot lie** (i.e. God is forever Holy, Loving, and Just)!!! He loves you, and He keeps his promises because **He is GOD: not a man**. Therefore, He always does what he says. ☺☺☺

<u>Simple Guidelines for Christian Growth:</u>
Study God's Mind-Set: Matt 22: 36 – 40; Luke 18: 16, 17; John 5: 39, 4.

Grow in God's Knowledge, Understanding, and Wisdom: Luke 24: 25 – 27; John 14: 26. John 5: 39

Live within God's Mind-Set: 1 Tim 1: 5; Rom 12: 1, 2; James 1: 22 – 25; Rom 2: 28, 29.

Lesson 25: Spiritual Values (V)/Morals (M)/Ethics (E) requires Jesus' Love

(Ref Prov 3: 5, 6; Rom 12: 1, 2; Jn 15: 3 to 5; Jn 14: 26)!

M - <u>God</u> is Agapa <u>Love</u> which is holy, loving, and just all the time. Ref 1 John 4: 7 to 10; 1 Pet 1: 16).

E - Jesus paid for everybody's <u>sin consequences</u>, cause He Loves you. (Ref Rom 5: 8; Heb 10: 10, 14, 17, 18; Titus 3: 4 to 7).

V - God created a simple, free, everlasting way for all to obtain <u>eternal life</u> right now. (Ref Rom 1: 16, 17; John 3: 15, 16; 1 John 5: 7 to 13).

E - You must <u>believe</u>, <u>repent</u>, confess, <u>accept</u> Jesus' Sacrifice to become <u>spiritually born again</u>. (Ref John 3: 3 – 8; Mark 1: 15; 1 John 1: 9; Rom 10: 9, 10: John 5:24).

V - God wants to <u>reconcile</u> with us right now and forever. (Ref 2 Cor 5:17 to 19; Col 1: 19 to 22).

M - What does it <u>profit</u> to gain all in this life, if we don't go to heaven? (Ref Matt 16: 26; John 3: 5 to 7; John 8: 23, 24; Rev 20: 10 to 15).

M - Heaven is filled with <u>eternal love</u> and Hell has no love in it. (Ref Rom 13: 10; Rom 14: 17; 2 Thess 1: 5 to 9; Luke 12: 4, 5).

E - We have to worship God in <u>Truth and Spirit</u>. (Ref John 4: 24; Rom 8: 1 to 4; 2 Tim 3: 16, 17: John 8: 31, 32).

M - God provides his Holy Spirit to help us <u>grow spiritually</u> through Bible study. (Ref Prov 3: 5, 6; 2 Tim 1: 7; John 14: 26; Luke 13: 3; Rom 12: 1, 2).

V - God promises to be <u>with us always</u> after we accept his Holy Spirit. (Ref Eph 4: 30; Heb 13: 5b, 6; Eph 1: 12 to 14).

V - Bible scripture is provided by God via specific men to convey his truth as he intended. (Ref 2 Tim 3: 15 to 17; Prov 25: 2; Heb 4: 12; Rom 7: 12).

M - The <u>Holy Spirit</u> of God provides us with knowledge, understanding, and wisdom. (Ref Titus 2: 11; 1 Pet 5: 5, 6; 1 Cor 12: 8).

E - Without <u>Faith</u> in God, you cannot please God. (Ref Heb 11: 6; Eph 2: 8, 9; Rom 5: 1 to 11; Rom 10: 17).

M - God want you to have a <u>heart attitude</u> like his. (Ref 1 Tim 1: 5; Eph 5: 20, 22 to 33; Deut 10: 12).

E - God blesses you according to your heart's <u>humble attitude, decision</u>, and actions. (Ref Jer 17: 5 to 10; Rom 8: 14 to 17; Eph 4: 1 to 7).

V - Spiritual blessings, growth, and <u>faith</u> come from <u>rejoicing, praying</u>, and <u>thanksgiving</u>. (Ref 1 Thess 5: 16 to 18; 2 Pet 1: 10; Phil 4: 6, 7).

M - God has shown his <u>grace</u> to all. (Ref Titus 2: 11; John 1: 16; Rom 1: 19, 20).

V - God's hope is for all to <u>Love God first and his neighbor as himself</u>. (Ref Matt 22: 36 to 40; 1 John 3: 22 to 24).

E - You <u>reap what you sow</u> in accordance with your good or bad decisions. (Ref Gal 6: 7, 8; Prov 23: 7; 2 Pet 1: 5, 6; 1 John 5: 14, 15).

V - God allows <u>trials to provide spiritual vision, training, and growth</u>. (Ref Heb 12: 10, 11; Eph 6: 11, 12; Jer 9: 23, 24).

E - Pray in Jesus' name to remain <u>humble, respectful, and wise</u>. (Ref Prov 22: 4: Matt 11: 28 to 30; Eph 5: 20; Prov 2:6).

V- - Grow where God has allowed you to be planted, and pollinate your brothers and sisters.

Note: Spiritual Checklist Regarding God's Values (V), Morals (M), Ethics (E)

A recommended/suggested prayer:
Dear Lord Jesus I confess that I am a sinner and unable to keep your standard of being Holy, Loving, and Just all the time, and I am sorry for all my sins which caused you to suffer greatly for me. I accept your love sacrifice on the cross to pay for the consequences of all my sins, and I ask you to come into my life and unite my spirit with your Holy Spirit again to help me to more closely follow your plan for my life. **Thanks you for coming into my life and re-uniting my spirit with your Holy Spirit now to provide me eternal life with you in heaven per your promise and love sacrifice.** I pray in Jesus name to let you know that I am eternally grateful for what you have just eternally done for me. Amen. ☺☺☺
If you were sincere with above prayer, then at this instance you were re-united with Jesus' Holy Spirit, and **you become children of God again, right now, and forever unconditionally** (i.e. being spiritually re-born again instantly

back into God's Holy Spirit forever per Jesus' unconditional promise to us -- which you can never, **never lose again**) (Ref Romans 10: 9, 10; Ephesians 2: 8, 9; Titus 3: 4 to 7). **How can you be sure you are spiritually born again right now, because Jesus cannot lie** (i.e. God is forever Holy, Loving, and Just)!!! He loves you, and He keeps his promises because **He is GOD: not a man**. Therefore, He always does what he says. ☺☺☺

Basic Bible Lessons

Lesson 26: Key Bible Truths Revealed
(Ref I John 3: 22 to 24; James 2: 8 to 10; 1 Tim 1: 5)!

Prov 25: 2	**Hidden Truth Search**
John 3: 15, 16	Ultimate Love Sacrifice
Rom 5: 8	**Commended Love**
John 15: 13	Greatest Love Proof
1 John 4: 7 to 10	**God's Agapa Love**
1 John 3: 18 to 24	Complete Commandment
1 John 4: 7 to 21	Love Mind Set
1 John 5: 7 to 15	**Eternal Life Record**
Rom 1: 16, 17	Gospel's Truth
1 John 3: 22 to 24	God's Mark
Rom 3: 9 to 28	**Sin, Faith, Law Dynamics**
James 2: 8 to 10	Whole Law Requirements
James 2: 26	**Body without Spirit is Dead**
Rom 2: 28, 29	Inward Spiritual Jew
2 Tim 1: 7	**HS: power, love, sound mind**
2 Tim 3: 15 to 17	Word of God Authority
Heb 4: 12	**Work of Scripture**
Peter 1: 20, 21	**Scripture Authority**
Rom 5 :1 to 11	Faith Justification
Rom 8: All	Law vs Spirit Salvation
Rom 10: 4, 9, 10-13,17	**Salvation Decision**
Rom 12: 1, 2; 1 Tim 1:5	**Correct Spiritual Attitude**
Titus 2: 11, 12	**Holy Spirit's Work**
Titus 2: 16, 25, 26	Holy Spirit's Seal
Isa 26: 3	God's Peace
Josh 1: 9	Meditate on God's Law
Deut 6: 31	**God's courage, peace, promise**
I Thess 5: 16 to 18	Rejoice, pray, be thankful
Phil 4: 4 to 9, 10, 11, 13, 17, 19	God's Peace

245

Humble Mind Benefits

Prov 16: 19	Isa 57: 15
James 4: 6	1 Pet 5: 5
Ps 34: 2	Ps 69: 32
Matt 18: 4	Luke 14: 11
Prov 2: 24	

Lesson 27: Verses related to Predestination
(Ref Rom Ch 8: All)!

-- Obtaining our Eternal Salvation is by God's Foreknowledge, His Fulfilled Salvation Promise, and Our Acceptance Choice of Jesus' price for our sins, not by some sort of absolute predestination idea based upon a single time decision made before we were born and before we accepted or rejected God's eternal salvation gift.)

- God used this foreknowledge to plan every body's existence to provide all a fair, equitable, and unforced decision making capabilities to enable all to reap their choices' consequences.

- Because God has the ability to have foreknowledge of our existence and our freewill decisions; He is able to plan a world where everyone is allowed to make their own unforced, freewill, and unconditional decisions for God's plan for their lives or their plan for their lives (Eph 2: 8,9). Because God is pure love, loves us, knows us, and cares for us; He has to allow us to make freewill decisions in order to be in line with his character of being holy, loving (caring), and just all the time. Otherwise, God is not pure love.

- In other words, we make our own decisions and receive the consequences accordingly. Our decisions determine our lives and also determine if we go to heaven or not. Because God knows our decisions before we are born does not predestinate our lives or if we go to heaven or not, rather it allows God to ensure our decisions are our own freewill decisions. The use of predestination in the Bible simply states that God knows where our final destination will be, which is contingent upon our own freewill decisions; and this destination is a result of our decision for or against his plan for our life made at a time during our lives, not as a result of God making a decision of our destination way back in the beginning of God's creation of our world.

Rom 8: 28	We choose God. God knows our choices. God plans around our choices to ensure all can have fair choices and consequences.
Rom 5: 8	Even when we were in sin, Jesus suffered for all of our sin consequences.
John 14: 6	Jesus said, I am the way, the truth, the life…no comes to the Father except through me.
Heb 11: 6	For without faith it is impossible to please God… we must believe He exists/rewards them who seek him.
Gal 6: 7, 8	We reap what we sow from our faithful/trusting/thankful choices.
Rom 2: All	We are judged according to truth, our deeds, our knowledge, and gospel.
Rom 10: 9 to 13	With our heart and mouth confession we gain salvation through Jesus.
John 1: 12	We must believe and accept Jesus to become part of his Holy Spirit (HS).
Eph 2: 8, 9	Our salvation is gained by faith (trust, belief, thanks), not by our works.
John 5: 24	We accept Jesus' suffering for salvation and our spiritual rebirth.
John 3: 16 to 18, 36	Accepting Jesus through trusting God's word gains eternal life.
Prov 3: 5, 6	Choose to seek God's will for your life daily to make good decisions.

Eph 1: 3 to 21 Until we repent, confess, ask, accept, and thank Jesus; we won't become a part of God's family via reuniting of our spirit with his Holy Spirit.

1 John 5: 2 to 12   We believe/trust/accept Jesus for our eternal life with him.

Matt 7: 24 to 27   We should build our life upon Jesus our rock.

1 John 1: 9   Confession of our sin nature opens the avenue to become a child of God.

Matt 16: 26, 27   What profit to gain world's treasures and lose your soul?

John 8: 23, 24   Our sins will not be forgiven/covered, unless we accept Jesus and his payment for our sins.

John 3: 3, 5   We will not be born again in God's Holy Spirit without accepting Jesus.

John 11: 25, 26   Whoever believes/accepts Jesus is resurrection... will never die.

1 John 4: 15   Confess Jesus is Son of God and God will live within you.

John 14, 1 to 4   Jesus prepares a mansion in heaven for his children - Matt 18:3,4.

1 John 5: 1, 4, 9-15   Whosoever accepts Jesus is the Christ is a son/daughter of God.

Ecc 12: 13, 14   We reverentially trust God and reap consequences.

Rom 10: 13   Whoever calls upon the name of Jesus, shall be saved.

Ps 50: 15   Call upon me in your day of trouble, and I will deliver you.

Matt 11: 28 to 30   Come unto me all that labor and are heavy laded…I will give you rest.

Rom 6: 15 to 18   If we are under God's grace, we are no longer under the law's shackles.

Rom 8: 13, 14   Those led by Holy Spirit are the sons and daughters of God.

Phil 4: 4 to 7   Be anxious for nothing rather pray, ask, thank God for his peace/wisdom.

I Thess 5: 16 to 18   Rejoice evermore, pray often, and being thankful is God's will for us.

Rev 20: 11 to 15   And the dead were judged out of the things written in the books.

Sincerely thanking God is the greatest action (proof) of our faith/belief/trust in Him, and we should thank him often for the good things in our lives as well as the adverse things in our lives. This mind set of exercising thankfulness in all life's circumstances will help us grow spiritually by providing more knowledge, understanding, and wisdom of God and of God's plan for us to reunite with him spiritually now and forever and to grow spiritually during our eternal lives in heaven as a result of our humble heart and resultant joy of receiving many associated blessings (Ref Matt 11: 28 to 30; Eph 5: 1 to 21; Phil 4: all; James 1: 1 to 25; Eph 5: 21).

Lessson 28: Recommended Christian Doctrinal Statement
(Ref 2 Tim 3: 16, 17; Dallas Theological Seminary Faith Doctrine)!

The Scriptures

We believe that "all Scripture is given by inspiration of God," by which we understand the whole Bible is inspired in the sense that holy men of God "were moved by the Holy Spirit" to write the very words of Scripture. We believe that this divine inspiration extends equally and fully to all parts of the writings—historical, poetical, doctrinal, and prophetical—as appeared in the original manuscripts. We believe that the whole Bible in the originals is therefore without error. We believe that all the Scriptures center about the Lord Jesus Christ in His person and work in His first and second coming, and hence that no portion, even of the Old Testament, is properly read, or understood, until it leads to Him. We also believe that all the Scriptures were designed for our practical instruction (Ref Mark 12:26, 36; 13:11; Luke 24:27, 44; John 5:39; Acts 1:16; 17:2–3; 18:28; 26:22–23; 28:23; Rom. 15:4; 1 Cor. 2:13; 10:11; 2 Tim. 3:16; 2 Pet. 1:21).

The Godhead

We believe that the Godhead eternally exists in three persons—the Father, the Son, and the Holy Spirit—and that these three are one God, having precisely the same nature, attributes, and perfections, and worthy of precisely the same homage, confidence, and obedience

(Ref Matt. 28:18–19; Mark 12:29; John 1:14; Acts 5:3–4; 2 Cor. 13:14; Heb. 1:1–3; Rev. 1:4–6).

Angels, Fallen and Unfallen

We believe that God created an innumerable company of sinless, spiritual beings, known as angels; that one, "Lucifer, son of the morning"—the highest in rank—sinned through pride, thereby becoming Satan; that a great company of the angels followed him in his moral fall, some of whom became demons and are active as his agents and associates in the prosecution of his unholy purposes, while others who fell are "reserved in everlasting chains under darkness unto the judgment of the great day" (Ref Isa. 14:12–17; Ezek. 28:11–19; 1 Tim. 3:6; 2 Pet. 2:4; Jude 6).

We believe that Satan is the originator of sin, and that, under the permission of God, he, through subtlety, led our first parents into transgression, thereby accomplishing their moral fall and subjecting them and their posterity to his own power; that he is the enemy of God and the people of God, opposing and exalting himself above all that is called God or that is worshiped; and that he who in the beginning said, "I will be like the most High," in his warfare appears as an angel of light, even counterfeiting the works of God by fostering religious movements and systems of doctrine, which systems in every case are characterized by a denial of the efficacy of the blood of Christ and of salvation by grace alone (Ref Gen. 3:1–19; Rom. 5:12–14; 2 Cor. 4:3–4; 11:13–15; Eph. 6:10–12; 2 Thess. 2:4; 1 Tim. 4:1–3). We believe that Satan was judged at the Cross, though not then executed, and that he, a usurper, now rules as the "god of this world"; that, at the second coming of Christ, Satan will be bound and cast into the abyss for a thousand years, and after the thousand years he will be loosed for a little season and then "cast into the lake of fire and brimstone," where he "shall be tormented day and night for ever and ever" (Ref Col. 2:15; Rev. 20:1–3, 10). We believe that a great company of angels kept their holy estate and are before the throne of God, from whence they are sent forth as ministering spirits to minister for them who shall be heirs of salvation (Ref Luke 15:10; Eph. 1:21; Heb. 1:14; Rev. 7:12). We believe that man was made lower than the angels; and that, in His incarnation, Christ took for a little time this lower place that He might lift the believer to His own sphere above the angels (Ref Heb. 2:6–10).

Man, Created and Fallen

We believe that man was originally created in the image and after the likeness of God, and that he fell through sin, and, as a consequence of his sin, lost his spiritual life, becoming dead in trespasses and sins, and that he became subject to the power of the devil. We also believe that this spiritual death, or total depravity of human nature, has been transmitted to the entire human race of man, the Man Christ Jesus alone being excepted; and hence that every child of Adam is born into the world with a nature which not only possesses no spark of divine life, but is essentially and unchangeably bad apart from divine grace (Ref Gen. 1:26; 2:17; 6:5; Pss. 14:1–3; 51:5; Jer. 17:9; John 3:6; 5:40; 6:35; Rom. 3:10–19; 8:6–7; Eph. 2:1–3; 1 Tim. 5:6; 1 John 3:8).

The Dispensations

- been gracious, regardless of the ruling dispensation, but that man has not at all times been under an administration or stewardship of grace as is true in the present dispensation (Ref 1 Cor. 9:17; Eph. 3:2; 3:9, asv; Col. 1:25; 1 Tim. 1:4, asv).

We believe that it has always been true that "without faith it is impossible to please" God (Heb. 11:6), and that the principle of faith was prevalent in the lives of all the Old Testament saints. However, we believe that it was historically impossible that they should have had as the conscious object of their faith the incarnate, crucified Son, the Lamb of God (Ref John 1:29), and that it is evident that they did not comprehend as we do that the sacrifices depicted the person and work of Christ. We believe also that they did not understand the redemptive significance of the prophecies or types concerning the sufferings of Christ (Ref 1 Pet. 1:10–12); therefore, we believe that their faith toward God was manifested in other ways as is shown by the long record in Hebrews 11:1–40. We believe further that their faith thus manifested was counted unto them for righteousness (Ref Rom. 4:3 with Gen. 15:6; Rom. 4:5–8; Heb. 11:7).

The First Advent

We believe that, as provided and purposed by God and as preannounced in the prophecies of the Scriptures, the eternal Son of God came into this world that He might manifest God to men, fulfill prophecy, and become the Redeemer of a lost world. To this end He was born of the virgin, and received a human body and a sinless human nature (Ref Luke 1:30–35; John 1:18; 3:16; Heb. 4:15).

We believe that, on the human side, He became and remained a perfect man, but sinless throughout His life; yet He retained His absolute deity, being at the same time very God and very man, and that His earth-life sometimes functioned within the sphere of that which was human and sometimes within the sphere of that which was divine (Ref Luke 2:40; John 1:1–2; Phil. 2:5–8).

We believe that in fulfillment of prophecy He came first to Israel as her Messiah-King, and that, being rejected of that nation, He, according to the eternal counsels of God, gave His life as a ransom for all (Ref John 1:11; Acts 2:22–24; 1 Tim. 2:6).

We believe that, in infinite love for the lost, He voluntarily accepted His Father's will and became the divinely provided sacrificial Lamb and took away the sin of the world, bearing the holy judgments against sin which the righteousness of God must impose. His death was therefore substitutionary in the most absolute sense—the just for the unjust—and by His death He became the Savior of the lost (Ref John 1:29; Rom. 3:25–26; 2 Cor. 5:14; Heb. 10:5–14; 1 Pet. 3:18).

We believe that, according to the Scriptures, He arose from the dead in the same body, though glorified, in which He had lived and died, and that His resurrection body is the pattern of that body which ultimately will be given to all believers (Ref John 20:20; Phil. 3:20–21).

We believe that, on departing from the earth, He was accepted of His Father and that His acceptance is a final assurance to us that His redeeming work was perfectly accomplished (Ref Heb. 1:3).

We believe that He became Head over all things to the church which is His body, and in this ministry He ceases not to intercede and advocate for the saved (Ref Eph. 1:22–23; Heb. 7:25; 1 John 2:1).

Salvation Only Through Christ

We believe that, owing to universal death through sin, no one can enter the kingdom of God unless born again; and that no degree of reformation however great, no attainments in morality however high, no culture however attractive, no baptism or other ordinance however administered, can help the sinner to take even one step toward heaven; but a new nature imparted from above, a new life implanted by the Holy Spirit through the Word, is absolutely essential to salvation, and only those thus saved are sons of God. We believe, also, that our redemption has been accomplished solely by the blood of our Lord Jesus Christ, who was made to be sin and was made a curse for us, dying in our room and stead; and that no repentance, no feeling, no faith, no good resolutions, no sincere efforts, no submission to the rules and regulations of any church, nor all the churches that have existed since the days of the Apostles can add in the very least degree to the value of the blood, or to the merit of the finished work wrought for us by Him who united in His person true and proper deity with perfect and sinless humanity (Ref Lev. 17:11; Isa. 64:6; Matt.

26:28; John 3:7–18; Rom. 5:6–9; 2 Cor. 5:21; Gal. 3:13; 6:15; Eph. 1:7; Phil. 3:4–9; Titus 3:5; James 1:18; 1 Pet. 1:18–19, 23).

We believe that the new birth of the believer comes only through faith in Christ and that repentance is a vital part of believing, and is in no way, in itself, a separate and independent condition of salvation; nor are any other acts, such as confession, baptism, prayer, or faithful service, to be added to believing as a condition of salvation (Ref John 1:12; 3:16, 18, 36; 5:24; 6:29; Acts 13:39; 16:31; Rom. 1:16–17; 3:22, 26; 4:5; 10:4; Gal. 3:22).

The Extent of Salvation

We believe that when an unregenerate person exercises that faith in Christ which is illustrated and described as such in the New Testament, he passes immediately out of spiritual death into spiritual life, and from the old creation into the new; being justified from all things, accepted before the Father according as Christ His Son is accepted, loved as Christ is loved, having his place and portion as linked to Him and one with Him forever. Though the saved one may have occasion to grow in the realization of his blessings and to know a fuller measure of divine power through the yielding of his life more fully to God, he is, as soon as he is saved, in possession of every spiritual blessing and absolutely complete in Christ, and is therefore in no way required by God to seek a so-called "second blessing," or a "second work of grace" (Ref John 5:24; 17:23; Acts 13:39; Rom. 5:1; 1 Cor. 3:21–23; Eph. 1:3; Col. 2:10; 1 John 4:17; 5:11–12).

Sanctification

We believe that sanctification, which is a setting-apart unto God, is threefold: It is already complete for every saved person because his position toward God is the same as Christ's position. Since the believer is in Christ, he is set apart unto God in the measure in which Christ is set apart unto God. We believe, however, that he retains his sin nature, which cannot be eradicated in this life. Therefore, while the standing of the Christian in Christ is perfect, his present state is no more perfect than his experience in daily life. There is, therefore, a progressive sanctification wherein the Christian is to "grow in grace," and to "be changed" by the unhindered power of the Spirit. We believe also that the child of God will yet be fully sanctified in his state as he is now sanctified in his standing in Christ when he shall see his Lord and shall be "like Him" (Ref John 17:17; 2 Cor. 3:18; 7:1; Eph. 4:24; 5:25–27; 1 Thess. 5:23; Heb. 10:10, 14; 12:10).

Eternal Security

We believe that, because of the eternal purpose of God toward the objects of His love, because of His freedom to exercise grace toward the meritless on the ground of the propitiatory blood of Christ, because of the very nature of the divine gift of eternal life, because of the present and unending intercession and advocacy of Christ in heaven, because of the immutability of the unchangeable covenants of God, because of the regenerating, abiding presence of the Holy Spirit in the hearts of all who are saved, we and all true believers everywhere, once saved shall be kept saved forever. We believe, however, that

God is a holy and righteous Father and that, since He cannot overlook the sin of His children, He will, when they persistently sin, chasten them and correct them in infinite love; but having undertaken to save them and keep them forever, apart from all human merit, He, who cannot fail, will in the end present every one of them faultless before the presence of His glory and conformed to the image of His Son (Ref John 5:24; 10:28; 13:1; 14:16–17; 17:11; Rom. 8:29; 1 Cor. 6:19; Heb. 7:25; 1 John 2:1–2; 5:13; Jude 24).

Assurance

We believe it is the privilege, not only of some, but of all who are born again by the Spirit through faith in Christ as revealed in the Scriptures, to be assured of their salvation from the very day they take Him to be their Savior and that this assurance is not founded upon any fancied discovery of their own worthiness or fitness, but wholly upon the testimony of God in His written Word, exciting within His children filial love, gratitude, and obedience (Ref Luke 10:20; 22:32; 2 Cor. 5:1, 6–8; 2 Tim. 1:12; Heb. 10:22; 1 John 5:13).

The Holy Spirit

We believe that the Holy Spirit, the Third Person of the blessed Trinity, though omnipresent from all eternity, took up His abode in the world in a special sense on the day of Pentecost according to the divine promise, dwells in every believer, and by His baptism unites all to Christ in one body, and that He, as the Indwelling One, is the source of all power and all acceptable worship and service. We believe that He never takes His departure from the church, nor from the feeblest of the saints, but is ever present to testify of Christ; seeking to occupy believers with Him and not with themselves nor with their experiences. We believe that His abode in the world in this special sense will cease when Christ comes to receive His own at the completion of the church (Ref John 14:16–17; 16:7–15; 1 Cor. 6:19; Eph. 2:22; 2 Thess. 2:7).

We believe that, in this age, certain well-defined ministries are committed to the Holy Spirit, and that it is the duty of every Christian to understand them and to be adjusted to them in his own life and experience. These ministries are the restraining of evil in the world to the measure of the divine will; the convicting of the world respecting sin, righteousness, and judgment; the regenerating of all believers; the indwelling and anointing of all who are saved, thereby sealing them unto the day of redemption; the baptizing into the one body of Christ of all who are saved; and the continued filling for power, teaching, and service of those among the saved who are yielded to Him and who are subject to His will (Ref John 3:6; 16:7–11; Rom. 8:9; 1 Cor. 12:13; Eph. 4:30; 5:18; 2 Thess. 2:7; 1 John 2:20–27).

We believe that some gifts of the Holy Spirit such as speaking in tongues and miraculous healings were temporary. We believe that speaking in tongues was never the common or necessary sign of the baptism nor of the filling of the Spirit, and that the deliverance of the body from sickness or death awaits the consummation of our salvation in the resurrection (Ref Acts 4:8, 31; Rom. 8:23; 1 Cor. 13:8).

The Church, A Unity of Believers

We believe that all who are united to the risen and ascended Son of God are members of the church which is the body and bride of Christ, which began at Pentecost and is completely distinct from Israel. Its members are constituted as such regardless of membership or non-membership in the organized churches of earth. We believe that by the same Spirit all believers in this age are baptized into, and thus become, one body that is Christ's, whether Jews or Gentiles, and having become members one of another, are under solemn duty to keep the unity of the Spirit in the bond of peace, rising above all sectarian differences, and loving one another with a pure heart fervently (Ref Matt. 16:16–18; Acts 2:42–47; Rom. 12:5; 1 Cor. 12:12–27; Eph. 1:20–23; 4:3–10; Col. 3:14–15).

The Sacrament or Ordinances

We believe that water baptism and the Lord's Supper are the only sacraments and ordinances of the church and that they are a scriptural means of testimony for the church in this age (Ref Matt. 28:19; Luke 22:19–20; Acts 10:47–48; 16:32–33; 18:7–8; 1 Cor. 11:26).

The Christian Walk

We believe that we are called with a holy calling, to walk not after the flesh, but after the Spirit, and so to live in the power of the indwelling Spirit that we will not fulfill the lust of the flesh. But the flesh with its fallen, Adamic nature, which in this life is never eradicated, being with us to the end of our earthly pilgrimage, needs to be kept by the Spirit constantly in subjection to Christ, or it will surely manifest its presence in our lives to the dishonor of our Lord (Ref Rom. 6:11–13; 8:2, 4, 12–13; Gal. 5:16–23; Eph. 4:22–24; Col. 2:1–10; 1 Pet. 1:14–16; 1 John 1:4–7; 3:5–9).

The Christian's Service

We believe that divine, enabling gifts for service are bestowed by the Spirit upon all who are saved. While there is a diversity of gifts, each believer is energized by the same Spirit, and each is called to his own divinely appointed service as the Spirit may will. In the apostolic church there were certain gifted men—apostles, prophets, evangelists, pastors, and teachers—who were appointed by God for the perfecting of the saints unto their work of the ministry. We believe also that today some men are especially called of God to be evangelists, pastors and teachers, and that it is to the fulfilling of His will and to His eternal glory that these shall be sustained and encouraged in their service for God (Ref Rom. 12:6; 1 Cor. 12:4–11; Eph. 4:11).

We believe that, wholly apart from salvation benefits which are bestowed equally upon all who believe, rewards are promised according to the faithfulness of each believer in his service for his Lord, and that these rewards will be bestowed at the judgment seat of Christ after He comes to receive His own to Himself (Ref 1 Cor. 3:9–15; 9:18–27; 2 Cor. 5:10).

The Great Commission

We believe that it is the explicit message of our Lord Jesus Christ to those whom He has saved that they are sent forth by Him into the world even as He was sent forth of His Father into the world. We believe that, after they are saved, they are divinely reckoned to be related to this world as strangers and pilgrims, ambassadors and witnesses, and that their primary purpose in life should be to make Christ known to the whole world (Ref Matt. 28:18–19; Mark 16:15; John 17:18; Acts 1:8; 2 Cor. 5:18–20; 1 Pet. 1:17; 2:11).

The Blessed Hope

We believe that, according to the Word of God, the next great event in the fulfillment of prophecy will be the coming of the Lord in the air to receive to Himself into heaven both His own who are alive and remain unto His coming, and also all who have fallen asleep in Jesus, and that this event is the blessed hope set before us in the Scripture, and for this we should be constantly looking (Ref John 14:1–3; 1 Cor. 15:51–52; Phil. 3:20; 1 Thess. 4:13–18; Titus 2:11–14).

The Tribulation

We believe that the translation of the church will be followed by the fulfillment of Israel's seventieth week (Ref Dan. 9:27; Rev. 6:1–19:21) during which the church, the body of Christ, will be in heaven. The whole period of Israel's seventieth week will be a time of judgment on the whole earth, at the end of which the times of the Gentiles will be brought to a close. The latter half of this period will be the time of Jacob's trouble (Ref Jer. 30:7), which our Lord called the great tribulation (Ref Matt. 24:15–21). We believe that universal righteousness will not be realized previous to the second coming of Christ, but that the world is day by day ripening for judgment and that the age will end with a fearful apostasy.

The Second Coming of Christ

We believe that the period of great tribulation in the earth will be climaxed by the return of the Lord Jesus Christ to the earth as He went, in person on the clouds of heaven, and with power and great glory to introduce the millennial age, to bind Satan and place him in the abyss, to lift the curse which now rests upon the whole creation, to restore Israel to her own land and to give her the realization of God's covenant promises, and to bring the whole world to the knowledge of God (Ref Deut. 30:1–10; Isa. 11:9; Ezek. 37:21–28; Matt. 24:15–25:46; Acts 15:16–17; Rom. 8:19–23; 11:25–27; 1 Tim. 4:1–3; 2 Tim. 3:1–5; Rev. 20:1–3).

The Eternal State

We believe that at death the spirits and souls of those who have trusted in the Lord Jesus Christ for salvation pass immediately into His presence and there remain in conscious bliss until the resurrection of the glorified body when Christ comes for His own, whereupon soul and body reunited shall be associated with Him forever in glory; but the spirits and souls of the unbelieving remain after death conscious of condemnation and in misery until the final judgment of the great white throne at the close of the millennium, when soul and body reunited shall be cast into the lake of fire, not to be annihilated, but to be punished with everlasting destruction from the presence of the Lord, and from the glory of His power (Ref Luke 16:19–26; 23:42; 2 Cor. 5:8; Phil. 1:23; 2 Thess. 1:7–9; Jude 6–7; Rev. 20:11–15).

Lesson 29: Some Key Bible Questions
(Ref Jn 14: 26)!

- Why does the Bible keep referring to Death when we will live forever either in heaven or hell? (Ref Jam 2: 26, Luke 9: 27, 1 John 3: 14, Rev 21: 4, John 11: 25, 26).
- How does predestination work in God's eternal plan for our lives? (Ref Rom 8: 29, John 5: 24).
- If God is a God of Love why are there so many problems, disasters, and misfortunes in life? (Ref Gal 6: 7, Heb 12: 10, 11, Jam 1: 2, 4, 12, Rom 5: 1 – 11, 1 Pet 1: 7).
- What are the elements of God's true love? (Ref 1 Cor 13: 4 – 8, John 15: 13, Titus 2: 11).
- Did Jesus' sacrifice cover the consequences of every one's sins even those that choose hell? (Ref Rom 5: 18, Rom 8: 1 – 17, Rom 10: 9 – 13, 1 Pet 3: 9).
- Are allowing people to go to hell a loving benefit? (Ref Gal 6: 7, Jer 17: 5 – 10).
- What does it mean when the verse states that if we transgress one part of God's Law that we are guilty of breaking all the laws? (Ref Jam 2: 1 – 10, 1 Tim 1: 5).
- How can we know if God accepts us as his children for eternity? (Ref 2 Pet 3: 9, 1 Pet 3: 9, Luke 18: 17).
- Can we ever lose our position as a child of God after we are spiritually born again? (Ref 1 Pet 1: 1 – 9, 1 Pet 2: 1 – 9, 1 Pet 1: 2 – 4).
- Is all of God's Law included in Love God with our whole mind, heart, and soul and Love our Neighbor as our self? (Ref 1 John 3: 23, Matt 22: 36 to 40).

- Is there any sin that we can commit that can never be forgiven? (Ref Heb 10: 26, 29, Mark 3: 28, 29).

- How can we grow spiritually strong to become a spiritual adult? (Ref 1Tim 1: 7, 2 Pet 1: 20, 21, 1 Pet 2; 1 – 9, 2 Tim 3: 15 – 17).

- What is the purpose of the believers after being spiritually born again? (Ref Col 1: 19 – 22, Rom 12: 1, 2, John 4: 24, John 15: 5, 6).

- Is the work of the believer to encourage, uplift, and edify our brothers and sisters? (Ref Eph 4: 1 – 16: 1 Cor 1:29 – 31, Isa 57: 15).

- What is sin, and what are the consequences of sin? (Ref Jam 2: 26, John 3: 3, 5, Matt 16: 26).

- What proof do we have that Jesus is God? (Ref 2 Tim 3: 15 – 17, John 8: 21, 24; Luke 24: 25 – 27: John 5: 39, 40, Mark 1: 9 – 11).

- Was every bodies name written in the Book of Life? (Ref 2 Pet 3: 9; Rev 20: 11 – 15, Rev 3: 5).

- Does God listen to people who are not spiritually born again? (Ref John 4: 24, Jam 2: 26, John 9: 31).

- Will God ever stop loving us? (Ref Rom 8: 35 - 39, Heb 13: 5b, Deut 6: 31: Rom 8: 35 – 39).

- What is the work of the Holy Spirit? (Ref John 14: 26, John 16: 13 – 16: Rom 8: 1 – 4 & 14 – 17).

- What is the work of Christians? (Ref Eph Ch 4: All; 1 John 3: 23, Matt 22: 36 – 40).

Lesson 30: God's Use of Three in Bible Verses
(Ref Luk 3: 21, 22)!

God is one God with three manifestations: God the Father, God the Son, and God the Holy Spirit (i.e. Holy Trinity) (Ref Gen 1: 26); and the similarities are that we have an individual soul/spirit/body, are a member of a family/church/clan, and have a vocation/job/business.

God's standard, character, and personality is always Holy, Loving, and Just always (Ref Isa 6: 3; Rev 4: 8; Ps 145: 17; 1 Jn 4: 8, 16; Rom 5: 8; Deut 32: 4; Deut 45: 21; Jer 9: 23, 24).

God made each of us as one person, in his image, and in his likeness with three manifestations: Soul, Body, and Spirit (Ref Gen 1: 26; 1 Thess 5:23).

God's Love for us is translated Agape: i.e. Eternal, Total, and Unconditional Love (Ref Rom 2: 32; Jer 31: 1 to 3; Eph 1: 13, 14; Rom 2: 28, 29; Rom Ch 3: All; 1 Tim 1: 5; Deut 31: 6).

God gave us his creation, his Son Jesus, and his word (i.e. bible); so we can receive his eternal love, his eternal salvation, and eternal family membership (Ref Rom Ch 1: All; Titus 2: 11; Gal 4: 5 to 7; Rom 5: 8; Jn 11: 25, 26; Gal Ch 3: All; 1 Tim 1: 9; 1 Tim 1: 5).

God's Son Jesus did a love sacrifice on the cross (i.e. his hell sacrifice – one time no love from his Father for 3 hours) for all of our sins (past, present, and future); spent 3 days in the grave; and Jesus is our Lord, Savior, and Mediator (Ref Rom 5: 8; Jn 3: 15, 16; 1 Tim 2: 3, 4; Deut 31: 6).

We can receive eternal salvation now by asking/accepting/thanking Jesus via repentant/sin nature confessional/appreciative prayer to come into our lives with his Holy Spirit **(i.e. trust by concent of my mind, act of my heart, and by my will) not just believe**, **to personally accept his free love gift** (i.e. free undeserved grace gift) **in order to live in heaven with him with my new body forever)** (Ref Rom 10: 9, 10; Jn 5: 24; Rom 1: 16, 17; Rom 3: 23; Jn 3: 3, 5, 6; Eph 1: 13: Titus 3: 5).

Jesus said that he is the way, the truth, and the life; no man comes to the father except by me (Ref John 14: 6; Eph 1: 13; Eph 4: 30).

Jesus said that the Holy Spirit is our comforter, teacher, and eternal life seal (Ref John 14: 26; Eph 1: 13; Eph 4: 30; Titus 3: 5; Gal 5: 14 to 16).

God made us personal, rational, and moral beings that need to learn how to bond with other folks, settle and respect personal and other folks boundaries, differentiate between good and bad issues, and grow into adults (Ref Gen 2: 19, 20; Gen 3: 8; Gen 3: 6; Gen 3: 6, 7; Eph 4: 23, 24; Col 3: 10; Rom 2: 11 to 16; Rom 2: 1 to 10).

God gave humans free, independent, and unforced decision making capability; therefore humans are responsible, accountable, and recipients of their decisions' consequences: (Ref Gal 6: 7 to 9 "… you reap what you sow…"; & Rom 6: 23; Jn 3: 36).

Lesson 31: Sample Love Letter to a Friend
(Ref Mark 16: 15)!

Hi, Trust you and yours are doing well. ☺☺☺

I want to share with you God's Loving Mind-Set of treating everyone with his Pure Love. In other words, God loves everyone, simply because they exist, not because He is demanding some form of compensation in return for his love toward us. In short, God loves everybody because they deserve it sorely as individual human beings.

God's Pure Love is not forced upon us, rather we have the right to make our own free, personal, and accountable choices and deserve to receive the results of our decisions; or we would be mere puppets.

As you know a viable, desired, and equitable love relationship must be founded upon free willing mutual reciprocal love, free willing mutual reciprocal action, and free willing mutual reciprocal respect. Unfortunately, humans' love is usually based upon receiving some form of compensation in return and usually under some type(s) of terms/demands/restrictions.

The most basic foundation of God's eternal salvation plan is to realize that our spirit and God's Holy Spirit were joined together at our birth. However, when we commit our first non-loving action; God's Holy Spirit and our spirit separate. This is because God cannot be connected to a non-loving spirit (i.e. sin is to transgress God's mark of being loving always). Therefore, we need to re-connect back to God's Holy Spirit with our spirit before our human body expires in order to insure eternal life with God in Heaven forever. Jesus said in John 3: 3, 5 that we must be spiritually born again (i.e. our spirit must be re-united to God's Holy Spirit); or we cannot enter into heaven. We all get a new body when our human body expires, and we are responsible to choose if we live in heaven or hell forever.

The above delineation of God's Pure Love is basically repeated over and over again in the Bible in many varied perspectives, so everyone can better understand the Concept of God's Pure Love for us with a little Bible research/study on our own part. God's Love is especially revealed through Jesus' sacrifice during the last 3 hours on the cross when the whole earth turned dark for 3 hours; because God the Father, during that time, had to turn his back against his son (i.e. God the Father stopped sharing his love with his Son for the first and last time). This love sacrifice between God the Father and his Son was so excruciating that it paid for the consequences of the sins of all humans (All), and the degree of Jesus' sacrifice is hinted when Jesus sweat blood in the Garden of Gethsemane the night before Jesus was placed on the cross (Luke 22; 39 - 44)

Since Jesus' last 3 hours on the cross sacrifice covered all humans' sin consequences, all we humans have to do now is realize we can't work our way into heaven, confess our sin nature, and accept Jesus' gift of eternal salvation with thanksgiving right now. Why must we accept this gift in order to obtain heaven, because we have the free right of making our own decisions without any demands on us from God. As part of God's Pure Love, we deserve the consequences of our free will decisions, or we are not really individuals responsible for our own decisions (puppets).

The Apostle Paul was very educated in the Old Testament from the best Bible Scholar available during his life; nevertheless, he failed to understand the above Pure Love Mind-Set of God until Jesus cast a light on him on his way to Damascus to kill Christians that blinded him and advised him to wake up. He then went to Damascus, so a Christian could show him that he did not understand Jesus purpose and to become a spiritually born again Christian. The result is that he discovered the true Pure Love God Mind-Set was based upon above delineated God Pure Love concept, not trying to obey all the commandments which we are not capable of doing; because study of the law reveals its foundation is based upon God's Love, not our works (i.e. Law is micro perspective of God's Macro Pure Love Standard) (Matt 22: 37 – 40, Eph 2: 8,9; Rom 10: 9, 10; Titus 3: 5; and I Tim 1: 5).

I have attached a lesson that provides more in-depth delineation of God's Pure Love Concept and His Simple Eternal Life Plan; as well as provides a more detailed way to obtain eternal life in heaven right now to include a recommended sealing prayer. Hope you take time to research my lesson, so you can be spiritually re-born now and share this with your loved ones to allow them to be spiritually re-born too now. I am not selling religion, rather a relationship with God on a very personal basis as he always wanted.

Recommend you study the Bible (start with the New Testament); and begin with the Books of Romans, Galatians, and Ephesians first with the understanding that each book of the Bible has a central theme and is written for various folks in different spiritual states. In short, it is not necessary to read any book as a prerequisite for reading other books of the Bible. Remember Paul the Apostle did not understand / comprehend / discern the spiritual messages in the Old Testament Bible scriptures at first until he did some Pure Love Concept perspective research/study of the Bible. In human language, don't miss the message because of the mechanics of the communications, and don't allow other humans or yourself to erode your faith in God (i.e. trusting God's Love for you). ☺

Sincerely in Jesus' Love for You and Yours,

Chuck a grateful and thankful saved sinner

Lesson 32: God's Fundamentals for Living a Successful Christian Life
(Ref Matt 22: 36 to 40; Micah 6: 8; Prov 3: 5, 6; Jn 15: 4, 5; Gal 5: 14 to 26)!

Remember God Loves You (Ref Rom 5: 8 – "But God commended his love toward us in that while we were yet sinners, Jesus Christ **died for us**") (Ref also Titus 2: 11; 2 Cor 5: 17 – 19; Col 1: 19 – 22; John 3: 15, 16; 1 John 4: 10). God kept his love from his son for 3 hours to show his love for us (i.e. **Jesus experienced hell for us during the 3 hours of darkness over the earth**)!!! (Sin is to do something non-loving, and our first sin separates our spirit from God's Holy Spirit. ☹)

Remember Jesus' love sacrifice on the cross (separation from his Father's love for 3 hours) **covered all our sins' consequences (past, present, future)** (Ref Heb 10: 14 – "For by one offering he has perfected forever them that are sanctified"). (Ref also Rom 8: 32; Titus 2: 11; 2 Pet 3: 9; Heb 13: 11; 1 John 2: 2). **However, we must choose to accept his gift of eternal salvation now with thanksgiving!**

Choose Believing/Trusting/Accepting Jesus' Vicarious Sacrifice/Promise gains eternal salvation instantly (Ref Eph 2: 8, 9 – "For **by grace** are you saved by faith; and that not of yourselves, it is the **gift of God**, **not of works** lest any man should boast"). (Ref also John 5: 24; Rom 10: 9, 10; Luke 18: 17; John 20: 31; John 14:6; Rom 7: 6; Mark 10: 26, 27). If Jesus had to suffer for our sins' consequences (i.e. did hell for us – Jesus was separated from his Father's Love for 3 hours on the cross during total darkness), how could we ever imagine to match his sacrifice by our works to cover all our sins consequences? **We must personally accept his free gift of salvation now on this earth while we can still make decisions about our fate (Ref Gal 6: 7, 8; Heb 9: 27; 2 Cor 6: 2).**

Thank Jesus Daily for his Love Sacrifice/Promise, not trying to satisfy all the law's prescriptive concepts to try to get into heaven via our works, gains **re-union** back into God's Holy Spirit **right now** (Ref Titus 3: 5 – "Not by works of righteousness which we have done, but according to his mercy he saved us, by the washing of **regeneration**, and **renewing of the Holy Spirit"**) (Ref also Rom 3: 20, 28; Rom 10: 9 – 13; Eph 1: 13, 14; Gal 2: 16; Matt 16: 26; John 3: 3, 5; John 4: 24; Jas 2: 26; 2 Tim 1: 7; Eph 4: 30; Mark 15: 15, 16; 1 John 3: 18 – 24; Rom 7: 6). God is a spirit, and we must commune with him in Truth and in his Holy Spirit!!! **We need to re-unite with God's Spirit now by our choice via our mind-set of repentance, confession, request, and thanksgiving to receive eternal life now** (Ref Romans 10: 9, 10; John 5: 24). God's Law is description of his Pure Love using many perspectives – (Ref Matt 22: 36 – 40).

Remember God's ultimate mind set and attitude for us is to be reconciled to him by employing his pure love mind set as much as possible (Ref I Tim 1: 5 – "Now the end of the commandment is **love** out of a pure heart, and of a good conscience, and of faith unwavering") (Ref also Matt 22: 36 – 40; Jer 17: 5 – 10; and 2 Pet 1: 20, 21). **If we employ God's love mind set in all we do (Ref Matt 22: 36 – 40), will we not receive many blessings** as will others that we have a relationship???

Remember Living a victorious Christian life requires daily use of Faith, Bible Study, Confession, Repentance, Prayer, Trust, Forgiveness, God's Wisdom, Rejoicing, Thankfulness (Ref Heb 11: 6 – "**But without faith, it is impossible to please God**, for he that comes to God **must believe** that He is, and that He is a rewarder of those that diligently seek him") (Ref also Rom 1: 16; Prov Ch 3; Eph 1: 13; 1 Thess 5: 16 -18; John 9: 31; Eph 4: 30; John 3: 5; Matt 11: 28 – 30; Matt 28: 19, 20; Prov 25: 2; Heb 4: 12; John 14: 26; John 16: 12 to 15). **If we can't trust God at his word, who or what can we trust???** Our eternal life depends on this trust!!!

Remember God allows us to experience trails and temptations to help us to make **good decisions for** improving **reconciliation** with God, **growing** spiritually, and **receiving** more blessings (Ref Heb 12: 11 – " Now no chastening for the present seems to be joyous, but grievous; nevertheless, afterward it yields the peaceful fruit of righteousness unto to them who are exercised by it") (Ref also James 1: 2 - 4, 12, 13 – 15; and Deut 31: 6, 8). **We get a new body in heaven** that will be perfect, never have illnesses, sickness, or shortcomings; and our new body will encase **our undying soul and spirit** for eternity,!!! **Our soul and spirit never die, otherwise why is there a heaven and hell??? The real question is where we will spend eternity???**

Remember God's promises are realized by daily Bible study with Holy Spirit's teaching because **God is pure Love (not a man) and can not lie** (Ref 1 John 5: 11, 12 – "And this is the record that God has given to us eternal life, and this life is in **his Son. He that has the Son has life; and he that has not the Son of God has not life**") (Ref also 2 Pet 3: 9; Heb 4: 12;

Prov 3: 5, 6; 2 Pet 1: 20, 21; John 5: 24; Ps 37: 3 – 5; 2 Tim 3: 15 – 17; Eph 4: 30; John 14: 6; Num 23: 19). Where will you spend eternity??? How can you be sure??? (Ref Gal 6: 7, 8). Shouldn't God's salvation plan be simple **so all can** understand??? If not, God is not a God of pure love (i.e. all-ways holy, loving, and just)!!!

A **recommended Prayer of Faith/Belief/Trust** to request/accept/thank Jesus **for your eternal salvation right now** (Sin means to miss God's mark of being holy, loving, just all the time):

Dear Lord Jesus I confess that I am a sinner and unable to always keep your standard of being Holy, Loving, and Just all the time (i.e. Loving all the time); and I am sorry for all my sin choices which caused you, others, and me to suffer greatly and needlessly. I accept your love sacrifice on the cross which paid for the consequences of all my sin choices (past, present, and future), and I ask you to come into my life and unite my spirit with your Holy Spirit again **right now** to help me to more closely follow your will/plan for my life. **I thank you** for coming into my life **right now**, forgiving all my sin consequences **right now**, and re-uniting my spirit with your Holy Spirit **right now, resulting in me receiving** eternal life with you **right now according to your word**. I pray in Jesus name to let you know that I am eternally grateful for what you have **just now** done for me and to remind me that I could not have been **spiritually re-born again** without your love sacrifice. Amen. ☺☺☺

If you were sincere with above prayer, then at this moment you were re-united with Jesus' Holy Spirit, and you became a child of God again, right now, and forever

unconditionally by your choice and Jesus promise (i.e. being spiritually born again back into God's Holy Spirit forever per Jesus' unconditional promise to us -- which we can never, never lose again per Jesus word) (Ref Romans 10: 9, 10; Ephesians 2: 8, 9; Titus 3: 4 to 7; John 14: 6). God does not lie like humans, because it is against his love nature!!!

How can you be sure you are spiritually born again right now: God is not a man and cannot lie (i.e. God is always Holy, Loving, and Just)!!! He loves you, and He keeps his promises because He is GOD: not a man. In addition, **God had to make sure that his eternal life plan was very simple, so that everyone could understand it no matter what their physical, mental, psychologically, social, cultural, moral, rational, man's training/condition's impacts, etc are.** Another example of God's true love!!! (Ref Rom 1: 16; Rom 1: 19, 20; Heb 11: 6; Gal 6: 7, 8; Rom 10: 9 – 13; Jer 17: 5 - 10; Eph 2: 8, 9; Isa 6: 3; 1 John 4; 8, 16). God keeps his promises!!! ☺☺☺

PS: Simple Guidelines for Christian Growth:

Study God's Mind-Set: (Ref Matt 22: 36 to 40; Luke 18: 16, 17; John 5: 39, 40).

Grow in God's Knowledge, Understanding, and Wisdom: (Ref Luke 24: 25 to 27; John 14: 26; John 5: 39; Prov 3: 5, 6).

Live within God's Mind-Set as much as possible: (Ref 1 Tim 1: 5; Rom 12: 1, 2; James 1: 22 to 25; Rom 2: 28, 29; Gal 6: 7, 8). ☺☺☺

Lesson 33: Spiritual Growth requires Jesus' Love
(Ref Matt 22: 37 to 40; 1 Thess 5: 16 to 18; Micah 6: 8)!

-- Seeking God's lessons from all good and bad decisions/circumstances produces our greatest spiritual training/growth/blessings – (Ref Heb 12: 1 to 15; Proverbs 22: 4; 1 Cor 10: 11 to 15; Prov 25: 2; 2 Cor 12: 9/10).

- Rejoicing and thanking God for all circumstances, regardless if they are good or bad, provides greatest knowledge/understanding/wisdom/rewards/spiritual adult growth (Ref 1 Thess 5: 17 to 19); as well as provides best transformation of our mind, soul, and spirit to God's Love concept – (Ref Romans 12: 1, 2; Rom 8: 31 to 39; Matt 7: 1, 2; Rom 1 All; Prov 25: 2; John 3: 11, 12; 1 Thess 5: 16 to 18).

- Praying to Holy Spirit daily and often to keep my mind on God's plan for me; so I can perform my best faith based thoughts, walk, and actions in order to provide the greatest blessings for me, my loved ones, and other humans – (Ref Prov 3: 5, 6; Ps 37: 3 to 7; Matt 11: 28 to 30; Rom 12: 1, 2; John 15: 5; Deut 31: 6; Micah 6: 8; Isa 40: 31; Matt 18: 28, 29; John 14: 26; 2 Tim 3: 16, 17; John 14: 6).

Grow where God has allowed you to be planted, and pollinate your brothers and sisters.

A recommended/suggested prayer:
Dear Lord Jesus I confess that I am a sinner and unable to keep your standard of being Holy, Loving, and Just all the time, and I am sorry for all my sins which caused you to suffer greatly for me. I accept your love sacrifice on the cross to pay for the consequences of all my sins, and I ask you to

come into my life and unite my spirit with your Holy Spirit again to help me to more closely follow your plan for my life. **Thanks you for coming into my life and re-uniting my spirit with your Holy Spirit now to provide me eternal life with you in heaven per your promise and love sacrifice.** I pray in Jesus name to let you know that I am eternally grateful for what you have just eternally done for me. Amen. ☺☺☺

If you were sincere with above prayer, then at this instance you were re-united with Jesus' Holy Spirit, and **you become children of God again, right now, and forever unconditionally** (i.e. being spiritually re-born again instantly **back into God's Holy Spirit forever per Jesus' unconditional promise to us** -- which you can never, **never lose again**) (Ref Romans 10: 9, 10; Ephesians 2: 8, 9; Titus 3: 4 to 7). **How can you be sure you are spiritually born again right now, because Jesus cannot lie** (i.e. God is forever Holy, Loving, and Just)!!! He loves you, and He keeps his promises because **He is GOD: not a man**. Therefore, He always does what he says. ☺☺☺

Lesson 34: A recommended Prayer of Faith/Belief/Trust
(Request/accept/thank Jesus for your eternal salvation right now and in heaven forever with Jesus (Sin means to miss God's mark of being holy, loving, just)!

Dear Lord Jesus I confess that I am a sinner and unable to always keep your standard of being Holy, Loving, and Just all the time (i.e. Loving all the time); and I am sorry for all my sin choices which caused you, others, and me to suffer greatly and needlessly. I accept your love sacrifice on the cross which paid for the consequences of all my sin choices, and I ask you to come into my life and unite my spirit with your Holy Spirit again **right now** to help me to more closely follow your will/plan for my life. **I thank you** for coming into my life **right now**, forgiving all my sin consequences **right now**, and re-uniting my spirit with your Holy Spirit **right now, resulting in me receiving** eternal life with you **right now according to your word**. I pray in Jesus name to let you know that I am eternally grateful for what you have **just now** done for me and to remind me that I could not have been spiritually re-born again without your help. Amen. ☺

If you were sincere with above prayer, then at this moment you were re-united with Jesus' Holy Spirit, and you became a child of God again, right now, and forever unconditionally by your choice and Jesus promise (i.e. being spiritually born again back into God's Holy Spirit forever per Jesus' unconditional promise to us -- which we can never, never lose again per Jesus word) (Ref Rom 3: 20 to 28; Rom 5: 1 to 11; Jn 14: 6; Jn 3: 3 to 7; Jn 11: 25, 26; Matt 22: 36 to 40; Matt 18: 3 to 5; Rom 10: 9, 10; Jn 5: 24; Eph 2: 8, 9; 1 Tim 1: 5; Eph 1: 13; Titus 3: 4 to 7; Rom Ch 8: All). God does not lie like humans, because it is against his love nature!!!

How can you be sure you are spiritually born again right now: God is not a man and cannot lie (i.e. God is always Holy, Loving, and Just)!!! He loves you, and He keeps his promises because He is GOD: not a man. Therefore, He always keeps his promises. In addition, God had to make sure that his eternal life plan was very simple, so that everyone could understand it no matter what their physical, mental, psychologically, social, cultural, moral, rational, and man's training/condition's impact was. Another example of God's true love!!! (Ref Rom 1: 16; Rom 1: 19, 20; Heb 11: 6; Gal 6: 7; Rom 10: 9 – 13; Jer 17: 5 -10; Eph 2: 8, 9; Isa 6:3; 1 John 4; 8, 16). God keeps his promises! ☺

Lesson 35: A Eternal Salvation Testimony Sample
(Ref Jn Ch 3: All; Rom Ch 8: All; Eph 1: 13; Titus 3: 5)!

Dearly Beloved

Hi! I hope you take the time to read this letter, because it may be one of the most important letters that you will ever read. Why? Because I am going to share with you how I found out how I could obtain eternal life before my body dies. You can obtain eternal life too, if you don't already have it; and you can secure your eternal life right now. Accepting God's free gift of eternal life through his son Jesus Christ is a gift from God, and it is simple step of childlike faith that secures the gift. Once you accept God's gift of eternal life, there is nothing that you or anyone else can do to change that destiny. Why, because it is an unconditional promise to us from God. Interested? Sure you are, who wouldn't you be! I was. Best of all, I am not selling a religion to you, or asking for money, favors, or anything else. So let's get started.

For 27 years I thought that I really knew God. But I had never read the Bible to see just exactly what God expected of me or promised to me. I found out when I began to read the Bible that I wasn't even close to understanding God, or his plan for me, or his plan for the entire human race in particular. Even the Apostle Paul did not understand God or his plan for him, until Jesus appeared to Paul who was on the road to Damascus where he was headed to kill more Christians. Paul was killing Christians, because he thought the Christians were working against God's will. After being struck blind, he proceeded into Damascus where he met a Christian appointed by God who taught him what God's real purpose and plan was for all humans. It took Paul years of Old Testament Bible study to understand where he went wrong. Then Paul wrote most of the New Testament Books (Epistles) to explain to the entire human race what God expected of us, and to explain God's hopeful plan for us to spend all of eternity in heaven with him. After reading the New Testament for about six months, I realized that I really did not understand God or his plan for me. I realized that if I did not accept his free, paid-for gift through Jesus Christ who made an atonement for all of my sins, past, present, and future that I would go straight to hell by my own choice when my body died. So I would like to share God's simple plan of acquiring eternal salvation and life with you now.

First of all, I realized that God's nature is that he is holy, loving, and just all the time, every time, in all circumstances no matter what. Secondly, I realized that he created us as free, independent, moral beings that have the responsibility and accountability to make decisions that will determine our lifestyle and eternal fate. Why are we free independent moral beings with decision-making capabilities, because God wants us to love him by our decision and not because we are puppets. Love has to be a two way street of fair give and take, as well as mutual, reciprocal, sharing between two beings, or it is not true love. When Adam committed the first sin, he inherited the nature to commit more sins; and God's Holy Spirit and his spirit separated at that moment. Adam's sin nature is passed unto everyone by our association with one another and our capability to make our own decisions. Sin means to miss the mark, and the mark is God's standard to be holy, loving, and just all the time, every time, no matter what. The world's standard is to be selfish, inconsiderate, and not-respectful. We as humans cannot hit the mark all the time, so God who is true, pure love (Ref. I John 4: All) had a dilemma.

God loves us, but he cannot have a relationship with us when we are living within our sin nature. He wants everyone to go to heaven and spend all eternity with him in pure, true love. But he cannot, and will not, force anyone to choose him or his plan for us, because that would not be loving. So we reap what we sow (either good or bad per our decisions) (Galatians 6:7, 8) which is a really loving and a just consequence of our own decisions. Pure love must be holy, loving, and just, or it is not pure love. Holy means simply to expect true, honest, and sincere love from someone, or from yourself toward someone. Because God could see into the future, he knew what decisions we would make. So he allowed us to be placed into the environment fit for us where we could make our own free will decisions without duress from anyone, especially the Devil and his demons. And, God sent his son, who was sinless, to pay the penalty for everybody's sins: past, present, and future sins. Yes, everybody's sins. When we stand before God at the Great White Throne Judgment after the end of the world, He will be able to tell everyone who ever lived, that he paid for all their sins because he loves everybody. All that they had to do was accept that free atonement gift. So he expressed his great love for everyone when he placed the penalty of all the sins in the world for all time on Jesus Christ. In essence, we will not be able to point a finger at him and say that he put us into an environment that prevented us from making the decision to accept his free eternal life gift. In addition, God will advise us that his Holy Spirit and our spirit were joined at birth. However, when we decided to commit our first sin, when we reached the age of understanding, our spirit and

God's Holy Spirit separated in accordance with the consequence of our decision.

After reading the New Testament, I realized that some day my body would die, but I would receive a new body. This new body would contain my existing soul and spirit. Therefore, I was going to spend eternity somewhere: either heaven or hell. In order to make the right decision, I needed to understand some very fundamental facts. When I committed my first sin, after I realized the difference between right and wrong and I understood why right is right and why wrong is wrong, my spirit became dead in God's sight (i.e. my spirit and God's Spirit separated). That is, God could not have a relationship with me until my spirit was made holy again, because God cannot have anything to do with anybody that is not holy, loving, and just. In the Gospel of John Chapter 14, Verse 6 Jesus said, "I am the Way, the Truth, and the Life, no man comes to the Father, except by me". In other words, when Jesus hung on the cross for the last 3 hours of the 6 hours that he was on the cross, (i.e. when the earth became dark); God the Father turned his back on his Son for the first time ever. This means that Jesus was without the Love of his Father for the first time ever, and he experienced the total effects of being in hell (i.e. a place without any love or hope). This torture of being without the Father's Love for 3 hours paid for all the sins of the world. That is why Jesus said, "It is finished" before he gave up his spirit on the cross. Now it was up to the Father to accept the payment, and he did accept it, which he showed us when he raised his son from the dead three days later as prophesied. Medical science believes that when a body is dead for three days, then it is really dead. That is why God allowed his Son to stay in the grave for three days. So what did I have to do to inherit eternal life? The Bible says that we cannot work our way into heaven; otherwise Jesus Christ (i.e. God) would not have had to die for my sins on the cross. Could I do better than God?

I had to believe (i.e. trust) that Jesus' sacrifice had covered the penalty (consequences) for all of my sins: past, present, and future (i.e. repent – admit that I was a sinner). Then I had to make my profession of childlike faith (i.e. trust) for God's atonement by accepting his gift and **thanking him** (my act of faith) for making a provision for covering my sins, without having any doubt that God really did what he said he did (Hebrews 11:6). At that moment, God's Spirit and my spirit re-united and become one forever. And I became holy again in God's eyes, because of what he did for me. Since God's Spirit will live with God forever, we will also (Ref John 3:15,16,36; Rom. 6:23; Romans 10: 9-13; John 5: 24; I John 5: 10-14; Romans 8: all.). Since God cannot lie, and his eternal life promise to me is unconditional (that means I can do nothing to work my way out of my newly received eternal life, because it is a free, everlasting gift from God based upon his actions, not my actions, to unite my spirit with his Holy Spirit (Ref Ephesians 2: 8,9). All I had to do was accept his eternal life promise based on Jesus ultimate love sacrifice. My eternal life began the moment that I accepted, and thanked, Jesus Christ for becoming my Personal Lord and Savior. Simple? Yes, it is, because if it were not simple, then many humans would not be able to understand it and become eternally saved. Really smart people and ego-centered humans will not accept the simple plan, because they want to show God that they can work their way to heaven! If God had to send his son down here to pay for all of our sins, who could possibly think that they could save themselves by doing the same work that Jesus did? Who: humans listening to the Devil's lies?

Make no mistake, the Devil hates us and wants us to go to hell. By the way, God does not choose hell for anyone, humans choose hell or heaven themselves because we are free will, moral, and independent beings. Think about it, isn't that loving to give someone what they choose! We will either spend our eternal existence in heaven or hell. Heaven is a place full of God's love, and Hell is a place devoid of God's love. Jesus experience hell during the 3 hours of darkness on the cross. Our earthly body will die someday, but our soul, spirit, and new body will spend eternity in either heaven or hell. These are our choices. Not to choose God's plan through Jesus Christ is the same as rejecting God and the result is hell forever. These are God's words, not mine. Yes, cold, hard, facts; but all we have to do is accept God's plan for escaping hell and we will live with him in heaven forever. Wouldn't it be foolish to reject God's free, already paid for plan? How do we know that this is God' plan, because He says so in the Bible. If the plan is true and we try it; we gain eternal life with him forever. If the plan is not God's plan, we lose nothing if we try it. If we don't want to believe that Jesus made it that simple for us: how do you explain why babies that die go to heaven; how mentally challenged people go to heaven when they die; how natives in the jungles get his plan in order to go to heaven; how folks in our concrete city jungles get the plan to go to heaven when they die; etc? (Ref Hebrews 11: 6 & Matthew 24: 25 to 27). God ensures we all get his plan and many opportunities to accept his simple plan of salvation: otherwise He is not a Holy, Loving, and Just God. If you were not ready to accept Jesus' Plan (i.e. Gospel means good news), would you stop your children from accepting the plan? I did all I could to ensure that my children understood the plan and accepted Jesus into their spirit, and God was merciful to allow them to understand and accept Jesus (i.e. become one with him through his Holy Spirit reuniting with our spirit again that sealed their eternal salvation). Yes, they are still saved sinners, but they are going to heaven no matter what because Jesus said so, not me.

I would not have had any joy in my eternal salvation if I knew that any of my children did not get to heaven. Now I want to share how your children can also have eternal joy starting now by understanding Jesus' plan and accepting his love sacrifice for all your sins, i.e. simply by asking/accepting/thanking God for the re-uniting of his Holy Spirit and your spirit now, so you receive your eternal salvation right now. You can't afford to wait, because you don't know what tomorrow holds for you or your children. You must accept Jesus' plan of salvation while you still have the ability to choose. After you die, your fate is sealed forever, because you can't make any decisions concerning your fate after your spirit and soul leave this life. Don't wait, you have eternal salvation to gain and nothing to lose by making your decision now. If you wait and your body dies before you make your decision, you can not make the decision after your body dies, cause you will stand before God instantly and be judged based upon your decision for or against him.

The moment that you accept Jesus Christ's Holy Spirit into your spirit again as your personal Lord and Savior, you enter into the first moment of your eternal life with him instantly. God says so, and He cannot lie. Doesn't the above really reflect a God who is holy, loving, and just all the time, every time no matter what the circumstances are. Yes it does, and your understanding of this simple concept (i.e. God's Act of Love toward us) will determine if you spend your eternal life in hell or heaven. You have nothing to lose by trusting God and taking that step of faith (trust) of accepting God's free gift of eternal life from Jesus' Spirit by thanking him (your eternal faith action) for providing the way to eternal love with God (Ref Ephesians 2:8,9).

The whole bible has the above message. It is a little harder to see in the Old Testament, because that is where God is giving humans the consequences of their not always so good decisions immediately. Read the New Testament at least five times before trying to read the Old Testament. Remember that Paul knew the Old Testament writings very well (he thought), and he missed the boat big time until Jesus stopped him on the road to Damascus where his mission was to kill Christians. You can be sincere in your heart and think you are on the right path, but you may find out too late that you were sincerely wrong. Be right, read the Bible where God tells you the right way through the men he picked to relate his plan. Don't study the counterfeit to see the real thing, go straight to the real source. Don't delay, for no one knows what tomorrow will bring. Does it make sense not to accept God's plan today, this instance; so you can begin your eternal life right now? The eternal life that no one can take away from you as God said. Thank God I am going to heaven because of Jesus' sacrifice and love for me. There is plenty of room and blessings in heaven for everybody. Yes I am still a sinner, and I will always be one as long as I am here on the Earth in my human body. But I am a saved sinner, and this means that when I sin that I need to confess my sin so I can restore my relationship, not my spiritual position as God's family member, with God. I always remain a saved sinner who will go to heaven, because no one can change that Jesus died for all my sins. In addition, I always have someone to pick me up when I fall. In short, once we accept Jesus' eternal salvation, our position, as a child of God will never change. But when I sin, my relationship with God is interrupted until I repent (i.e. with remorse change my attitude to do my life God's way, not my way).

Our position with God can never change when we accept Jesus' Holy Spirit into our spirit again as our Lord and Savior, but our relationship can change for a while when we sin. To amplify, our children will always be our children. Nothing can change their family position, however, we can be angry with them when they do wrong to us (i.e. the relationship is changed for a time). In short, no matter what the relationship, they will always be our children. This is the same thing that occurs after we are saved, when we sin, our relationship with God is changed until we mend the relationship with our desire to please our Father in heaven.

Confirm you eternal salvation now if you have not already done so, so God can start showering you with his love and blessings now, and forever. I recommend that you read the Books of Romans, Galatians, Ephesians, I John, and the Gospel of John first. Then read the other books in the New Testament, and the Holy Spirit will show you what I realized is really true, really simple, and almost too good to be true; except for a Loving, Holy, and Just God. If you don't believe the above, I challenge you to try to disprove it using your Bible.

PS: I have referenced scriptures above which you can find in the Catholic and Protestant Bibles, since both Bible versions have the same relevant scriptures. Otherwise, God will not provide his truth to all without bias.

Ref Matthew 16: 25;
"For what will it profit a man, if he gains the whole world and forfeits his life. Or what shall a man give in return for this life?" (i.e. or how will he live with the eternal thought that his family and friends may not have made it into heaven, and he could have helped them?)

Ref 1 John 5: 11 & (Romans 10: 9 to 13);
"And this is the testimony that God gave us eternal life, and this life is in his Son. <u>He who has the Son has life</u>; he who <u>has</u> not the Son of God has not life."

Ref Matthew 18: 3, 4;
"Jesus said, Truly, I say to you, unless you turn and have the faith in me like children, you will never enter the kingdom of heaven. Whoever humbles himself like this child, he is the greatest in the kingdom of heaven."

Ref John 14: 6;
"Jesus said to him, I am the way, the truth, and the life; no one comes to the Father, but by me."

Ref Titus 2: 5 to 8;
"he saved us, <u>not because of deeds done by us</u> in righteousness, <u>but in virtue of his own mercy</u>, by the washing or regeneration and <u>re-newal in the Holy Spirit</u> (i.e. being born again spiritually), which he poured out upon us richly

through Jesus Christ our Savior, so that we might be justified by his grace and become heirs in hope of eternal life."

A recommended/suggested salvation prayer:
Dear Lord Jesus I confess that I am a sinner and unable to keep your standard of being Holy, Loving, and Just all the time, and I am sorry for all my sins which caused you and others to suffer greatly. I accept your love sacrifice on the cross to pay for the consequences of all my sins, and I ask you to come into my life and unite my spirit with your Holy Spirit again to help me to more closely follow your plan for my life. **Thanks you for coming into my life and re-uniting my spirit with your Holy Spirit now to provide me eternal life with you in heaven per your promise and love sacrifice.** I pray in Jesus name to let you know that I am eternally grateful for what you have just eternally done for me. Amen. ☺☺☺
(Ref 1 John 4: 8; Rom 5: 8; John 3: 3, 5, 6, 7, 15, 16; Rom 10: 17; 1 John 1: 9, 10; John 14: 6; Heb 11: 6; Matt 19: 14; Rom 10: 9, 10; John 5: 24; Eph 1:13; Titus 3: 5; Heb 13: 5b; 1 Tim 1: 5; 1 John 5: 10 to 14; John 14: 26; Rev 20: 15: Rom Ch 8: All).

If you were sincere with above prayer, then at this instance you were re-united with Jesus' Holy Spirit, and **you become children of God again, right now, and forever unconditionally** (i.e. being spiritually re-born again instantly **back into God's Holy Spirit forever per Jesus' unconditional promise to us** -- which you can never, **never lose again**) (Ref Romans 10: 9, 10; Ephesians 2: 8, 9; Titus 3: 4 to 7). **How can you be sure you are spiritually born again right now, because Jesus cannot lie** (i.e. God is forever Holy, Loving, and Just)!!! He loves you, and He keeps his promises because **He is GOD: not a man**. Therefore, He always does what he says. ☺

Lesson 36: God's Standard: TO BE HOLY, LOVING AND JUST ALL THE TIME
(Ref Jn 15: 1 to 17; 1 Jn 4: 7, 8; Mark 12: 33; 2 Cor 4: 4 to 8)!

HOLY:

(Holy means to be without sin (i.e. being Loving and Just). Sin is the transgression of God's Standard of being Holy, Loving, and Just all the time, every time, no matter what).

Ref Proverbs 9: 10 – "The reverential trust of the LORD is the beginning of Wisdom, and the Knowledge of the Holy One is Understanding".

Ref Hebrews 11:6 – "But without faith it is impossible to please him; for he that comes to God must believe that he is, and that he is a rewarder of them that diligently seek him".

Ref Hebrews 13: 5b – "Jesus said, I will never leave you, nor forsake you".

Ref Romans 5:1 to 5 – "... We have peace with God through our Lord Jesus Christ, we rejoice in our sufferings, knowing that suffering produces endurance, and endurance produces character, and character produces hope".

LOVING:

(Loving has to come from a free, independent, and selfless/considerate/respectful moral being (i.e. being Holy and Just) that has the capability to make its own decisions without being under duress).

Ref Romans 5: 8 – "But God commended his love toward us in that, while we were yet sinners, Christ died for us".

Ref John 15:13 – "Or, Greater love has no man than this that a man lay down his life for his friends".

Ref Mark 12: 33 – "Thou shall love the LORD thy God with your whole heart, your whole soul, and your whole mind, and your neighbor as thy self".

Ref John 15: 12 – "Jesus said: This is my commandment that you shall love one another as I have loved you".

Ref 1 John 4: 7, 8 – "Beloved let us love one another; for love is of God, and everyone that loves is born of God, and knows God; … For God is Love".

Ref 1 Cor 13: 4 to 8 – "Love is patient and kind,… it always protects, it always trusts, it always hopes, it always preservers. Love never fails".

JUST: (Just means to treat yourself and to treat others as you would like to be treated based upon Holy, Loving, and Mutually Reciprocal and Equitable morals).

Ref Galatians 6: 7, 8 – "For whatever a man sows, that shall he reap".

Ref John 14: 6 – "I am the way, the truth, and the life; no man comes to the Father except by me".

Ref Hebrews 12: 1 to 11 - "…; for the LORD disciplines him whom he loves, and chastises every son whom he receives, … for the moment discipline seems painful rather than pleasant; later it yields the peaceful fruit of righteousness to those who have been trained by it".

Ref Matt 16: 26 – "For what will it profit a man, if he gains the whole world and loses his soul? Or what shall a man give in return for his soul".

Ref Matthew 11: 28 to 30 – "Come unto me all you that labor and are heavy laden, and I will give you rest. Take my yoke on you, and learn of me; my heart is gentle and lowly, and your soul will find rest. My yoke is easy and my burden is light".

Ref Isaiah 40: 31 – "They that wait upon the LORD shall renew their strength; they shall mount up with wings like eagles; they shall run, and not be weary; and they shall walk, and not be faint".

Ref Philippians 4: 6, 7 – "Be anxious for nothing, but in everything with thanksgiving, let your requests be make known to God, and the peace of God which passes all understanding, shall keep your hearts and minds through Christ Jesus".

Ref 1 Thessalonian 5: 16 – 18 "Rejoice evermore. Pray without ceasing. In everything give thanks for this is the Will of God in Christ Jesus concerning you: (i.e. giving thanks is your faith/trust put into action)".

Lesson 37: 66 Books of the Bible (39 OT and 27 NT)
(i.e. God's Plenary Inspiration: 1 Tim 1: 5; 2 Tim 3: 15-17; Heb 4: 12)!

Spiritual Themes - Prov 25: 2
Titles   Themes   Meaning
(Books on God's Perfect Will of Love, Salvation by Choice, Sanctification by our Actions)

Titles	Themes	Meaning
Genesis	Origins-	God is Creator
Exodus	Deliverance-	God is Savior
Leviticus	Holiness-	God's Love Standard
Numbers	Wilderness-	Choice Consequences
Deuteronomy	Law Revisited-	Love is God's Mark

(Books on Man's History relative to God's Will for us, our Choices, and Consequences)

Titles	Themes	Meaning
Joshua	Conquering Canaan-	Obedience
Judges	Defeat/Deliverance-	Consequences
Ruth	Kinsman Redeemer-	Jesus' Purpose
I Samuel	Samuel/Saul/David-	Trusting God
II Samuel	David/Solomon's-	God' Wisdom is Best
I Kings	United/Divided-	Prov 3: 5, 6
II Kings	Israel and Judah-	Seek God's Plan
I Chronicles	Genealogy/History-	Remember God's Plan
II Chronicles	Judah's Greatness-	Keep close to God
Ezra	Return of Remnant-	Salvation thru Jesus
Nehemiah	Rebuild of Jerusalem	Sanctification in Jesus
Esther	God's Care-	Trust God is all things

(Books on Knowledge, Understanding, and Spiritual Wisdom relative to God's Will for us)

Titles	Themes	Meaning
Job	Problem of Suffering-	Discipline trains us
Psalms	Praise-	Rejoice with Thanks

Basic Bible Lessons

Proverbs	Wisdom-	Seek God's Viewpoint
Ecclesiastics	Man's Reasoning-	God's Wisdom is best
Song of Solomon	The Beloved-	God Loves his People

(Books on Prophecy relative to God's Plan for us, Will for us, and Choice Consequences)

Isaiah	Israel's Messiah-	God keeps promises
Jeremiah	Warning, Judgment-	Understand The Word
Ezekiel	Judgment & Glory-	Follow God's Plan
Daniel	Rise & Fall-	God is Just
Hosea	Redeeming Love-	God will provide
Joel	Day of the LORD-	God has provided
Amos	Judgment & Sin-	Love is just
Obadiah	Doom of Edom-	Reap what you sow
Jonah	God's Mercy-	God fosters mercy
Micah	Judgment/Kingdom-	Salvation by His Will
Nahum	Nineveh's Doom-	Love is Just
Habakkuk	From Doubt to Faith-	Heb 11: 6
Zephaniah	Day of the LORD-	God is Faithful
Haggai	Rebuilding the Temple	Seek God's Purpose
Zechariah	Messiah's Advents-	Jesus is Faithful
Malachi	Formalism Rebuked-	1 Tim 1: 5

(Books on 4 Perspectives of Jesus the Christ (Gospels – Good News))

Matthew	Christ, the King-	God is in control
Mark	Christ, the Servant-	Matt 11: 28 to 30
Luke	Christ, the Man-	God Love us
John	Christ, the Deity-	Jesus is Lord

(Repeat of God's Perfect Will of Love, Salvation by Choice, Sanctification by our Actions)

Acts	First Century Missions- The Saved in Action

Romans	Gospel of God-	Salvation by Choice
I Corinthians	Christian Conduct-	Be humble/faithful
II Corinthians	Paul's Authority-	2 Tim 5: 6, 7
Galatians	Salvation by Grace-	choices and works
Ephesians	The Church-	Christians Purpose
Philippians	Christian Experience-	Learn from Discipline
Colossians	Christ's Pre-eminence-	Reconcile to God
I Thessalonians	Christ's Return-	God is Faithful
2 Thessalonians	Day of the Lord-	God keeps his word
1 Timothy	Church Order-	Follow Jesus example
2 Timothy	Holding the Truth-	Keep close to Jesus
Titus	Church Order-	Order is Loving/Just
Hebrews	Priesthood of Christ-	Jesus is our advocate
James	Practical Living-	Keep God's Will for us
I Peter	Suffering and Glory-	Growth is by discipline
2 Peter	Last Days-	Keep close to Jesus
I John	Fellowship-	Practice Jesus Walk
2 John	Christ's Commandment-	Agape Love
3 John	Walking in Truth-	Keep God's Wisdom
Jude	Faith-	Stay close to God
Revelation	Jesus' Glory-	Jesus is Deity

Lesson 38: God's Concept of Love Perspective
(Ref Rom 13: 11 - "Love works no ill to its neighbor; therefore, love is the filling of the law";

1 Tim 1: 5: - "**Now the end of the commandment (i.e. Mosaic Law) is love out of a pure heart, and of a good conscience, and of faith unwavering**";

Heb 11: 6 – "But without faith it is impossible to please him; for he that comes to God must believe that He is, and that He is a rewarder of them that diligently seek him")!

-- Be advised: according to Jesus and the bible, God in Love created all humans (i.e. their souls, spirits, and new spiritual bodies) to live forever in either heaven or hell contingent upon their own independent, free will, accountable faith (i.e. trust) decision (Ref 1 Tim 2: 4 to 6 – "Who will have all men to be saved, and to come unto the knowledge of the truth. For there is one God, and one mediator between God and men, the man, Jesus Christ. Who gave himself a ransom for all, to be testified in due time".

(Ref also 1 John 4: 8, 16; Luke 24: 25 to 27; 2 Tim 5: 16 to 17; Heb 4: 12; Matt 22: 37 to 40; Romans 3: 23; Romans 5: 8; John 3: 3, 5, 6; John 14: 6; John 11: 25, 26; John 14: 26; John 11: 25, 26; Gal 6: 7, 8; Eph 1: 13, 14; Romans 10: 9, 10; John 5: 24; Eph 2: 8, 9; Jer 17: 10; Romans Ch 8: All; 2 Cor 5: 17 to 19; Eph 1: 13; Mark 16: 15; Romans 12: 1, 2; 1 Tim 1: 5; 1 John Ch 4: All; Gal 2: 16; Josh 1: 8, 9; Eph 4: 30; Gal 5: 16; Eph Ch 4: All; 1 John 5: 10 to 14; Phil 4: 4 to 7; 2 Tim 3: 16, 17; 22 Peter 1: 20, 21; 1 Thess 5: 16 to 18; Micah 6: 8).

- God created humans with a soul, body, and spirit like his self-manifestations (Ref Gen 1: 6; 1 Thess 5: 23); and He gave all humans the capability to make free, independent, unforced decisions (Ref Jer 17: 10). All decisions have consequences (e.g. blessings, results, accountability) (Ref Gal 6: 7, 8). The requirement of a true personal love connection, relationship, and associated value should be based upon an acceptable, equivalent, and reciprocal personal, rationale, and moral standard in my opinion (Ref Eph Ch 4: All; 1 John Ch 4: All). Otherwise, the relationship is of little value, fosters little self-worth and self-esteem, and produces little beneficial consequences (Ref 1 Tim 1: 5).

- Pure Love requires a giving and receiving between two individuals with the highest expectations that the relationship will continue to grow, flourish, and satisfy both parties for all time; and each person in the relationship will support each other to develop into the best person that we are capable of achieving if we follow the Holy Spirit's leading (Ref 1 John Ch 4: All; Eph Chs 4 & 5: All; Eph 4: 11 to 15).

- I determined through my bible studies that God is Holy, Loving, and Just all the time no matter what (i.e. his pure love standard which reflects his character, personality, and temperament) (Ref Matt 22: 37 to 40; Eph 1: 13; Romans 5: 1 to 11). He loves everyone, and would like everyone to spend their eternity in heaven with him (Ref 1 Tim 2: 4 to 6; John 3: 16, 17; Titus 2: 11; Heb 10: 10 to 18). God however knew that humans will not always make wise decisions, and therefore our spirit will be separated from his Holy Spirit when we commit our first sin (i.e. first non-loving thought, word, or actions) (Ref Romans 3: 23). <u>This above spiritual separation places humans in a "spiritually dead" condition in</u>

God's mind-set (Ref John 3: 3, 5; Romans 6: 23; Col 2: 13). I determined that I needed to spiritually reconcile myself with God through Jesus Christ in order to become spiritually alive again (Ref Eph 1: 13; 2 Cor 5: 17 to 19; Romans 3: 23; Col 2: 13; John 3: 3, 5, 6; John 5: 24; Romans 5: 8; Romans 10: 9, 10; John 11: 25, 26; Gal 6: 7, 8; Eph 2: 8, 9; 1 John 1: 9; Rom 8: 1 to 4; Jer 17: 10; Titus 3: 5; Eph 4: 30; 1 Tim 1: 5).

- My bible studies confirmed that God provides me with the knowledge, understanding, and wisdom to help me to strive to achieve connection with his above love standard (Ref 2 Tim 3: 16, 17; Heb 4: 12); as well as, I would receive many associated blessings by employing a faithful, mature, spiritual loving decision making process in my life as reflected in the bible verses delineated in parenthesis regarding God's Concept of Love Perspective (Ref Matt 22: 36 to 40; Romans Ch 8: All; Gal 5: 16). For example, our family bible studies also helped our children to become spiritually born again Christians early in their lives; and the bible studies also helped our children to read better, comprehend concepts better, and express themselves better as evidence by their good grades in school and by getting along with one another in the our family setting (Ref Heb 4: 12).

- In summary, I concluded that a God of Love would surely want me to have many blessings; and God would provide encouragement, uplifting, and edification in his word (i.e. bible) to show that the purpose of his commandants were to provide loving opportunities for many blessings if I made wise decisions (i.e. not to give-up mind-less control of my life to him (i.e. make me a mere puppet)) (Ref Eph Ch 4: All; Josh 1: 8,9; Mich 6: 8; Matt 11: 28 to 30; Phil 4: 4

to 8; Rom 8: 31 to 39; Gal Ch 5: All; Deut 31: 6; Jer 9: 23, 24; 2 Tim 1: 6, 7; 2 Cor 12: 9, 10; Prov 3: 5, 6).

- In essence, I needed to commit to Jesus to repent in my life, confess my sins and sin nature, and ask/accept/trust Jesus' eternal salvation promise with thanksgiving in order for me to be re-united (i.e. spiritually born again) with him and his Holy Spirit immediately (Ref Jn 3: 36; Jn 5: 24; Rom 10: 9, 10; Phil 4: 4 to 8; Prov 22: 4; Eph 1: 13; Titus 3: 5; Eph 4: 30).

- Therefore, I have to choose (i.e. trust by concent of my mind, act of my heart, and by our will with thanks), not just believe, to personally ask/accept his free love gift (i.e. free undeserved grace gift) of eternal salvation in order to live in heaven with him withour new body forever; or we have to choose to reject his free gift and live in a place devoid of God's presence and love forever with our new body (Ref Prov 22: 4; Heb 11: 6; Prov 3: 5, 6; Romans 3: 23; Romans 10: 9, 10; John 3: 15, 16; Eph 2: 8, 9; Eph 1: 13; Luke 20: 34 to 38).

A **recommended Prayer of Faith/Belief/Trust** to request/accept/thank Jesus **for your eternal salvation right now** (Sin means to miss God's mark of being holy, loving, just all the time no matter what):

Dear Lord Jesus I confess that I am a sinner and unable to always keep your standard of being Holy, Loving, and Just all the time (i.e. Loving all the time); and I am sorry for all my sin choices (past, present, and future) which caused you, others, and me to suffer greatly and needlessly. I accept your love sacrifice on the cross that paid for the consequences of all my sin choices, and I ask you to come into my life and unite my spirit with your Holy Spirit again **right now** to help me to more closely follow your will/plan for my life. **I thank you** for coming into my life **right now**, forgiving all my sin consequences **right now**, and re-uniting my spirit with your Holy Spirit **right now; resulting in me receiving** eternal life with you **right now according to your word**. I pray in Jesus name to let you know that I am eternally grateful for what you have **just now** done for me and to remind me that I could not have been **spiritually re-born again** without your help. Amen. ☺☺☺

After all, **eternity is** a long, long, long, **never-ending** time!
PS: I need to also ensure that my loved ones become "spiritually born again" by their own faith-action decision, so they too can live eternally in heaven with Jesus and me.

Lesson 39: Fundamental Bible Truths - Life's Purpose
(Ref Matt 22: 36 to 40; Micah 6: 8; Mark 16; 15; Eph Ch 4: All)!

My life purpose (i.e. finding my "missing part") comes from relational reconciliation between God's Pure Love, Jesus' Love Sacrifice, and Holy Spirit and my spirit;
My life meaning and love comes from understanding/accepting/sharing Jesus' Love-Sacrifice with others; and
My life fulfillment comes from living in God's love via Holy Spirit through prayer, faith actions, grace living, thankful/humble/grateful attitude; and knowing that my soul and spirit will never die and will exist eternally in a new body in heaven.
(Ref Jn Ch 3: All; Eph Ch 4: All; Micah 6: 8; 1 Tim 1: 5; 1 John 4: 13 to 16)

Searching for the "Spiritual Missing Part" in My Life
(Ref Prov 25: 2; Prov 3: 5, 6; Gal 6: 7 to 9)!
-- God is Pure Love (i.e. Holy, Loving, and Just all the time) – (Ref 1 John 4: 5b).
- God's Law is to Love God first with whole mind/heart/soul and your neighbor as yourself – (Ref Matt 22: 37 to 40; Rom 8: All; 1 John Chs 4 and 5).
- Sin is a non-loving thought/talk/walk action – (Ref Eph 2: 1 to 3; Jer 17: 5 to 10).
- Understand my first sin separated my spirit from God's Holy Spirit (i.e. Spiritual Death in God's eyes) – (Ref Rom 3: All; Rom 3: 19 to 28; Jam 1: 10; Rom 10: 4; Jam 2: 26).
- All have sinned, and must repent and confess sin nature to obtain eternal salvation – (Ref Rom 3: 10; 23; 1 John 1: 9; Eph 2: 8, 9; Rom 10: 9, 10; Rom 6: 15 – 18; Jn 3: 3, 5).

- God created us to be personal, rationale, and moral beings that are responsible for our decisions, and will be judged according to the truth, our deeds, light enjoyed, gospel – (Ref Romans 2: 1 to 16; Matt 7: 2; 1 John 1: 9, 10; 1 John 2: 15 to 17 & 22 to 25; John 5: 24).

My Decision to Research the Bible
(Ref John 3: 3, 5 to 7; John 3: 15, 16; John 6: 40)!
-- What evidence was there that God really cared about me and loved me? (Ref Rom 5:8).
- If Jesus, God's Son, had to endure a love sacrifice for my sins, then I obviously could not accomplish the same results to cover my sins' consequences? (Ref John 14:6).
- What proof would I have that God would keep his promises? (Ref 1 John 5: 10 to 14).
- My life's purpose needs to come from a relational reconciliation with God's Holy Spirit and my Spirit (Ref 2 Cor 5: 17 to 19; James 2: 26).
- My life's meaning needs to come from understanding/requesting/accepting by my sincere faith in Jesus' Love-Sacrifice for all my sins' consequences (Ref Matt 16: 26).
- My life's self-fulfillment needs to stem from my spiritual growth in order to exercise God's Love daily with humble thanksgiving (Ref Prov 3: 5, 6; Josh 1: 8, 9).

Conclusions from my Past Life
(Ref Bible Book of Romans All Chapters)!
-- Searching for the "missing part' in my past life resulted in little success (Ref John Ch 3: All; Romans Ch 1: All; Romans Ch 3: All).

- Neither religion, grade school, high school, sports, girl friend, world travel, military service, family, or college helped me to find my "missing part" (Ref Matt 16: 26, 27).
- Joining a bible study opened my eyes to what my "missing part" might be (Ref John Ch 3: All).
- Learning about God's Pure Love Concept lead me to determining what my "missing part" probably was (Ref Romans 5: 8).

Bible Study Revelations
(Ref John 5: 39; Luke 24: 25 to 27; Eph 1: 12 to 14)!
-- God wants to reconcile with me – (Ref 2 Cor 5: 17 - 19; Jam 2: 26; Rom 8: 11; Rom 8: 14-17).
- God's Love and Grace (free gift) provided a sinless Jesus love sacrifice to cover all of my sins – (Ref Rom 5: 8; Heb 10: 10 to 18; Eph 2: 8, 9; Rom 2: 28; Eph 4: 30/ 1: 13; 2 Tim 3).
- Jesus covered all humans' sin consequences when his Father turned his love from his Son for the first and last time during Jesus' last 3 hours on the cross when the earth was covered by darkness and Temple Veil split – (Ref Matt 27: All; Titus 2: 11; 1 Jn 1: 8 to 10).
- However I must choose to repent/confess our sin nature, believe/trust/ask/accept Jesus Love sacrifice for us, and thank Jesus to become spiritually born again into God's Holy Spirit for eternity (i.e. a child of God forever); cause we are not puppets – (Ref John 3: All; Rom 10: 4, 9 to 13; Rom 2: 28/29; Matt 11: 28 to 30; John 3: 15/16; Eph 1: 12 to 14).

Decision to Obtain Eternal Life
(Ref John Ch 3: All; Romans 10: 9, 10; Eph 1: 13)!
-- Bible study provided answers concerning my life questions about life, love, and death.

- Jesus' love sacrifice on the cross covered all my sins' consequences.
- God's Pure Love was the key for finding my "missing part" life question.
- Realized that I had to choose to accept Jesus' Love sacrifice, not just believe in it.
-I determined that Jesus' Holy Spirit is essential to being "spiritually born again".

Lesson 40: Fundamental Bible Truths - Life's Meaning
(Ref Jn 3: 1 to 21; All; Jn 11: 25, 26; Jn 6: 35 to 40; Rom Ch 5: All; Jn 5: 24)!

My life purpose (i.e. **finding my "missing part") comes from relational reconciliation between God's Pure Love, Jesus' Love Sacrifice, and Holy Spirit and my spirit;** My life meaning **and love comes from understanding / accepting / sharing Jesus' Love-Sacrifice with others; and My life fulfillment** comes from living in God's love via Holy Spirit through prayer, faith actions, grace living, thankful / humble / grateful attitude; and knowing that my soul and spirit will never die and will exist eternally in a new body in heaven .

(Ref Jn Ch 3/ Eph Ch 4/Micah 6: 8/1 Tim 1: 5; 1 John 4: 13 to 16)

Understanding the Value of God's Love
(Ref Rom 5:8; Rom 8:32; John 11:25, 26; 1 John 4:13- 16)!
-- God's Love consists of allowing me: free decisions / consequences; confessing of my sins / sin nature; believing/trusting Jesus' love sacrifice covered all of my sins consequences; asking/accepting Jesus' and his Holy Spirit into my life/spirit; thanking Holy Spirit for returning into my life and sealing my eternal salvation now; and sharing God's simple plan of salvation; otherwise, I am just puppet, and God is not a God of Pure Love - (Ref Rom 5:8; John 3: 15, 16; John 5: 24; Rom 10: 9, 10; 1 John 5: 11 to 13; Titus 3: 4 to 7; Titus 2: 11; John 4: 24; Heb 11:6; John 14: 6).
- I can only connect to God/Eternal Salvation/Heaven through Jesus' Holy Spirit – (Ref Eph 2: 8, 9; Rom 8: 14 to 17; Titus 2: 11; Col 1: 19-22; Jam 2: 26; Rom 8: 11; Jn 11: 25/26).

- Understand that my faith/trust in God's word is strengthened by studying the Bible (i.e. God Talking to us) – (Ref Rom 10: 17; 2 Pet 1: 20, 21; Heb 4: 12; Heb 11: 6; 2 Tim 3: 15 – 17).
- Comprehend that God's Law (i.e. 10 Commandments / Judgments / Ordinances), reveal that I have a sin nature, and I cannot obtain eternal salvation by my actions – (Ref Rom 3: 20).
- Personally accepting God's Grace gift of Salvation releases me from the shackles of my sinning past, sin nature, and world's sin standards, if I choose; so I can now live daily in God's grace, joy, peace, love, wisdom, humility, gratefulness, trusting prayer, thankfulness, mature spiritual growth, and successful living for me which is the ultimate blessing - (Ref 1 Thess 5: 16 to 18; Prov 3: 5, 6; Prov 1: 7; Romans Ch 8; Eph Chs 4 & 6; Matt 11: 28 to 30; Gal 6: 7, 8; Ps 37: 3 to 7).
- Heaven is a place full of God's Love that is the ultimate reward from reuniting my spirit with God's Holy Spirit - (Ref Romans 14: 17; Ecc 5: 2; John 5: 24; John 3: 3, 5; John 14: 2, 3).
- My soul/spirit will exist forever in Heaven by my choice – (Ref Eph 1: 13; Titus 3: 4 to 7).

How to obtain maximum blessings daily
(Ref Jer 9: 23, 24; Gal 5: 13 to 26; Prov 22: 4; Ps 37: 4 to 7)!
-- Employing God's Knowledge, Understanding, and Wisdom should be my daily spiritual goal – (Ref Psalm 37: 3 to 5; 1 Pet 1: 20, 21; Prov 1: 7; Prov 2: 1 - 6; Prov 3: 1 - 35; 1 John 2: 15 – 17).
- Realize that God's Standard/Law/Mark is based upon loving God first and my neighbor as our self – (Ref Matt 22: 37 to 40; 1 John: 4 All; 1 John 3: 11 to 24; John 11: 25, 26).
- God wants me to have maximum blessings, because He loves me and wants me to make wise decisions, not as a puppet, to receive maximum blessings – (Ref Gal 6: 7, 8).
- Understand that my good/bad choices/actions/experiences, with God's help, are meant to help me adjust my

attitude/actions/thoughts, so I can receive many blessings for me and others – (Ref Gal 6: 7, 8; Heb 12: 6 to 15; Heb 11: 6) (i.e. I receive blessings for all our faith actions: e.g. prayer, bible study; thanking, rejoicing, sharing, listening, serving, growing).
- Pursue God's goal that I try to love all humans, even myself; but not our non-loving actions – (Ref Eph Ch 4; Josh 1: 8, 9; Deut 31: 6; Col 3: 12, 13; 2 Cor 12: 9, 10).
- Being aware that Human's philosophy "What's In It For Me" stems from Selfishness, Inconsideration, and Non-respect (i.e. Sin) – (Ref Rom 3: 23; Rom 12: 1, 2; John 5: 3).

Lesson 41: Fundamental Bible Truths - Life's Fulfillment
(Ref Rom Ch 8: All; 1 Jn Ch 4 & 5: All; Prov 3: 5, 6; Eph Ch 4: All)!

My life purpose (i.e. finding my "missing part") comes from relational reconciliation between God's Pure Love, Jesus' Love Sacrifice, and Holy Spirit and my spirit;
My life meaning and love comes from understanding/accepting/sharing Jesus' Love-Sacrifice with others; and
<u>My life fulfillment comes from living in God's love via Holy Spirit through prayer, faith actions, grace living, thankful/humble/grateful attitude; and knowing that my soul and spirit will never die and will exist eternally in a new body in heaven</u>.
(Ref Jn Ch 3/ Eph Ch 4/Micah 6: 8/1 Tim 1: 5; 1 John 4: 13 to 16)

Adjusting my life's purpose toward God's Love concept
(Ref 1 Tim 1: 5; Eph 5: All; 1 Jn 4: All)!
-- My Bible study stated that my life's purpose was to reconcile with God through Jesus, grow spiritually through the Holy Spirit, and share my eternal life news with others via Holy Spirit's divine appointments – (Ref 2 Cor 5: 17 to 19; John 14: 16; Mark 16: 15; 1 John Chs 1 to 4; Eph 4: Ch 4: All).

- Faith actions provide blessings/consequences/spiritual growth- (Ref Heb 11: 6; Phil 4: 4 to 9; Prov 25: 2; 2 Tim 3: 16, 17) (i.e. all choices/actions require/receive consequences).
- Trusting God with the faith of a child is key to real faith/trust/belief in God, and our faith strength comes from understanding how God's Love is essential for our life salvation – (Ref Mark 10: 15; Prov 3: 5, 6; Psalm 37: 3 to 7; John 14: 26).
- Protection/growth of our faith in God is essential to receiving blessings as opposed to not receiving blessings from employing our sinful past, our sin nature, and the world's standards – (Ref Rom 12: 1, 2; Matt 16: 24 to 28; Prov 3: 5,6; Heb 11: 6).
- Understand/employ God's Love equation (i.e. "You Reap What You Sow") which is the foundation of God's love; because it requires an overall trust, average 50/50% love relationship, and loving God first and our neighbor as our self – (Ref Col 3: 12, 13; Rom 7: 4; Rom 6: 14; 2 Pet 1 to 10) (e.g. for every action, there is an equal and opposite reaction/consequence).

Adjusting my Mind-Set to follow God's will for me (Ref Rom Chs 12, 5, 8)!
-- Seeking God's love and lead in all of my decisions provides peace/joy/happiness – (Ref Prov 3: 5, 6; 1 John 3: 23; 1 John Chs 4, 5 All; 1 John 4: 16).
- Since Jesus had to cover my sins, why would I think that I could do better – (Ref John 14: 6).
- To follow Holy Spirit's leading in all of my thoughts/decisions/actions is my only true source of power, love, and self-discipline – (Ref John 14: 26; 2 Tim 1: 6, 7; Gal 5: 16 to 26).
- Realize that I should be seeking to share eternal salvation/heaven with everybody when the opportunities occur per Holy Spirit's divine appointments to help us share God's Love – (Ref Matt 28: 19. 20; 1 Tim 2: 1 to 4).
- Praying daily with thanksgiving for Holy Spirit to set up divine appointments for me with others – (Ref Matt 28: 19, 20 (i.e. Great Commission Direction); Eph Ch 4 All).

- Good spiritual mind-set comes from studying God's word, trusting him, sharing his love; a pure heart/good conscience, and strong faith – (Ref Romans 12: 1, 2; Romans 4: 10; 1 Tim 1: 5; Rom 10: 17; Micah 6: 8; Eph 4: 2; Psalm 37: 3 to 7).

Growing daily into a Mature Spiritual Being (Ref Matt 22: 37 to 40; 1 Thess 5: 16 to 18; Micah 6: 8)!
-- Seeking God's lessons from all good and bad decisions/circumstances produces our greatest spiritual training/growth/blessings – (Ref Heb 12: 1 to 15; Proverbs 22: 4; 1 Cor 10: 11 to 15; Prov 25: 2; 2 Cor 12: 9/10).
- Rejoicing and thanking God for all circumstances, regardless if they are good or bad, provides greatest knowledge/understanding/wisdom/rewards/spiritual adult growth - (Ref 1 Thess 5: 17 to 19); as well as provides best transformation of our mind, soul, and spirit to God's Love concept – (Ref Romans 12: 1, 2; Rom 8: 31 to 39; Matt 7: 1, 2; Rom 1 All; Prov 25: 2; John 3: 11, 12; 1 Thess 5: 16 to 18).
- Praying to Holy Spirit daily and often to keep my mind on God's plan for me; so I can perform my best faith based thoughts, walk, and actions in order to provide the greatest blessings for me, my loved ones, and other humans – (Ref Prov 3: 5, 6; Ps 37: 3 to 7; Matt 11: 28 to 30; Rom 12: 1, 2; John 15: 5; Deut 31: 6; Micah 6: 8; Isa 40: 31; Matt 18: 28, 29; John 14: 26; 2 Tim 3: 16, 17; John 14: 6).

Adjusting my Behavior to God's Love concept in my daily life (Ref Col 3: 12, 13; Matt 16: 26; Matt 11: 28 to 30)!
-- Remember daily that God's commandments, ordinances, and judgments are based on loving God first and my neighbor as myself, and I should try to emulate God's Love Concept – (Ref Exodus Chs 19 to 40; Leviticus All; 1 John 3: 23; Matt 22: 37 to 40).
- Loving/Encouraging everybody, but not their sinful actions, should be my primary life goal/attitude – (Ref 1 John 4: 1 to 10; Gal 6: 7 to 9; Eph 4: 12).

- Praying daily for God's will/ plan for me is a great act of faith – (Ref 1 Thess 5: 17; Gal 3: 3).
- Using God's Word in all my encounters (i.e. divine appointments) with others – (Ref Heb 4: 12/2 /Tim 1: 7/Col 3: 17; 2 Tim 3: 15 to 17; Phil 4: 4 to 7; Prov 3: 6, 7; Psalm 37: 4 to 8).
- Striving to increase my faith/belief/trust in God daily by Bible study, prayers, thoughts, actions – (Ref Heb 11: 6; Rom 10: 17; Josh 1: 8, 9; 1 Thess 5: 17; Eph Ch 4: All).
- List of daily spiritual considerations to assist in maintaining God's Love Perspective.

Bible Verses to Support Spiritual Growth
(Ref Eph Ch 4: All; Jn 14: 6; Prov 3: 5, 6; Gal Ch 3: All; Gal 6: 7 to 9; 2 Tim 3: 15 to 17: 2 Pet 20, 21); Jn 11: 25, 26; Jn 5: 39; Jn 14: 26; Matt 28: 19, 20)!

Lesson 42: Best Christmass Gift Ever Letter Sample
(Ref Jn Ch 3: All; Jn 11: 25, 26; Jn 5: 24; Jn 5: 39, 40)!

Hi Y'all,
Pray you and yours a very blessed Christmas and Eternal Life. Below are bible verses that reveal how you can secure your eternal salvation in heaven today (i.e. right now) via your faith action decision of requesting asking / accepting / thanking Jesus the Christ and his Holy Spirit for coming into your life right now. Trust you will accept Jesus free eternal salvation today, and become a part of his Christ-Mass forever. In Jesus Love for you and yours. ☺☺☺

The ultimate Christ-Mass gift available for all humans is to secure your eternal salvation in heaven right now by your child-like faith in Jesus and in his love sacrifice on the cross (i.e. Jesus suffered hell (i.e. not knowing his Father's love for 3 hours) by his vicarious (i.e. substitute) love sacrifice for us)). Heaven is a place full of God's Love forever, and Hell is a place without any love forever (Ref Rom 5: 8; Jn 14: 6; Heb 11:6; Jn 3: 15, 16; Jn 5: 24; Rom 10: 9, 10; Eph 1: 13).

(Below Bible verses are in the Catholic Bible Douay-Rheims Translation, Catholic Confraternity Bible Translation, Schofield Reference Bible Translation, and Bible New and Old Testaments)

Love is foundation/redemption for God's Mosaic Law (i.e. 10 Commandments, Worship Ordinances, Social Judgments) – (Ref Matt 22: 37 – 40: 1 Tim 1: 5; Books of Exodus, Leviticus, Deuteronomy). **God's eternal salvation is based upon our choice and God's grace**, not our works; and we must ask/accept his eternal salvation plan by

trust/faith/thanks (otherwise Jesus would not have been required to do his love sacrifice on the cross for us (Ref Eph 2: 8, 9; Gal 6: 7, 8; Jer 17: 10; John Ch 3: 11, 12)).

God's Free "Christ-Mass" Grace Gift (i.e. eternal salvation) can be obtained right now by your decision to Repent/Confess your sin nature-sins / Request / Trust / Accept and Thank Jesus' for his Love Sacrifice on the cross for us (i.e become a part of God's "Christ-Mass" again by **re-union right now with his Holy Spirit forever** through Jesus the Christ) (Ref 1 Tim 2: 1 to 6; Rom 8: 1 to 17).

John 3: 3, 5 – "Jesus answered, Verily, verily, I say unto thee, **except a man be born** of water (i.e. human birth) **and of the Holy Spirit (choose to re-unite with Jesus' Holy Spirit – become "spiritually alive again"), he cannot enter into the kingdom of God**" (Ref Jam 2: 26; Jn 5: 24).

Romans 3: 3:10 – "As it is written, there is none righteous, no, not one". (**Our sin nature and sins** cause us to miss God's mark (i.e. Pure Love) of being holy, loving, and just that **results in the separation of our spirit from God's Holy Spirit**" (i.e. "spiritual death" in God's eyes (Ref Eph 2: 1 - 10)).

Romans 3: 20 – "Therefore, **by the deeds of the law there shall no flesh be justified in his sight**; for by the law (i.e. God's Mosaic Law) is the knowledge of sin" (Ref Eph 2: 1 to 10).

Romans 5: 8 – "But God commended his love toward us in that, while we were yet sinners, Christ died for us". (God's Mark/Standard is Holy/Loving/Just. **Sin is** to commit a non-loving thought/word/action that **separates** our spirit from God's Holy Spirit, and interrupts our spiritual relationship with God.

Salvation is only achieved by asking/receiving/reuniting our spirit with Jesus' Holy Spirit via our sincere sins confession and childlike faith-trust/thanks to Jesus.) (Ref John 3: 3, 7; Romans 10: 9, 10; Rom 8: 11; Eph 4: 30; 1: 13; John 5: 24: Heb 11: 6; Titus 3: 5).

John 3:15, 16 – "**Jesus said**, whosoever believeth in him should not perish, but have eternal life. For God so loved the world, that he gave his only begotten Son, that whosoever believes in him (i.e. **with childlike faith** (Ref Matt 22: 37 to 40/Hebrews 11: 6) **should not perish, but have everlasting life**" (Ref also John 5: 24; Rom 8: 32; Deut 31: 6).

John 3: 36 – "He that believes on the Son has everlasting life; and he that believes not the Son shall not see life, but the wrath of God abides on him". If Jesus had to sacrifice for our sins, how could we ever expect to out do him/his sacrifice: (i.e. Jesus was without his father's love for the 3 hours of darkness on the cross which covered the sin consequences for all humans sins as verified by the tearing of the veil in the temple when Jesus declared on the cross that it is finished (Ref 2 Cor 3: 6 to 18)).

Romans 10: 9, 10 – "If you **confess with your mouth** the Lord Jesus, and **believe in your heart** that God raised him from the dead, you shall be saved. For with the heart man believes unto righteousness; and with the mouth confession is made unto salvation". (i.e. **believe/ask/accept/thank Jesus** for our receiving his Holy Spirit again and being re-born spiritually **for all eternity** at that moment per Jesus promise). We have to choose to accept (i.e. trust by concent of my mind, act of my heart, and by my will with thanksgiving), not just believe, to personally accept his free love gift sacrifice on the cross) (i.e. free undeserved grace gift) in order to live in heaven with him forever with my new spiritual body (Ref Prov 22: 4; Rom 10: 9, 10, 13; Luke 20: 34 to 38).

John 14: 6 – "Jesus said, I am the way, the truth, and the life; no man can come to the Father except by me". Jesus paid for everybody's sins; but we have to believe/ask/accept his love sacrifice on the cross with a child-like repentant/contrite/thanksgiving heart in order to redeem our soul and spirit forever. **Why, cause Jesus will not force us to accept his free love eternal salvation gift, because that would not be holy, loving, and just**).

Titus 3: 5 – "**Not by works of righteousness** which we have done, **but according to his mercy he saved us**, **by the washing of regeneration, and the renewing of the Holy Spirit**". We have to choose to ask/accept/thank Holy Spirit through Jesus to come back into our lives in order to receive the gift of eternal salvation right now (Ref Romans 10: 9, 10; Eph Ch 4: All; Romans Ch 8: All).

Here is a recommended prayer/choice/action to use to obtain your eternal spiritual salvation right now:

Dear Lord Jesus I confess that I am a sinner and unable to always keep your standard of being Holy, Loving, and Just all the time. I am sorry for all my sins which caused you, others, and me to suffer greatly/needlessly. I accept your love sacrifice on the cross which paid for the consequences of all my sins; and I ask you to come into my life and unite my spirit with your Holy Spirit again right now to help me to more closely follow your will/plan for my life. I thank you for coming into my life right now, forgiving all my sin consequences right now, and re-uniting my spirit with your Holy Spirit right now to give me eternal life right now with you in heaven per your promise, your forgiveness, and your great love sacrifice for me. I pray in Jesus name to let you know that I am eternally grateful for what you have just now done for me and to remind me that I could not have been spiritually born again without your help. Amen.

If you were sincere with above prayer, then at this instance you were re-united with Jesus and his Holy Spirit, and you became a child of God again, right now, and forever unconditionally (i.e. being spiritually re-born again instantly back into God's Holy Spirit forever per Jesus' unconditional promise to us -- which you can never, never, never lost again *) (Ref Romans 10: 9, 10; Ephesians 2: 8, 9; Titus 3: 4 to 7; John 14: 6). How can you be sure you are spiritually born again right now, because God is not a human being and cannot lie (i.e. God is forever Holy, Loving, and Just)!!! He loves you, and He keeps his promises – (Ref Romans Ch 8: All; 1 Tim 1: 5).

Sincerely in Love,
Chuck Pringle (a very grateful saved sinner, Thank you Jesus!)

Lesson 43: Bible Verses that support God's Love Concept
(Ref Heb 4: 12; 2 Pet 20, 21; Rom 8: 1 to 4)!

-- The following bible verses support that living via God's Love Concept promotes spiritual growth; direct personal relationship with God; access to God's knowledge, understanding, and wisdom from the Holy Spirit; membership in God's family forever; eternal salvation in heaven; and abundant holy, loving, and just blessings:

2 Pet 1:20, 21 – "Knowing this first, that no prophecy of the scripture is of any private interpretation. <u>For the prophecy came not at any time by the will of man, but holy men of God spoke as they were moved by the Holy Spirit</u>".

Luke 24:25, 27 – "Then he (i.e. Jesus) said unto them, O foolish ones, and slow of heart to believe all that the prophets (i.e. Old Testament) have spoken! Ought not Christ to have suffered these things, and to enter into his glory? And beginning at Moses and all the prophets, <u>he expounded unto them, in all the scriptures, the things concerning himself</u>".

2 Tim 3:15 to 17 – "And that from a child thou has known the holy scriptures, which are able to make thee wise unto salvation through faith which is in Christ Jesus. <u>All scripture is given by inspiration of God</u>, and it profitable for doctrine, for reproof, for correction, for instruction in righteousness, that the man of God may be perfect, thoroughly furnished unto all good works".

Heb 4:12 – "<u>For the word of God</u> is living, and powerful, and sharper than any two-edged sword, piercing even to the dividing asunder of soul and spirit, and of the joints a marrow, and <u>is a discerner of the thoughts and intent of the heart</u>".

Rom 1:16, 17 – "<u>For I am not ashamed of the gospel of Christ, for it is the power of God unto salvation to everyone the believes</u>; to the Jew first, and also to the Gentile. For in it is the righteousness of God revealed from faith to faith; as it is written, the just shall live by faith".

Rom 8:1to 4 – "There is, therefore, now no condemnation to them who are in Christ Jesus, who walk not after the flesh, but after the Spirit. <u>For the law of the Spirit of life in Christ Jesus has made me free from the law of sin and death.</u> For what the Mosaic Law could not do, in that it was weak through the flesh, God sending his own Son, in the likeness of sinful flesh and for sin, condemned sin in the flesh. That the righteousness of the law might be fulfilled in us, who walk not after the flesh, but after the Spirit".

Jn 11:25, 26 – "Jesus said unto her, I am the resurrection, and the life; he that believes in me, <u>though he were "dead" (i.e. spiritually dead),</u> yet shall he live. And whosoever lives and believes in me shall never "die" (i.e. never die an eternal spiritual death and spend eternity in hell). Believe thou this"?

Matt 22:29 to 32 – "Jesus answered and said unto them, you do error, not knowing the scriptures, nor the power of

God. For in the resurrection they neither marry, nor are given in marriage, but are like the angels of God in heaven. But as touching the resurrection of the dead, have ye not read that which was spoken unto you by God saying, I am the God of Abraham, and the God of Isaac, and the God of Jacob. God is not the God of the dead, but of the living".

Jeremiah 17:9, 10 – "The heart is deceitful above all things, and desperately wicked, who can know it? I, the LORD, search the heart, I test the conscience, even to give every man according to this ways, and according to the fruit of his doings".

Jn 5: 24 – "Verily, verily, I say unto you, He that hears my word, and believes on him that sent me, has everlasting life, and shall not come into judgment, but is passed from death (i.e. spiritual death) unto life (i.e. spiritual life)".

Luke 18:16 – "Verily I say unto you, Whosoever shall not receive the kingdom of God like a little child (i.e. with the pure faith of a child) shall in no way enter it."

Rom 4:3– "For what says the scripture? Abraham believed God, and it was counted unto him for righteousness".

Rom 10:17– "So, then, faith comes by hearing, and hearing by the word of God".

Jn 3: 5 to 7 – "Jesus answered, Verily, verily, I say unto thee, Except a man be born of water and of the Spirit (i.e. Holy Spirit), he cannot enter into the kingdom of God.

That which is born of the flesh is flesh; <u>and that which is born of the Spirit is spirit</u>. Marvel not that I said unto thee, You must be (i.e. spiritually) born again".

<u>Jam 2:26</u> -"<u>For as the body without the Holy Spirit is dead</u>, so faith without works is dead also".

<u>Ephesians 1:13</u>– "In whom ye also <u>trusted</u>, after you heard <u>the work of truth</u>, the gospel of your salvation; and in whom also <u>after you believed, you were sealed with the Holy Spirit</u> of promise".

<u>Titus 3:5</u> –" <u>Not by works</u> of righteousness which we have done, but according to his mercy he saved us, by <u>washing of regeneration, and renewing of the Holy Spirit</u>" (i.e. our first sin separates our spirit from the Holy Spirit, and we need to re-unite with the Holy Spirit to become spiritually alive again in God's eyes).

<u>Jn 14:26</u> – "But the Comforter who is the Holy Spirit, by whom the Father will send in my name, he shall teach you all things, and bring all things to your remembrance, whatever I have said unto you".

<u>Ephesians 4:30</u> – "And grieve not the <u>Holy Spirit of God, by whom you are sealed</u> unto the day of redemption".

<u>Ephesians 4:4 to 6</u> – "There is one body, **and one Spirit (i.e. Holy Spirit)**, even as you are called in one hope of your calling: One Lord, one faith, one baptism, One God and Father of all, who is above all, **and through all and in you all**." (**Note**: <u>all spiritually born again christians' spirits are re-united into God's Holy Spirit forever, and the Holy</u>

Spirit will live forever and never be rejected from living in heaven for all eternity).

Rom 8:14 – "For as many as are led by the Spirit of God, they are the sons of God".

Rom 8:16 – "The Holy Spirit himself bears witness with our spirit, that we are the children of God".

1 Cor 3:16 – "Know you not that you are the temple of God, and that the Spirit of God dwells in you"?

2 Tim 1:7 – "For God has not given us the spirit of fear, but of power, and of love, and a sound mind".

1 Tim 1:5 – "Now the end of the commandment is love out of a pure heart, and of a good conscience, and of faith unwavering".

Micah 6:8 – "He has shown thee, O man, what is good; and what does the LORD require of thee, but to do justly, and to love mercy, and to walk humbly with thy God".

Deut 31:6 – "Be strong and of good courage, fear not, nor be afraid of them; for the LORD thy God, He it is who does go with thee; he will not fail thee, nor forsake thee,"

1 Cor 13:4 to 7 – "Love is patient. Love is kind. It does not envy. It does not boast. It is not proud. It is not rude. It is not easily angered. It keeps no records of wrongs. Love does not delight in evil, but rejoices with the truth. It always protects, always trusts, always hopes, and always perseveres. Love never fails".

1 Cor 13: 13 – "And now abides faith, hope, and love; but the greatest of these is love".

1 Jn 4:8b, 16b – "... God is love...".

Ps 46:10 – "Be still, and know that I am God".

Lesson 44: Free Will Choice versus Mosaic Law Mandates

(Ref Gal 6: 7, 8; Gal 3: 10 to 12, 22, 24, 25; Heb 10: 10 to 18: James 2: 10; Rom 3: 20; Matt 22: 37 to 40; Jn 11: 25, 26; Heb 11: 6; Luke 13: 3; Rom 10: 9, 10; Eph 1: 13; 1 Tim 1: 5)!

-- During my past life research I considered that If God is really the God of pure and true Love, then his solution for me to obtain eternal life in heaven should be very "simple" and easy to understand; because God knows that I am not the brightest light bulb in this life.

- In addition, a God of Love's eternal salvation plan should be the same for all humans regardless of their life's circumstances (e.g. mental, psychological, ideological, economic, physical, spiritual, geographical, educational, social, philosophical, religious, atheistic beliefs, ethic, cultural, etc).

- Further, I should be able to understand God's simple plan of eternal salvation and be able to choose, or not choose, his plan with my own God given independent, free will, and accountable decision-making capability; or God is not really a God of Love (Ref 1 Tim 2: 4 to 6; Heb 10: 10; Titus 2: 11; Jn 3: 15, 16).

- Otherwise, I considered that I might have no other choice other than to accept and to try to comply with God's Mosaic Law's (i.e. 10 Commandants and associated 600+ Worship Ordinances and Social Judgments) mandates and consequences respectively as spelled out in the first five books of the Old Testament.

- But I knew from my past life experiences and sin nature that I would not be able, or even want, to comply with all of the Mosaic Law mandates (Ref Gal 3: 10 to 12, 22, 24, 25; Heb 10: 10 to 18: James 2: 10; Rom 3: 20; Matt 22: 37 to 40; Jn 11: 25, 26; Heb 11: 6; Luke 13: 3; Rom 10: 9, 10; Eph 1: 13; 1 Tim 1: 5).

- So it was important that I determine what were my life choice options and their consequences were, if I expected to make the best decision concerning the eternal destiny of my soul and spirit.

Heb 11: 6 – "But without faith it is impossible to please him; for he that comes to God must believe that he is, and that he is a rewarder of them that diligently seek him".

Romans 5: 7 to 11 – "For scarcely for a righteous man will one die; yet perhaps for a good man some would even dare to die. But God commended his love toward us in that, while we were yet sinners, Christ died for us. Much more then, being now justified by his blood (i.e. assurance that my sins consequences are covered by Jesus' love sacrifice on the cross), we shall be saved from God's condemnation (i.e. **only if I choose** – Ref Rom 10: 9, 10; Jn 3: 15 to 18; 1 Pet 3: 18; Rev 20: 15; Jn 5: 24).

Romans 3: 23 – "For all have sinned, and come short of the glory of God (i.e. to sin is to have a thought, word, or action that is non-loving)."

Ephesians 2: 8, 9 – "For by grace are you saved through faith; and that not of yourselves, it is the gift of God – not of works, lest any man should boast (i.e. God's grace means a free, undeserved gift!)".

Rom 8: 32 - " He that spared not his own Son, but delivered him up for us all, how shall he not with him also freely give us all things"?

John 3: 15, 16 – "That whosoever believeth in him should not perish, but have eternal life. For God so loved the world that He gave his only begotten Son, that whosoever believes in Him should not perish, but have everlasting life."

Matthew 18: 3 to 5 – "Jesus said, Verily I say unto you, except you be converted, and become as little children (i.e. in your faith/belief/trust toward and in Jesus Christ), you shall not enter into the kingdom of heaven. Whosoever, therefore, shall humble himself as this little child, the same is greatest in the kingdom of heaven. And whosoever shall receive one such little child in my name receives me."

Titus 2: 11 – "For the grace of God that brings salvation has appeared to all men" (e.g. God's universe creation, earth's creation and environmental balance, and his creatures creations supplemented with their basic living needs).

Ephesians 1: 13 – "In whom ye also trusted, after you heard the work of truth, the gospel of your salvation; and in whom also after you believed, you were sealed with the Holy Spirit of promise".

Ephesians 4: 4 to 6 – "There is one body, **and one Spirit** **"(i.e. Holy Spirit)"**, even as you are called in one hope of your calling: One Lord, one faith, one baptism, One God and Father of all, who is above all, **and through all and in you all**." (**Note**: all spiritually born again christians' spirits are re-united into God's Holy Spirit forever, and the Holy Spirit will live forever and never be rejected from living in heaven for all eternity).

Lesson 45: Considerations regarding Heaven and Hell
(Ref Jn 5: 24; Ps 16: 10; Eph 4: 30; Ecc 12: 7; Jn 6: 63; 1 Thess 5: 23; Jn 3: 36; Rom 8: 14 to 17; Rev 20: 10 to 15; Matt 23: 33 & 43)!

-- Most religions and the bible assert that there is an eternal heaven and an eternal hell; and everyone will ultimately exist eternally in one of these places.

- Therefore according to the bible, I will live eternally in either heaven or hell with a new spiritual body (i.e. my earthly body will eventually die); and my soul and spirit will never die (Ref Jn 5: 24; Ps 16: 10; Eph 4: 30; Ecc 12: 7; Jn 6: 63; 1 Thess 5: 23; Jn 3: 36; Rom 8: 14 to 17; Rev 20: 10 to 15; Matt 23: 33 & 43).

- In essence, according to the bible, I will transition some day from my earthly living to either heaven or hell respectively for eternity contingent upon my decision to: (1) ask/accept by my own free will Jesus' love sacrifice on the cross for all of my sins consequences in accordance with my understanding of God's Love Concept (i.e. **my spirit will re-unite with God's Holy Spirit through Jesus (i.e. being spiritually born again)), and I will live in heaven forever with the understanding that God's Holy Spirit will never die** (Ref Jn 14: 6; Jn 6: 63; Rom 3: 20 to 31; Gal 5: 13 to 18; Eph 4: 1 to 7); or (2) I can choose to personally try to comply and to satisfy all of the Mosaic Law (i.e. 10 commandments and over 600+ worship ordinances and social judgments) with my life decisions and associated deeds in order to try to cover the consequences of all of my sins (**note: the bible states that it is impossible for any human to cover/redeem their sins' consequences through their own efforts or religion**) (Ref Jn

14: 6; 1 Tim 2: 5, 6; Jn 11: 25, 26; Eph 2: 8, 9; James 2: 10; Gal 3: 10 to 12; Gal Ch 3: All; Matt 5: 17 to 20; Rev 20; 15; Gal 2: 16; Gal 6: 7, 8; Rom 1: 16, 17; Luke 13: 3; Rom 2: 1 to 16; Rom 1: 18 to 20; Rom 3: 20 to 31; Titus 2: 11; 1 Tim 1: 5; Eph 1: 13; 1 John 5: 10 to 14).

- In other words, I questioned if it were possible to personally cover/redeem all of my sins consequences; why did Jesus (God's Son) have to come to earth to cover/redeem my sins consequences (e.g. note that Jesus name translates to God's Salvation)? I concluded based upon my life experiences with other humans and human religions that I researched that maybe I was not the only one confused about the true spiritual meaning and definitions regarding Jesus purpose, biblical words, parables, and spiritual concepts (Ref Jn 3: 1 to 21; Jn 5: 24; Jn 5: 39 to 40; Luke 24: 25 to 27; Jn 4: 24; Acts 9: 1 to 23).

- Relative to heaven and hell, I considered the Apostle Paul's (formerly named Saul) conversion to Christianity after being reproached by Jesus in a vision from heaven for killing Christians and subsequently being filled with the Holy Spirit during his trip to Damascus to kill christians. Paul had received an in-depth education concerning the Old Testament (i.e. Jewish Prophets teachings); nevertheless, Paul did not understand that the OT bible truths are based upon God's Love Concept (Ref Matt 22: 36 to 40; Jn 3: 7 to 15). He was advised by Jesus to go to Damascus to be retrained by Christian teachers. He consequently spent time in Damascus with Jesus' disciples to learn the true purpose of Jesus' Love, death on the cross, earthly purpose, words, parables, and spiritual concepts; and these bible revelations stopped him from continuing to kill Christians. In addition, Paul after his conversion subsequently wrote the majority of the New Testament books to reveal what he had learned in Damascus concerning God's Love Concept (Matt 22: 36 to 40; Gal 3: 10 to12; Jn 14: 6; Eph 2: 8, 9; Rom 10: 9, 10; Rom 3: 20 to 25; Titus 3: 5).

- I concluded that there was a lot of confusion regarding how to obtain eternal salvation in heaven (Ref Acts 9: 17 to 23; Jn 5: 24; Eph 2: 8, 9). Whereas, the bible simply delineated and repeated often that all I had to do to obtain eternal salvation in heaven was to make a personal decision to ask, accept, thank Jesus' for his love and love sacrifice on the cross by simply trusting him with a child like faith (Ref Jn 3: 11 to 21; Jn 5: 24; Rom 10: 9, 10; Eph 1: 13).

- A Recommended Eternal Salvation Prayer
Dear Lord Jesus I confess that I am a sinner and unable to always keep your standard of being Holy, Loving, and Just all the time (i.e. Loving all the time); and I am sorry for all my sin choices which caused you, others, and me to suffer greatly and needlessly. I accept your love sacrifice on the cross which paid for the consequences of all my sin choices, and I ask you to come into my life and unite my spirit with your Holy Spirit again **right now** to help me to more closely follow your will/plan for my life. **I thank you** for coming into my life **right now**, forgiving all my sin consequences **right now**, and re-uniting my spirit with your Holy Spirit **right now, resulting in me receiving** eternal life with you **right now according to your word**. I pray in Jesus name to let you know that I am eternally grateful for what you have **just now** done for me and to remind me that I could not have been spiritually re-born again without your help. Amen. ☺

- If you were sincere with above prayer, then at this moment you were re-united with Jesus' Holy Spirit, and you became a child of God again, right now, and forever unconditionally by your choice and Jesus promise (i.e. being spiritually born again back into God's Holy Spirit forever per Jesus' unconditional promise to us -- which we can never, never lose again per Jesus word) (Ref Rom 3: 20 to 28; Rom 5: 1 to 11; Jn 14: 6; Jn 3: 3 to 7; Jn 11: 25, 26; Matt 22: 36 to 40; Matt 18: 3 to 5; Rom 10: 9, 10; Jn 5: 24; Eph 2: 8, 9; 1 Tim 1: 5; Eph 1: 13; Titus 3: 4 to 7; Rom Ch 8: All). God does not lie like humans, because it is against his love nature!!!

- How can you be sure you are spiritually born again right now: God is not a man and cannot lie (i.e. God is always Holy, Loving, and Just)!!! He loves you, and He keeps his promises because He is GOD: not a man. Therefore, He always keeps his promises. In addition, God had to make sure that his eternal life plan was very simple, so that everyone could understand it no matter what their physical, mental, psychologically, social, cultural, moral, rational, and man's training/condition's impact was. Another example of God's true love!!! (Ref Rom 1: 16; Rom 1: 19, 20; Heb 11: 6; Gal 6: 7; Rom 10: 9 – 13; Jer 17: 5 -10; Eph 2: 8, 9; Isa 6:3; 1 John 4; 8, 16). God keeps his promises! ☺

Lesson 46: A Easter Story Letter Sample
(Ref Rom 5: 7, 8; Jn 3: 3 to 7; Heb 11: 6; Eph 2: 8, 9; Rom 10: 9, 10; Eph 1: 13)!

Hi Friend,
Pray you and yours a very blessed Easter Holyday season and life.

Forwarded for your blessing is some background on the real meaning of the Easter Holyday; as well as, I am forwarding the greatest gift that you can receive from Jesus which is how to obtain eternal salvation in heaven today.

<u>The Easter holyday should not be about Eostra the Goddess of Fertility</u> (i.e. symbolized by the easter bunnies), rather that God established 7 Holy Days (i.e. Feasts) (Ref Leviticus Ch 23) to remind us of the purpose of Jesus' love sacrifice on the cross for the redemption of all of our sins consequences. Who would divert our attention from the true spiritual meaning of Easter?

God's Holy Days: <u>Passover</u> (Jesus death); <u>Unleavened Bread</u> (Humans available redemption); <u>First Fruits</u> (Jesus' Resurrection from Death); <u>Weeks</u> (Holy Spirit becomes available to christians for spirit re-uniting); <u>Trumpets</u> (Second Advent of Jesus); <u>Atonement</u> (Regathering of Jews); <u>Tabernacles</u> (Restoration of God's Children).

<u>The Easter Holyday emphasis should be about</u> the Passover, Feast of Unleavened Bread, and the First Fruits Holy Days (i.e. and in particular on the last 3 hours when darkness covered all the earth while Jesus suffered on the cross). The Easter emphasis should be that <u>Jesus suffered literal hell</u> (i.e.

no love from his father during the 3 dark hours) for us, and Jesus was raised from the dead 3 days later to show that God the Father accepted Jesus sacrifice for our sins consequences. Why? God will not force us to love him, because that would make us puppets, and God would not be a God of Love (Ref 1 John 4: 8, 16). Rather, we must ask and accept Jesus' love sacrifice with thanksgiving in order to re-unite our spirit with Jesus' Holy Spirit and receive eternal salvation in heaven forever.

Romans 5: 7, 8 – "For scarcely for a righteous man will one die; yet perhaps for a good man some would even dare to die. But God commended his love toward us in that, while we were yet sinners, Christ died for us" (Ref Rom 10: 9, 10; Jn 3: 15 to 18; 1 Pet 3: 18; Rev 20: 15; Jn 5: 24). Sin is to do a non-loving thought/word/action.

John 3: 3 to 7 – "Jesus answered, and said unto him, Verily, verily, I say unto you, Except a man be born again, he cannot see the kingdom of God. Nicodemus said to him, How can a man be born when he is old? Can he enter the second time into his mother's womb, and be born? Jesus answered, Verily, verily, I say to you, Except a man be born of water and of the "Holy Spirit", he cannot enter in the kingdom of God. That which is born of the flesh is flesh; and that which is born of the "Holy Spirit" is spirit. Marvel not that I say unto you, you must be born again". Our first sin separated our spirit from God's Holy Spirit.

Jn 14: 6 – "Jesus said, I am the way, the truth, and the life; no man come to the Father but by me (i.e. we must re-unite our spirit with Jesus' Holy Spirit via faith and trust to be spiritually born again and become a child of God again forever and live in heaven forever)".

John 3: 15, 16, 17 – "That whosoever believeth in him (i.e. Jesus Christ) should not perish, but have eternal life. For God so loved the world that He gave his only begotten Son, that whosoever believes in Him should not perish, but have everlasting life (note: Jesus Christ translated is "God Saved his Anointed One"). For God sent not his Son into the world to condemn the world, but that the world through him might be saved (i.e. a true love relationship requires both parties to have a faith, trust, and reciprocal holy, loving, and just attitude/thoughts/actions toward one another based upon their own free will decisions, not because of forced decisions".

Romans 10: 9, 10 – "That if you shall confess with your mouth the Lord Jesus, and shall believe in your heart that God has raised him from the dead, you shall be saved. For with the heart man believes unto righteousness, and with the mouth confession is made unto salvation". **This is the greatest gift that God can give to you: eternal salvation in heaven.**

Ephesians 2: 8, 9 – "For by grace are you saved through faith; and that not of yourselves, it is the gift of God – not of works, lest any man should boast (i.e. God's grace means a free, undeserved gift!)".

Ephesians 1: 13 – "In whom ye also trusted, after you heard the work of truth, the gospel of your salvation; and in whom also after you believed, you were sealed with the Holy Spirit of promise".

Hebrews 11: 6 – "But without faith it is impossible to please him; for he that comes to God must believe that he is, and that he is a rewarder of them that diligently seek him."

Titus 3: 5 –" Not by works of righteousness which we have done, but according to his mercy he saved us, by washing of regeneration, and renewing of the Holy Spirit" (i.e. our first sin separates our spirit from the Holy Spirit, and we need to re-unite with the Holy Spirit to become spiritually alive again in God's eyes (Ref John 3: 5 to 7).

Romans 8: 16 – "The Holy Spirit himself bears witness with our spirit, that we are the children of God (i.e. if we become spiritually born again)".

Here is the prayer that I used to obtain my eternal salvation in heaven (i.e. be spiritually born again) right now:

"Dear Lord Jesus I confess that I am a sinner and unable to always keep your standard of being Holy, Loving, and Just all the time (i.e. Loving all the time); and I am sorry for all my sin choices which caused you, others, and me to suffer greatly and needlessly. I accept your love sacrifice on the cross that paid for the consequences of all my sin choices, and I ask you to come into my life and unite my spirit with your Holy Spirit again **right now** to help me to more closely follow your will/plan for my life. **I thank you for coming into my life right now, forgiving all my sin consequences right now, and re-uniting my spirit with your Holy Spirit right now, resulting in me receiving eternal life with you right now according to your word. I pray in Jesus name** to let you know that I am eternally grateful for what you have

just now done for me and to remind me that I could not have been spiritually re-born again without your help Amen."

Lesson 47: All Decisions have Consequences
(Ref Rom 2: 1 to 16; Rom 1: 16; Gal 6: 7, 8; Rom 8: 2; Rom 10: 9, 10)!

-- <u>It would be prudent for my decisions to be holy</u> (i.e. have the mind-set to not transgress any of God's Mosaic Law – i.e. sin), <u>loving</u>, and <u>just</u> to receive the best consequences of my decision(s) (i.e. either good or bad consequences), if God's Love Concept is real and pure.

- <u>Decisions require consequences; otherwise, how could I determine the benefits, quality, and value of my decisions (Ref Gal 6: 7, 8)</u>! I felt that allowing me to make my own decisions and receive the consequences of my choices concerning my life decisions has to be the fundamental personal mind-set, attitude, and subsequent related actions that generate true unconditional love between two persons.

- **A God of Love would surely want me to have many blessings; and God would provide encouragement, uplifting, and edification in his word (i.e. bible – Ref Eph Cp 4: All) to show that the purpose and understanding of his Mosaic Law (Ref Matt 22: 36 to 40; Rom Ch 5: All; Rom 3: 20) was to provide loving opportunities for many blessings (Ref Rom Ch 8: All; Heb 12: 1 to 15) which are directly contingent upon my wise decisions and their consequences, as opposed to me not making wise decisions and simply becoming a mere indecisive puppet** (Ref Gal 6: 7, 8; Eph Ch 4: All; Josh 1: 8, 9; 1 Tim 1: 5; Mich 6: 8; Matt 11: 28 to 30; Phil 4: 4 to 8; Rom 8: 31 to 39; Gal Ch 5: All; Deut 31: 6; Jer 9: 23, 24; 2 Tim 1: 6, 7; 2 Cor 12: 9, 10; Prov 3: 5, 6).

- Also, God's love for me should provide me with a permanent spiritual relationship (i.e. spiritually born again forever), positional relationship (i.e. saved sinner going to heaven forever), and self-worth relationship (i.e. eternal member of the family of God) with Him.

- Additionally, I appropriately needed to remember that God's Love Concept always requires me to be responsible, accountable, and deal with the consequences of my life decisions relative to, or not to, God's hopeful eternal salvation plan for me (Ref Gal 6: 7 to 9); because a true love relationship requires both relational parties to be considerate, respectful, and caring of each other and be willing to work through the consequences of their decisions for the benefit of both (Ref Col Ch 3: All; Eph Ch 4: All; 1 John Ch 4: All).

Gal 6: 7 to 9 – "Be not deceived, God is not mocked, for whatever a man soweth, that shall he also reap. For he that soweth to his flesh shall of the flesh reap corruption; but he that soweth to the Spirit shall of the Spirit reap life everlasting. And let us not be weary in well doing; for in due season we shall reap, if we faint not" (i.e. the Golden Rule – decisions require just consequences if love, or non-love, is to be realized, understood, and employed in our lives).

Matt 7: 1, 2 – "Judge not, that ye be not judged. For with what judgment ye judge, ye shall be judged; and with what measure ye measure, it shall be measured to you again" (i.e. Ref Rom 2: 1 to 16 – i.e. judged according to the truth; my deeds; my knowledge, understanding and wisdom of the truth; and the gospel) (i.e. asking/receiving/thanking Jesus' for his free eternal salvation gift allowing me to re-unite my spirit with his Holy Spirit).

Matthew 22: 37 to 40 – "Master, which is the great commandment in the law? Jesus said unto him, Thou shall love the Lord, thy God, with all your heart, and with all your soul, and with all your mind. This is the first and great commandment. And the second is like it, Thou shall love your neighbor as your self. On these two commandments hang all the law " (Ref Rom 8: 2 & Rom 3: 20 to 25).

Rom 8: 2 – **"For the law of the Spirit of Life in Christ Jesus has made me free from the law of sin and death"** (Ref Rom Ch 8: All vs Mosaic Law respectively – i.e. Mosaic Law refers to 10 commandments, and 600+ worship ordinances and social judgments spelled out in the bible books of Exodus, Leviticus, Numbers, and repeated in the book of Deuteronomy). (Note: Use of the word Law in the bible refers to teachings/instruction (Ref Ps 19; 7; Ps 119: All).

Heb 11: 6 – "But without faith it is impossible to please him; for he that comes to God must believe that he is, and that he is a rewarder of them that diligently seek him".

Matt 6: 33 – "But seek ye first the kingdom of God, and his righteousness, and all these things (i.e. life's spiritual and basic needs) shall be added unto you".

Romans 10: 9, 10 – "That if you shall confess with your mouth the Lord Jesus, and shall believe in your heart

Basic Bible Lessons

that God has raised him from the dead, you shall be saved. For with the heart man believes unto righteousness, and with the mouth confession is made unto salvation".

Matt 11: 28 to 30 – "Come unto me all ye that labor, and are heavy burden, and I will give you rest. Take my yoke upon you, and learn of me; for I am meek and lowly in heart, and ye shall find rest unto your souls. For my yoke is easy, and my burden is light".

Jn 5: 24 – "I tell you the truth, whosoever hears my word, and believes **(i.e. choose by your own free will and faith (i.e. trust by concent of my mind, act of my heart, and by my will with thanks (i.e. not just believe)** to personally ask/accept his free love gift (i.e. free undeserved grace gift) of eternal salvation in order to live in heaven (i.e. a place with God's eternal love) with him with my new body forever; or choose to reject his free gift and live in a place devoid of God's love forever with my new body (Ref also Heb 11: 6; Rom 3: 23; Rom 10: 9, 10; Jn 14: 6; Jn 3: 15, 16; Eph 2: 8, 9; Eph 1: 13; Titus 3: 5; Eph 4: 30)) him who sent me has eternal life and will not be condemned; **he has crossed over from "death" to life**".

Lesson 48: Jesus' Love and Reconciliation Bible Verses
(Ref Jn 15: 13; Rom 8: 32; Heb 11: 6; Titus 3: 5; Rom 10: 9, 10 ; Col 1: 20 to 22; 2 Cor 5: 14 to 21)!

-- The following bible verses confirmed how much Jesus loved me; and these bible verses helped me to understand how important it was to understand what part Jesus' Love played in my eternal salvation in heaven.

- These bible verses also helped me to reconcile with God through Jesus by believing (i.e. trusting) Jesus' Love for me and his love sacrifice on the cross to cover my sin consequences (Ref Col 1: 20 to 22; 2 Cor 5: 14 to 21).

- My reconciliation with God through Jesus Christ was achieved when I became a "spiritually born again" Christian (Ref Jn 3: 3 to 7; Jn 3: 15 to 18; Col 1: 20 to 22) as explained in the following bible verses.

> Rom 8: 32 - " He that spared not his own Son, but delivered him up for us all, how shall he not with him also freely give us all things"?

> John 15: 13 – "Greater love has no man than this, that a man lay down his life for his friends."

> Jn 14: 6 – "Jesus said, I am the way, the truth, and the life; no man come to the Father but by me (i.e. we must re-unite our spirit with Jesus' Holy Spirit to be spiritually born again and become a child of God **again** forever)".

> Romans 10: 9, 10 – "That if you shall confess with your mouth the Lord Jesus, and shall believe in your heart

that God has raised him from the dead, <u>you shall be saved</u>. For <u>with the heart man believes unto righteousness</u>, and with the mouth <u>confession is made unto salvation</u>".

<u>Titus 3: 5</u> – "<u>Not by works</u> of righteousness which we have done, but according to his mercy he saved us, <u>by washing of regeneration</u>, and <u>renewing of the Holy Spirit</u>".

<u>Hebrews 11: 6</u> – "<u>But without faith it is impossible to please him</u>; for he that comes to God must believe that he is, and that he is a rewarder of them that diligently seek him."

<u>Ephesians 2: 8, 9</u> – "<u>For by grace are you saved through faith</u>; and that not of yourselves, it is the gift of God – <u>not of works</u>, lest any man should boast" (i.e. God's grace means a free, undeserved gift!).

<u>John 3: 15, 16</u> – "<u>That whosoever believeth in him should not perish</u>, but have <u>eternal life</u>. For God so loved the world that He gave his only begotten Son, that whosoever believes in Him should not perish, but have <u>everlasting life</u>."

<u>Matthew 18: 3 to 5</u> – "Jesus said, Verily I say unto you, except you be converted, and become as little children (<u>i.e. in your faith/belief/trust toward and in Jesus Christ), you shall not enter into the kingdom of heaven</u>. Whosoever, therefore, shall humble himself as this little child, the same is greatest in the kingdom of heaven. And

whosoever shall receive one such little child in my name receives me."

Ezekiel 36: 26, 27 – " A new heart also will I give you and a new spirit will I put within you; and I will take away the stony heart out of your flesh, and I will give you a heart of flesh. And I will put my Spirit within you, and cause you to walk in my statues, and you shall keep mine ordinances, and do them" (Ref 2 Cor 5: 17; 2 Cor 6: 16).

2 Cor 5: 17 to 19 – "Therefore, if any man be in Christ, he is a new creation; old things are passed away; behold, all things are become new. And all things are of God, who has reconciles us to himself by Jesus Christ, and has given to us the ministry of reconciliation. To wit, that God was in Christ reconciling the world unto himself, not imputing their trespasses unto them, and has committed unto us the word of reconciliation".

Col 1: 21 – "And you, that were once alienated and enemies in your mind by wicked works, yet now has he reconciled".

For more information, contact Charles Pringle via email at info@advbooks.com

To purchase additional copies of this book, visit our online bookstore at advbookstore.com

www.advbookstore.com